Nelson
A Debt of Honour

Ken Vernon

Copyright © 2023 by Ken Vernon

All rights reserved. No part of this publication may be reproduced, distributed or transmitted in any form or by any means, without prior written permission.

 A catalogue record for this book is available from the National Library of Australia

Cataloguing in Publication Data: 2 April 2024
Author: Ken Vernon
Title: Nelson A Debt of Honour
Published: Australia, Maverick Publications 2024
Subjects: Historical, biographical, British Colonial history

Debt of Honour Ken Vernon.
Print: 978-0-9942962-3-8
Ebook: 978-0-9942962-4-5

The moral right of Ken Vernon to be identified as the author of this work has been asserted by him under the Copyright Amendment (Moral Right) Act of 2000.
This work is copyright. Apart from use as permitted under the Copyright Act of 1968, no part may be reproduced, scanned, copied, stored in a retrieval system, recorded, or transmitted in any form or by any means, without the prior written permission of the copyright holder.

Layout and design by Kassandra Patrick

Acknowledgements

A great many people have had a hand in bringing this book to term after, as one 'kind' friend said, 'such a long pregnancy' following its conception over four years ago.

It would be impossible to name all who lent a hand in that time, but some do deserve a special mention; my wife Daniele who has supported me - literally - through this madness; my daughter Kassandra, who jumped on board at a crucial time. To friends John and Karen Leahey who read the early drafts and managed to catch most of my misspellings; to Stacey King who offered some sage advice on final construction; To Charles Hanson for believing and Nick Denbow for his technical knowledge. Last but far from least, to a whole raft of librarians - too many to name individually - who toil at libraries stretching from the Britain's Caird Library at the Royal Museums, Greenwich, to the Australian National Library, the state libraries of Victoria and News South Wales and the University of Newcastle Library, and even my local Broadbeach City Council Library here on the Gold Coast of Queensland.

Without librarians there would be very few books.

Ken Vernon.
Gold Coast. Queensland.

1 Black Swans on the Hunter River circa 1820. Original sketch by Captain James Wallis, 46th Regiment. University of Newcastle.

Prologue

Morpeth. Colony of New South Wales. August 1881

None of the few residents of the Australian outback village of Morpeth out and about in the wintery afternoon chill gave the shrivelled old man a second glance as he carefully picked his way toward the Commercial Hotel. The grey-bearded figure moved slowly, considering each step carefully, knuckles showing white on his walking stick as he slowly navigated what passed for a footpath in the frontier town.

The short pilgrimage from his home to the pub was a daily ritual for William Thomas "Old Cookie" Cooke, one of the longest-surviving inhabitants of what had once been a bustling port at the navigable end of the Hunter River, second only to Sydney Town 90 miles to the south. In August 1881 Morpeth was once more just a village clinging stubbornly to life atop the south bank of the Hunter River in the colony of New South Wales.

Stopping for an moment to catch his breath in the sheltered entrance of the hotel, the old man looked out across the main street. Swan Street it was called, named by the first settlers for the black swans which, back when the town was first established, had glided imperiously along the river's deep, pristine waters.

Now both the bustle and the swans were long gone. In between the Hunter's uneven banks the river was a sliver of silver glinting in the afternoon sun, pointing westward into the hazy blue foothills of the Great Dividing Range. Old Cookie never tired of the view.

Stepping into the hotel lobby, he eased himself into a tattered leather armchair with a long sigh. Barely had he accomplished this carefully considered manoeuvre than young James the bar-keep appeared with the old man's first rum of the day, overproof rum of course, to be followed sometime afterwards, as always, by his second and then by the third and last tipple.

Good service and an extra finger of rum assured because Old Cookie always paid four and a half pence instead of the ruling thruppence, the extra penny and a half for James' pocket.

Old Cookie was early for his tipple on that day because he had agreed to meet a journalist, John Haynes, who wanted to interview him.

He remembered Haynes from many years ago when the boy had been one of the town's young ragamuffins who, when not in school – which was most of the time – would gang together to cause childish mayhem in their endless search for something exciting to do in an isolated village at the end of nowhere in a far-flung corner of the British Empire.

From deep in their wrinkled lair Old Cookie's eyes twinkled as he recalled how he and the village kids had waged a good-humoured war over the fruits of Cookie's orchard - literally.

Victory for the kids was to steal as much fruit as they could eat – which wasn't a lot – and to avoid being caught by Old Cookie. The old man's less than serious defence aimed to stop their plundering, if possible by catching them, scolding them, and then letting them go with the threat to tell their parents ringing in their ears. If he felt especially warlike he would set booby traps for the kids, a favourite being to paint low-hanging ripe apples with the long-lasting, foul-tasting juice of the ballart berry, sniggering as he listened to their howls of disgust as they bit into the tainted fruit.

It was a harmless, even good-humoured war, one with few victories or defeats and no casualties.

Haynes had gone on to work for the local Morpeth Leader newspaper, Cookie recalled, learning his craft first as compositor and then journalist, before leaving the town those many years ago to seek his fortune. A few days ago he had returned on a visit to his old home-town as a suit-wearing newspaper owner and just that morning, after renewing their acquaintance the day before, he had knocked on Old Cookie's door to ask if he would mind being interviewed for *The Bulletin*, the news magazine Haynes had recently co-founded.

"It will be a bit of fun" young Haynes had quickly added when Old Cookie had involuntarily stepped backwards, ready to demur and decline, but no words came from his mouth.

Haynes, like any good reporter, seized the moment.

"I think you might have a good story to tell behind that quiet exterior" Haynes joshed.

"What do you say? I'll even buy the drinks while we talk!"

Old Cookie did have a story to tell and recently, as he perceived his life was drawing to an end, he had begun to toy with the idea that perhaps the time had come to tell it.

"I will meet you at the Commercial Hotel tomorrow," he eventually said. "At 3pm. Sharp. Don't be late."

2. John Archibald (left) and John Haynes, co-founders of The Bulletin circa 1882.
SLNSW. Photographer unknown.

PART ONE

NELSON'S NAVY

Chapter One

Old Cookie had just taken the second sip of his first rum when Haynes blundered through the front door, standing for an instant burbling his lips and shaking his shoulders, trying to shed the cold the way a dog sheds water.

Spotting Old Cookie he strode over to shake his quarry's hand, at the same time signalling the bar-keep, indicating he would also have a rum and placing his leather satchel on the table - all in one economical movement.

"I'm glad you could make it, its bloody cold out there today" he said, carelessly taking a notebook and a few pencils out of the satchel, too busy to notice the reproving glance the old man gave to the use of a word he regarded as profanity.

Old Cookie had never uttered a swearword in his life. Young James appeared with the rum which Haynes quickly put to his lips without a word of thanks.

"Shall we begin"? he said, at the same time examining a pencil, draining his rum and signalling for another two glasses.

'Where exactly to begin' Old Cookie pondered silently, a silence that lasted for a full minute.

He looked at Haynes squarely in the eye for so long even the seasoned journalist began to feel a bit uncomfortable, though he was smart enough to let the silence linger.

Eventually the old man spoke, so quietly that Haynes initially thought he must have misheard the old man: "I suppose you want to hear about my time with Admiral Nelson".

Cape Trafalgar
October 21, 1805

From the mid-morning moment the drummer began to beat out the bouncy notes of '*Hearts of Oak*' - the call to arms in his majesty's navy - young Will Cooke and the other powder monkeys were pitched into a whirlwind.

"Move you little bastards, move now! Run! Run! If'n I catch a one of you standin' still again you'll be feedin' the bloody fish."

The rasping bellow belonged to John Ebbs, oldest and most feared quarter gunner on the *Victory* who, now action was imminent, had taken effective control of the upper gun deck in his gnarled hands. As one all the boys launched into a dead run to either the fore or aft 'hanging' magazines on the Orlop deck where a cache of canvas gunpowder cartridges were kept after being hoisted up from the main powder magazine deep in the bowels of the ship. With the boys gone, Ebbs turned his lone beady eye to the gun crews.

"And you, you lazy worthless pieces of shit, what you waitin' for, a bleedin' invitation from Napoleon! You'll be bleedin' all orl right unless you get those guns tackled up, 'cause I'll lay a fist to the lot o' you. You bin talkin' a fight for months and now you're all standin' there lookin' scared shitless. C'on, move, move, move!"

Each gun crew sprang to work like finely tuned pieces of clockwork, taking just minutes to loosen the guns from the bindings which kept them in place when not in use and secure each into its carriage.

That done, a canvas cartridge of gun powder was taken from one of the small storage boxes spaced along centre of the deck for each gun, placing it into a half-round copper cylinder at the end of a long-handled ladle which was then inserted into the barrel and twisted, neatly dropping the cartridge in the correct position beneath the primer hole. A wad of rope yarn was then driven onto the charge by the rammer.

Next a cannon ball was dropped in, another rope wad was then rammed in on top of the shot, and the cannon was almost ready to be fired. All that remained to be done, nearer firing time, was for the gun captain to take a long copper needle he carried and 'prick' the powder cartridge, releasing a spill of black powder to assure instant ignition. The gun readied, the gun captain would carefully fill his personal powder horn with highly refined priming powder, a little of which he would pour into the touch hole directly above the powder cartridge. Finally, when action was certain, he would light his 'match wick' - a length of twisted cotton soaked in lye which burned very slowly and was used to ignite the firing charge. The burning end of the wick was placed in a notch cut in the top of the gun's 'match tub' - a large bucket filled with wet sand - with the glowing end of the wick hanging a fraction of an inch above the wet sand, safely away from any powder, but still ready for use.

When the order to fire was given, the gunner would sight the cannon before touching the match wick to the priming powder, instantly igniting the main charge. With the guns ready for action, the gun crews prepared to deal with the main threat to the safety of the ship – fire - the worst fear of all sailors.

Water buckets, filled and placed near each gun, had the dual role of being used wet the swabs and blankets used to douse the almost inevitable sparks or small fires, as well as to quench the thirst of the gunners once the work became hot. Lamb's wool swabs were wetted and placed close to hand; water hoses were connected to the hand pumps and laid along the decks and wetted blankets were hung around each hatchway and wet sand was sprinkled on the decks – all designed to stop that one spark which could doom the entire ship.

"To soak up the blood" a gunner's mate had said in reply to Will's question about why the sand was being spread. "Don't want your bloody young guts sloshing about and making us slip and fall on our arses, do we," he had laughed, keen to shock the lad and delighted when Will visibly winced at the thought. With the 'wet' work done, the last task was for pistols and cutlasses to be issued to those members of the gun crews designated to board any enemy ship the *Victory* might close with.

As the gun crews had worked the powder monkeys had been running back and forth, collecting cartridges as quickly as they could be hoisted up from the main magazine and racing back to the gun deck to carefully place them in the 'salt boxes' - so called because the bottom of the box was spread with a layer of salt to prevent the cartridges becoming damp and so possibly misfire. The boxes were spaced down the centre of the deck as far as possible from any 'huff' or spit of fire that often accidentally leapt backwards from the touch hole when the cannon was fired. If a 'huff', or any hot ember, touched black powder it could spark a catastrophic explosion that could be end of the ship and all the men upon her.

Only when all the 'salt' boxes had been refilled could Will and the other ship's boys - all of who had been pressed into service as 'powder monkeys' for the battle, no matter what their usual position - were able to take a moment to catch their breath.

Will stood at his post beside the first four 12 pounders of the top gun deck, body taunt with fear and anticipation, his back aching and his bare feet stinging from running across the gritty wet sand. Only then did he notice the silence. Once the commands of the quarter-gunners and the swearing of the gun crews had died down, the lower decks of the ship became strangely silent, the creaking of wood and rope dominating the muted commands still being shouted by officers on the quarter deck to the 'topmen' tasked with manning the sails. The order to open the gun hatches came shortly before midday and once that had been done a running commentary commenced from those nearest the openings as they drew back the wet blankets to report on what they could see, which wasn't much, but just enough for the below decks crew to understand that once again Nelson was leading his men from the front and aiming straight at the line of French ships strung across *Victory's* bows.

"I'm wagering we'll take a bit of a pasting before we get anywhere near close enough to let the Frenchies taste our reply" intoned Ebbs. A natural actor, the old tar slowly cast his one eye around the men gathered about to hear his orders, waiting to let the tension build, "but when it starts, it'll be hot work me hearties, mark my words. Hot work indeed.

"But woe betide any man who touches wick to powder afore the order is given. D'ye all hear" he shouted, his dark eye moving slowing across the line of lamp-lit faces looking back at him, before adding in a whisper, "don't worry, there'll be plenty of work for everyone. There be no need to rush".

For the next half hour Will listened to the storm of enemy cannon fire grow. At the beginning it had been a low sound, but now, as the *Victory* closed with its fate, the sound was like thunder punctuated with the lightning strikes of French cannon balls cracking into the thick oak sides of the mighty *Victory* or whistling through its rigging. All the while the *Victory's* guns remained silent, even after the gun crews began hearing occasional screams of the wounded from above as *Victory* was raked as it ploughed straight at the enemy. Below decks, blind to the actions of the enemy, hardly a man stirred, each feeling their own terror but saying not a word as they awaited what fate would bring. Discipline was the watch word in his Majesty's navy in 1805.

"Don't concern yourselves, the Admiral has 'em fixed" said Ebbs as the men began to exchange worried glances, "we're running with the swell so our shots will be true, mark my words. But the bloody French are side on to the swell, so their guns are rising and falling with the waves and their guns be firing either high or low," he laughed, looking at each of his crew, his own mania forcing them to join in the laughter, the crazy laughter barked by men working themselves into the frenzy needed to fight to the death.

Looking down the length of the gun deck at the guns furthest from the Admiral's cabin, Will's eyes widened as he saw the first gunner adjusting the elevation of his gun, his action quickly copied by all the other gunners in turn. Suddenly the order to "prepare to fire" rolled up the deck and the wetted hatch curtains were drawn aside. A blinding light flooded in through the open hatchways, eclipsing the dim glow from the rows of purser's glims, the heavy fire-proof battle lanterns secured to the ship's side beside each gun, which for hours had been the only light the tars could see by.

The Battle

Without warning the big 32-pounders on both sides of the *Victory's* lower gun deck let loose a rolling volley to cheers and huzza's from the entire crew of more than 800 men, a full-throated war-cry that drowned out even the roar of the cannons.
A minute later the middle gun deck let loose a volley from their 24 pounders, followed a minute later by the 12 pounders on the upper deck, followed another minute later by a second volley from the 32 pounders.

3 Battle of Trafalgar. Painting by John Schetky.

With the Victory's guns firing regular volleys from both sides of the ship almost every minute, the noise became a constant overwhelming reverberation that left Will disoriented, his ears ringing.

A thick acrid smoke quickly filled the space between decks, changing daylight into a hazy twilight and setting Will's throat ablaze.

The first rolling blasts were the starter's gun for the powder monkey's second race to begin. Without waiting to be ordered they took off back and forth from the guns to the magazine hoist and back to the guns. Running as fast as they could, they needed all their barefooted, nimble-toed agility to dodge the shadowy human figures rushing across their path and avoid the dangerous tangle of buckets, ropes, boxes and discarded clothing that had quickly littered the gun decks.

Bent almost double, arms safely cradling their deadly cargo clutched beneath their jackets, each boy knew that one fall, one cartridge broken and spilt, one careless strike of metal on metal, could achieve what all the Frenchmen on the planet would never achieve – Victory's destruction. It was on his seventh run that Will came face to face with death.

He had just reached the last tread on the steps to the upper gun deck when a blinding flash and massive shock wave lifted him from his feet and hurled him back down the stairs, only a lucky landing on the two boys close behind him saved him from serious injury.

Those two were less lucky.

Laying dazed on the middle gun deck, still carefully cradling his cartridge with one arm, Will at first had no idea of what had happened. Using his free hand to feel his body, he decided he was not injured. Nothing seemed broken and he couldn't see any blood anywhere, but as he stood up the ship began to spin and he would have gone reeling away had he not managed to grab hold of a stanchion to steady himself. Standing unsteadily for a few long seconds, his head slowly cleared.

Looking down at the two other boys, he saw neither was moving.

'They're dead' was his first thought. His next thought being 'I must get the powder'.

Carefully sitting down to steady himself, he slid over to the boys. Turning over the first body he saw it was his best friend Rob Twichett. Rob had a huge swelling over one eye and there was blood running from his hair; a lot of blood. Gently turning him over he took the cartridge Rob had been carrying from beneath his jacket and slipped it into his own jacket.

The second boy was little Johnnie Saunders, the only boy on Victory shorter than Will. He didn't seem to be bleeding and when Will turned him over he groaned. Not knowing what else to do, he dragged the boy half under the stairs where he hoped he would be safe, added his cartridge to the two beneath his jacket, and headed gingerly back up the stairs. Carefully peeking over the last step, all he could see was smoke, but as he set one foot on the deck, the 12-pounders fired another rolling broadside, the thunderous noise hitting him with such force that he dropped down, falling back a step, just managing to catch himself.

As the noise faded and the smoke cleared a fraction, he dared a second look which showed the way to the salt boxes was open. As quickly as he could he wobbled onto the deck, staggering under his extra load of cartridges. Slowly edging his way from stanchion to stanchion, he made it to his station where he found himself looking at a hellish scene of bloody carnage. In the dark haze unseen men were shouting madly. One walked slowly past him dazed, another stood still, seemingly oblivious to the maelstrom going on around him. One man sat leaning back on an empty blood red gun carriage, his arm missing and blood spurting from the hole. Peering through the gloom Will could see there was a huge jagged hole where the gun hatch had been and realised the gun must have been blown off its carriage. Through the hole Will could see part of a ship wreathed in smoke. As he looked the ship belched flame and smoke as it fired a broadside toward him. He ducked involuntarily, but all the shots seemed to miss because nothing happened.

'How could they miss the whole side of the *Victory*' he thought, 'they must be terrible shots'. From his hiding place behind a stanchion he was jolted to see two small fires were burning on the deck not far from him. He clutched the cartridges beneath his jacket closer in fear, but even as he watched the fires were doused, by who he couldn't see. The main danger contained, now he saw there was an even bigger terror to fear.

As the *Victory* rolled gently to starboard, the 'missing' dismounted larboard side cannon began to roll, slowly at first, but quickly gathering speed as it rolled at an angle across and along the deck. Men screamed warnings and ran in all directions as the iron monster threatened to devour all in its path. Luckily it ran up against one of the massive support stanchions, stopping before it could reach the other gun crews. Will knew cannons weighed tons and it had been drummed into his head that once rolling about on a deck, a loose cannon could cause a huge amount of damage, easily smashing a hole in the side of the ship, killing or maiming anyone in their path. Even as he stood paralysed wondering what to do – and where to hide – the seasoned Ebbs sprang into action. Screaming at the men nearest to him to 'come with me' he grabbed a number of rolled up hammocks which had been stowed amidships and without wasting a second to explain, ran to the momentarily motionless cannon and wedged a hammock beneath the behemoth. Instantly understanding, all the men in the area did the same, followed quickly by other men who saw what was happening. One sailor then managed to wedge parts of the broken gun carriage under the cannon while the cool-headed Ebbs grabbed some rope and lashed the monster front and rear to the stanchion.

As quickly as it had begun the danger had been neutralised.

Quickly assessing the damage to the ship, Ebbs sent one tar off to find a carpenter's mate to seal the gaping hole, then ordered two men to arm themselves with wet swabs in case of any further fire and to secure any cartridges or loose powder. Only then did he turn his attention to the men who had been manning the gun when it was hit. The shot had smashed into the ship next to the gun hatch, smashing the hatch before hitting and dismounting the cannon from its carriage, showering deadly metal and wood splinters through the gun crew.

Will decided to stay where he had taken cover - just in case. Peeping out from behind the stanchion he could now see fallen men scattered round the gun position like rag dolls. The armless man sitting up against the gun carriage had stopped moving. Two other men lay on the deck near him; one wrapped backwards around a stanchion, his back clearly broken, the other seemingly untouched except that his head lay at an unnatural angle.

Again Ebbs acted decisively. Deciding three men were either dead or beyond help he ordered some men to help and simply picked the bodies up and slid them unceremoniously through the gaping hole to a watery grave. Another man whose chest had been sliced open and his innards hanging out was also pitched into the sea even as he struggled and screamed.

Four other wounded and bleeding men sitting or lying on the deck, seeing what had happened to their comrades, struggled to their feet, each looking fearfully at Ebbs.

"Right, you lot, get yourselfs off to the sawbones - now!" They didn't argue.

As soon as they hobbled away Ebbs gathered the remaining crew members of the disabled cannon and divided them between the other gun crews.

Swinging his eye around to see what else had to be done, he spotted Will peeking out from his hiding place. Quick as a flash he had him by the scruff of the neck.

"Wot you at then you cowardly little cur?" he spat.

Will could only stare back wide-eyed. Then, seeing the bulge under the lad's jacket, Ebb ripped the jacket open, revealing the three cartridges.

"Why you carryin' so many?" Again Will could only stare back, terror written all over his face. A quick look of comprehension swept Ebbs face and he looked around.

"Where the other monkeys?" Barely managing to hold a sob that threatened to break out of his throat, Will pointed toward the stairs.

"They're dead" he managed to get out.

Ebbs was a hard man, but not a brute. Suddenly realising why Will had the extra cartridges his visage softened just a bit.

"Orl right. Get these cartridges stowed and get back to work. Now!"

Shocked out of his stupor, in a flash Will stowed the cartridges in salt boxes and was off and running. Reaching the bottom of the stairs he stopped, bewildered. Both the boy's bodies were gone! For an instant he wanted to call out their names, or stop one of the men rushing by to ask if they had seen them, but fear of Ebbs overwhelmed his concern and so he continued his run - desperately trying to clear from his mind the probability that the two young bodies had been heaved overboard.

That was the last thought he had for nearly an hour as he ran himself to the point of exhaustion back and forth from cannon to hoist, hoist to cannon. After carefully looking around to make sure Ebbs was nowhere in sight, he sat down on one of the salt boxes to catch his breath. Around him gun crews continued their steady rhythm of fire, worm, swab, load, prime, aim, fire. There was barely a sound from them and no need for orders - each man knew his role and performed it quickly and efficiently. Will was about to head off on another cartridge run when suddenly the ship shuddered violently and a loud grinding noise ran down the larboard side, instantly hurling boys and men on the starboard side off their feet, cursing and screaming and shouting all at once. The men on the larboard side must have known what was going to happen because from where he lay Will could see most of them had managed to find a grip to hang on to and were still standing, but their guns were not firing. He had no idea what had happened, but with absolute certainty he knew he had to get to Lord Nelson's side. Jumping to his feet he ran as fast as his legs could carry him, this time away from the powder hoist and toward the steps leading up to the poop deck, from where he knew he should be able to see Lord Nelson. Clearing the last three steps in one leap he turned toward the railing overlooking the quarter deck, but his run petered out and he stood stock still, eyes wide open, his mind unable to compute what he was seeing.

Hard up against the side of the *Victory* was a huge ship and even as Will stared at it in disbelief, the yardarms of the ship sheared into the rigging of the *Victory*, breaking sheets, shredding sails, smashing yardarms and sending deadly splinters spearing to the deck below. In a state of total shock he could only stand as the deadly shower landed all around him, missing him completely. Looking around dumbly, he could see men on the other ship just a few yards away, their faces contorted with rage. Some were waving cutlasses, some were firing muskets and some were throwing grenades, all seemed to be screaming, but Will couldn't hear a sound. Pulling his eyes away he dumbly looked down the long length of the *Victory* toward the fo'c'sle and saw the crew of the *Victory* were doing the same thing as the men on the other ship - waving cutlasses and pikes and throwing grenades.

A volley of shots rang out and he turned, seeing for the first time some marines who had just fired their muskets.

'It's the French' he shouted to no one. He saw the other ship rise slightly, as if by magic, before crashing into the side of *Victory* and then moving slowly away. It took just an instant for Will to understand that the French ship had risen on a wave and, having crashed into the side of the *Victory*, was now slowly ricocheting away. As it did so the *Victory* blasted a volley point blank into the ship's side and a wall of smoke rose up between the ships like a curtain on a stage bringing an end to a play.

As Will tried to understand what had happened, a massive blast let loose a shockwave which burst over him, sending him crashing to the deck. A huge short-barrelled carronade called a 'smasher' had been fired from behind him directly into the French ship, sending a wall of shot screeching across the French decks, ripping almost everything and everyone on it to shreds.

Will lay on the deck, eyes screwed shut, his body curled up into a foetal position, his hands covering his ears so tightly he couldn't hear his own screams. He didn't even know he was screaming. After what seemed a long time he slowly opened his eyes - and looked straight into sightless grey eyes staring back at him. The eyes belonged to a dead marine and the realisation of how close he was to death sent Will scrambling upright then falling backwards and screaming, all in one move.

From behind him, somehow cutting through the endless roar, Will heard a calm military voice giving orders.

"Fire! Reload! Steady lads. Steaaady. Take your time and pick your target - them bloody Frenchies ain't goin' nowhere."

The old soldier's stern voice brought Will back to reality and he remembered why he had fled from his post - to find Lord Nelson. Standing unsteadily, he made his way to the handrail which looked out over the rest of the ship. Immediately in front of him was the quarter deck and much further up front, the fo'c'sle. Over the long length of the ship men were moving every which way like a swarm of ants, each fighting their own battle. For one instant the swarm parted and he saw Lord Nelson. His Lordship was lying on his back, a knot of officers kneeling around him, all of them standing stock still as if time had stopped. As Will tried to make sense of what he was looking at, a pair of midshipmen took to their heels, waving their arms and shouting to get the attention of officers further along the ship. A wave of horror and fear surged through his body and he began to pray, but the instant he closed his eyes a massive explosion of noise and light hit him, sending him reeling backwards into darkness.

"I'm dead" he had time to think.

Will awoke in hell. Shadowy figures slid by in the near total darkness. From the gloom came sounds unlike any he had ever heard, deep groans of pain, screams of agony, the death rattle of teeth shaking - all rising from bundles around him that quivered and shook unnaturally. A vision of himself as a child sitting in the church in Burnham Thorpe listening to Rev Nelson came to him and he knew then that he was dead and had to repent.

"My Lord" he whispered clamping his eyes in fear, "forgive me for I have sinned".

"Shaddup" said the bundle next to him.

Ignoring the bundle, he slowly sat up.

"My Lord" he continued, "forgive me ..."

Again the bundle spoke. "Shaddup or I'll slap ya, ya little bastard".

4 Admiral Nelson lies wounded on the quarter deck of Victory at the height of battle. Print: The Wellcome Centre.

Opening his eyes and looking around, he saw there were bundles squeezed in all around him and he could make out the occasional face. Slowly he understood he must be alive, but surrounded by wounded men somewhere deep in the bowels of the ship. A place so deep that he could no longer hear the sounds of battle.

"Is the battle is still going?" he asked, but no one answered.

As he tried to sit up an explosion of pain in his head confirmed he was definitely still alive, though maybe living among the dead. He slid back to blackness. It was a succession of small noises that woke him. He lay quietly on his back, afraid to try to move in case he couldn't. He opened his eyes and as his sight adjusted to the gloom he saw he was in a smallish room packed with men, some sitting up, some standing, some laying and not moving, some completely covered with blankets and some not.

Further away at the top end of the room a yellow light played over a knot of officers and sailors, all looking down at something.

Sitting up very slowly, he had to close his eyes again to stop the room swaying. The sound that made him open his eyes came from the knot of men at the end of the room. It was the sound of crying and soon the sound swelled to fill the room and then Cooke heard the dread words he would never forget.

"Lord Nelson is dying".

As the realisation swept from through the crowded room, one by one those men who could do so rose from their sick beds to inch closer to where the great man lay.

Will, his pain forgotten, was helped to his feet by someone he never saw and, being the smallest in the room, managed to squeeze close to the scene.

What he saw broke his heart. In the dim light cast by a cluster of Purser's Glims held by members of the crew, Will could see Lord Nelson.

He had been stripped of his uniform - the very uniform Will had helped him into that morning - but which now lay in a bundle at his feet, his nakedness covered by a large signal flag, a 'Blue Peter', ironically a flag used to signal a ship was about to leave port.

The Admiral's body was propped up and lying half on his side. Will could see Captain Hardy standing, looking down over the scene. *Victory's* Chaplain Doctor Scott knelt on one side of the Admiral, his eyes closed in prayer, while the ship's purser Mr Burke, knelt on the other side, crying unashamedly.

Surgeon Beatty was examining his Lordship, and even as Will watched the surgeon stood up, bowed he head, and quietly declared that Lord Nelson was dead. Then he knelt and lifted the Blue Peter to cover the Admiral's face. Crouching next to the body was Will's mentor, William Chevaillier, Lord Nelson's private steward, and spying Will peeping out from the edge of the light, Chevaillier signalled him to come nearer. Will crawled close and the valet gently laid his hand on the lad's shoulder.

No one said a word.

5 The death of Nelson and the birth of a legend.
Engraving by William Hullard after A Davis.
The Wellcome Collection.

Chapter Two

Old Cookie had finished speaking for several minutes before Haynes could utter a word. He had long since stopped writing and was sitting open-mouthed at the story he had just heard.

"You fought on the Victory and were with Nelson when he died?" he asked incredulously.

"That's Lord Nelson to you" Cooke bristled.

Haynes almost bristled in return. He was one of a new generation, born in Australia and proudly calling himself Australian and, as a journalist, agitating for the colony to become the independent country of Australia. In later years he would go on to become a member of parliament and a tireless advocate, not only of an independent Australia, but also of the rights of the Australian working man, campaigning against the privileges the British upper class had brought with them to Australia.

But he recognised this was not the time to push his own views.

"I beg your pardon. I meant no disrespect, it's just that... that. Well, that is such a fantastic story. In fact, it is one of the most fantastic stories I have ever heard. How is it that no one else has ever told me this? Do other people know this about you?"

Cooke was quiet, clearly considering what he was to say.

"No. No one knows. Only my family, and they are sworn to secrecy."

"But why?" insisted the reporter before once again knowing he had crossed a boundary when Cooke gave him a blistering look.

"Once again Mr Cooke" he said - himself missing the change in his mindset that had transformed 'old Cookie' into 'Mr Cooke' - "I mean no disrespect, but this is a remarkable story and one that the good people of Morpeth, and indeed of Australia, would love to hear.

"In fact, I think it's a story they NEED to hear. That a good solid citizen such as yourself, who once sailed with Nelson and knew the great man, is here in Morpeth. That shows so clearly the kind of people who live in this great new land called Australia."

Cooke said nothing. In his mind the phrase 'good solid citizen' echoed. 'Am I a good solid citizen' he asked himself. 'What dare I tell this young man? What would he say - what would he write - if I told him my story? My whole story? What if everyone knew what I really am?'

Being a good reporter, Haynes had let the silence stretch on, hoping the tension created by the silence would lead to Cooke saying more, but the old man kept his tongue and Haynes was the first to break.

"Can I ask, Mr Cooke, how did it all come about? How did you get to be on the Victory and how did you know Nelson, sorry, Lord Nelson, so well?"

Cooke was quiet for a long minute. "Do you have the time for this Mr Haynes, because if I am going to tell you the story, and you are going to tell everyone else the story, it needs to be told properly and it's a long story. A long, long story." In reply Haynes merely smiled, picked up his pencil and poised it over his journal.

Burnham Thorpe. Norfolk
August 1801

"For a time, when I was but a boy, my family lived at Burnham Thorpe, in Norfolk, at the parsonage of the Reverend Edmund Nelson and it was through the intervention of the Reverend - one of the finest men I have ever met" Cooke said, looking fiercely at the journalist, daring him to disagree - "that I eventually came to know his son, Lord Admiral Horatio Nelson."

Old Cookie said he never learnt exactly why he ended up at Burnham Thorpe along with his mother, his sister Ann and brother Tom, to live with 'uncle' Abraham - at least that is what Cooke called the man who had served the Reverend for many years - though what his actual relationship to his mother was he never really understood.

"I never found out what had happened to my father or why he wasn't with us," he said. "Whenever I asked, my mother just refused to talk about it, so eventually I just stopped asking. She said the family came from a place far to the south called Bishops

Waltham, in Hampshire, but for some reason when I was just a child we moved to Bristol.

"We lived in Bristol for a time and I remember my father used to go to work every day and mother stayed home. I played with other kids in a little alley between a group of houses where everyone knew everyone. Then one day my father didn't come home. Not that night, nor the next nor the one after that. He just disappeared and no one knew what had happened. My mother and brother went out looking for him day after day, but they never found him.

"One day he was there and we were a family, then the next day he was gone and never returned. Looking back I think he was probably taken by the press gang - it happens all the time. I know that now, but back then I was just a child and no one told me anything."

Growing up in the rural backwater of Burnham, the young Will loved nothing better than to sneak away from his main chore of tending the Glebe - the Reverend's private land by right of his tenure of the parsonage - to go fishing in the nearby river Burn or hunt waterbirds and rabbits in the woods, fens and the multitude of creeks and streams in the area - haunting the same fishing spots and secret boy places that Lord Nelson may well have found in his youth many years earlier.

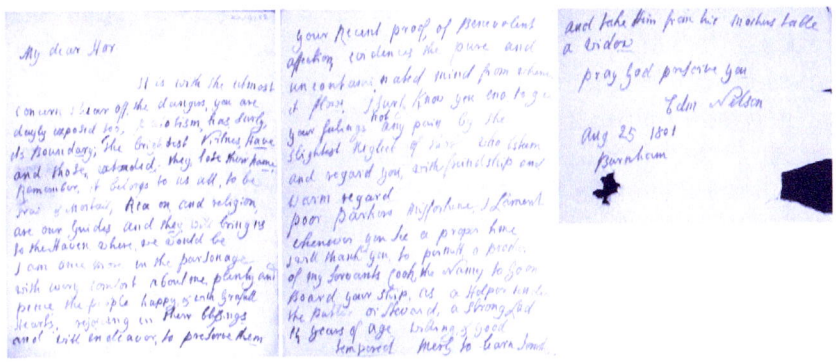

6 *Letter from Rev. Edmund Nelson to his son Admiral Nelson, pleading with 'my dear Hor' to find a place for Will aboard his ship. Phillips-Croker Collection. Caird Library. British Museum.*

He was about the age boys were expected to head out to make their own way in the world, but for a lad with no connections and no family, the chances of success were small, and that is when fate first stepped in to change Will's life.

Approached for help by Will's mother, who assisted the elderly Reverend, he wrote to his already famous son, newly appointed Admiral of the Blue, asking if he could find a place for young Will. After expressing his concern for the dangers his son faced and wishing him well, he interceded on behalf of the young lad, the transcription of the key passage reading:

"... I will thank you to permit, a brother of my Servants Cook the Nanny to Go on board your ship, as a Helper under the public, or Steward, a strong lad 11, years of age willing and good tempered verily to learn something and take him from his mothers table a widow.
Pray God preserve you
Edm Nelson. Aug 25 180.
Burnham"

The letter had been addressed simply to *"Viscount Nelson. Deal"* and when it finally reached Nelson it could not have arrived at a worse time because the Admiral was being almost overwhelmed by crises both public and private. Nelson had retreated to the port of Deal to handle the consequences of a rare failure, a disastrous failed attack on the French port of Boulogne which left his force of 'fencibles' decimated and dispirited. At the same time he was in the final throes of leaving his dutiful but dull wife Frances in favour of the notorious courtesan and 'actress' Emma Hamilton, who was unfortunately still married to and living with Sir William Hamilton, the eccentric British ambassador to the Kingdom of Naples. To further complicate the matter Sir William was a good friend of Nelson's.

The Admiral had rescued Sir William and Lady Emma from a deadly rebellion in the Kingdom of Naples and the odd trio had been together ever since.

The explicitly illicit love affair between the naval hero and the married and reformed courtesan, conducted in the open and with the apparent knowledge and possibly even contrivance of the cuckolded husband, was the scandal and the talk of British society, high and low alike. After first missing Nelson when he transferred from the

Medusa, his father's letter was finally delivered into his hands aboard the frigate *Amazon*, and it presented him with yet another conundrum he did not need. He not seen his father for some time but, knowing the Reverend was ill, perhaps deathly ill, he desperately wanted to do so.

He also wanted his father to meet and approve of his relationship with his lover Emma, but at the same time was well aware that, together with much of his family, the Reverend strongly disapproved of his relationship with a married woman, especially given the Admiral himself was also still married!

The final complication of this convoluted dilemma was that Nelson's wife Frances was both loved and admired by the Reverend and she in turn doted on the old man and spent much of her time caring for him.

Even though he was worshipped by the common people of Britain as a fighting Admiral and a war hero, Lord Nelson nevertheless needed and sought the approval of his father.

The rift between them was a raw wound he desperately needed to heal.

It was all devilishly complicated, but as he did with most of the complicated situations he had encountered in his life, Nelson determined to confront the problem head on. He wrote to his father saying he would do all he could to help the boy and suggested that his father should visit him at his new home, Merton, near Wimbledon just outside London, and to bring the boy so he could meet him - adding that he only expected to be back at the mansion late in October.

The shrewd tactician then enclosed the letter to his father inside a letter he wrote to Emma Hamilton, who with her husband was living at Nelson's country estate of Merton, near Wimbledon, just outside London. In the letter to Emma he explained that he 'could not say less' to his father than offer to have the boy stay at Merton while he tried to find the lad a suitable post As a sop to his fun-loving mistress, who he knew was dreading meeting his father, he told her his father would then have to visit Merton as *her* guest, thus putting her in a dominant position, an option he believed Emma would find difficult to refuse.

He wrote that, after reading his letter to his father, if she agreed, she should on-post his father's letter to him at Burnham Thorpe.

During October 1801 Nelson and Emma exchanged letters discussing his tangled relationship with his father. Nelson then received a letter from him dated October 8th in which the Reverend asked his son outright *"where it is likely your generall (sic) place of residence may be"* which Nelson rightly saw as his father trying to divide him from Emma, to who he wrote saying the letter had "hurt me."

For Emma the battle lines with the Reverend had now been drawn.

Nelson, trapped in the middle, wrote to Emma he was thinking of replying to say he *"shall live at Merton with Sir William and Lady Hamilton"*, and there would always be *"a warm room and cheerful society"* for his father there. Referring to young Cooke, Nelson wrote to his father saying; *"the boy will come of course,"* possibly to tempt the Rev. to also visit.

Confident in his ability to control the situation, he felt if he could just get the two together Emma would charm his father, allowing him the chance to convince the old gentleman that the love that he had for Emma was real and thus honourable, dissipating the tension between the strictly conventional Reverend and his totally unconventional son. Deep down he knew his plan amounted to playing with fire and that if it all went wrong, mollifying his irate lover would be much harder than dealing with a French invasion.

The Reverend was equally trapped between his love and regard for his son and his distaste for the 'liaison' - for that is the word he used to describe it - with Mrs Hamilton. Torn between wanting to see his son, but not his son's lover, in the end the Reverend bowed to the reality of a situation beyond his control and accepted the invitation, with a caveat.

On November 2nd he wrote back to Lord Nelson saying that he would visit him and Lady Hamilton *"before taking up my winter residence at Bath"*, but added his journey to London would be *"very slow, not only due to infirmities, but by necessary and pleasing visits with my children, whose kindnesses are a cordial for an age such as few parents can boast of."*

A few days later the Reverend and Will, the boy carrying all of his meagre possessions in a sack, stood beside a dusty road in Norfolk waiting for the mail coach. The Reverend felt he had to accompany the boy to the coach stop because his mother had stayed away, fearing she would break down and add to the anxiety of the moment, but like any mother she had done her best to send her boy away looking as good as she could manage.

Will was wearing a pair of corduroy breeches tied at the knee and strapped to a tight fit around his waist. The breeches weren't new, but had been cunningly repaired so as no one would know their secret. Beneath a light linen blue jacket he wore a collarless white shirt, also second-hand, while atop his unruly mop of sun-bleached hair he wore a cloth cap she had sewn herself. His most important piece of apparel was a pair of new lace up boots which had been supplied by the Reverend. They were the first that Cooke had worn, let alone owned, and they were already chafing the back of his heels and tops of his toes beyond tolerance. All too soon the coach arrived, four big horses thundering down the main street before coming to a stop in a shower of flying lather and dust that scattered bystanders. The arrival of the mail coach was still a novel and exciting event in many places in Norfolk and a crowd had turned out to welcome it.

The coach itself was a vision of shiny splendour, its upper parts painted black, while the lower panels were maroon and the wheels red. Each coach featured the royal coat of arms embossed in gold paint on the doors, along with the title 'Royal Mail'. Each had its own unique number, embossed in gold paint on the back boot. The driver wore a fine scarlet coat and black top hat while on the back boot stood a Post Office guard, also dressed in a black hat, but with a gold band and a scarlet coat with blue lapels and gold braid.

Of more interest to the boys gathered around was that he carried two pistols tucked into a red sash covering his considerable girth, atop which rested a blunderbuss. Before the boy climbed aboard the Reverend placed his hand on his shoulder.

"Alright my son, now be off and don't be worrying. I have written to 'Hor' and he has promised he will find a place for you. And I will see you soon. Be sure to be a good lad and do as my son bids.

"You are not a bad lad, though a bit on the adventurous side, and you must learn to curb that. I strongly bid you listen to what you are told.

"Do what you are told. Do your duty. Do your best at all you do.

"Trust your fate to the Lord and all will be well."

The boy looked around again and again for his mother, but she was nowhere to be seen. Looking up at the Reverend tears began to well up despite him trying as hard as he could to stop them. Soon they were rolling down his cheeks and deep sobs escaped from his chest.

"Where is mother?" he sobbed. "Why doesn't she want me anymore? I promise I will be good and go to school an ..." Desperate to avoid a scene he had neither control over or desire for, the Reverend bent down and gently shook the boy by the shoulders.

"Now, now, my boy, enough of that. A time comes in each boy's life where he has to take those first steps to manhood by himself. My own son did it at your age, as did I, and now it is your time to do so. There is nothing else to be done for it. Your mother loves you and, ah ... wishes you well. I am sure she will soon be in touch. OK, off you go and fare thee well."

Mother and son never saw each other again.

The coach to London normally bypassed Lord Nelson's newly acquired love nest by a few miles, but in part awed by the Nelson name and in part out of sympathy for his clearly bewildered young passenger, the driver made a detour past the home of the most famous man in Britain.

Merton sat in solitary splendour in a quiet rural setting eight miles East of London. The road to the mansion meandered through villages and fields below the forested area known as the Wimbledon Common. As it neared Merton the coach eased to a trot passing the track that turned off to the corn mill perched beside the River Wandle, then slowed to a walk past Cowdrey's Lane and down to the rickety bridge spanning the Wandle, giving everyone a good view of Admiral Nelson's house on a rise on the other side.

Merton was a fine, doubled-story red brick building featuring a triangular pediment over a portico linking into one what had originally been two separate buildings. Large urns sat atop the points where the pediment and the two buildings met, while statues scattered about the grounds and a small lake near the house gave the estate a Greco-Roman appearance.

7 Merton Place circa 1800. Copperplate engraving by Edward Hawke Locker. Wikimedia Commons.

To a young lad from country Norfolk, Merton seemed the perfect palace to house Britain's hero, but neither the driver or passengers - cynical Londoners used to far more striking structures - were impressed and didn't bother hiding their disappointment.

The driver quickly turned the coach and thundered off, leaving the lad clutching his sack before the imposing main gates and high brick wall which ran the length of the property.

Will walked slowly - crept might be a better description - to the main gate and, peering cautiously through the surrounding foliage, saw a short circular drive leading up to the front of the house.

After a few minutes, losing his caution, he stepped out, standing spellbound, but was soon torn from his reverie when two members of the garden staff hailed the lad, one jogging down waving and shouting to send the unwanted visitor packing.

Only the intervention of Sir William Hamilton saved Will from a hasty ending to his first adventure into independence. Sometime beforehand Sir William had been informed in a casual aside by his wife that the lad was on his way, and as luck would have it he was walking down the drive, fishing rod in hand to try out a new fishing hole when he witnessed Will being chased away and divined immediately what was happening.

He shouted to the gardener to run after the boy and bring him back at once, but Will had set off down the road like Napoleon himself was after him, stopping only briefly to shuck his new shoes. It took almost half an hour for the gardener to catch up to the runaway and convince him to return.

Back at Merton Sir William managed to calm the lad, but having calmed him and ushered him through the gates, had no idea of what to actually do with him. His confusion didn't last long, he was after all a patrician and thus adept at ordering things to be done, so he simply handed the problem to the gardeners to arrange a bed for him and then continued on his way. Unfortunately Merton had no functioning servants quarters at the time, the servants living on neighbouring farms. Neither Nelson nor Lady Hamilton were at Merton – his Lordship occupied in the channel fighting the French, while Mrs Hamilton was in London pining for his return, but still managing to party most nights. Left to his own devices Will bunked down on a bed of hay in a disused dairy and, ignored by everyone, in the coming days did what he liked to do best, which was explore his surroundings.

The quick flowing River Wandle backed onto the Merton property and Will soon discovered it was a fine place to fish. Local boys rarely fished the Wandle because, while it wasn't exactly illegal, it was frowned upon by the local gentry. Being a newcomer Will was ignorant of such restrictions and being a country boy, he always carried a roll of fishing twine and some hooks in his bag and within a day had found a number of fine fishing holes.

Downstream of Merton was a dye factory so there was little fishing to be had there, the water being full of chemicals. Upstream there were a number of flour mills where mill wheels had gouged deep holes where fish loved to congregate to feed off particles of grain washed off the mill stones. Another good spot was beneath the big willow tree on the western side of the river, just upstream of nearby Merton Abbey, but the best spot of all was the mouth of the canal which had been dug from the river to feed an ornamental lake in front of Merton. The river had scoured out the bank downstream of the canal entrance and trout loved to hide under the bank waiting for tasty morsels. A fresh grasshopper dangled over the edge of the bank by a patient boy was a sure recipe for success, and it was at that spot a week after he had arrived that Will bumped into Sir William for the first time since the old gentleman had rescued him. Sir William had completely forgotten the incident and without so much as a 'bye your leave' the elderly patrician simply sat down beside the boy and began to fish.

He soon discovered that his expensive rod and fantastically contrived lures were no match for Will's twine and grasshoppers. Sensing he might be intruding on the old man's territory, Will picked up his few trout and, begging his Lordship's pardon, went back to his dairy bedroom.

Two days later the pair met again, but this time the old man had arrived early and had already caught two fine fish by copying Will's ploy, dangling an expensive imitation of an actual grasshopper, and so was in a friendly mood. Will reminded him of their meeting and told him how he had been sent by the Reverend Nelson. Assured the boy was not a thief or vagabond, the young boy and the old man were soon chatting amiably. The isolated and lonely old aristocratic scholar and the young boy with a knack of catching fish had become, if not friends, then at least friendly, though not friendly enough for the old man to enquire about where Will actually slept or how he survived.

Cooke had also become friendly with a young lad who lived nearby, Henry Lancaster, son of the local Reverend, and it was through Henry that Will met some of the locals who worked at Merton. It was they who had come to the lad's rescue, taking pity on him and inviting him in turns to share what little they had, as those who have very little often do. Once his story became known, local families vied to share their table - Will bringing an exotic touch to their small, unchanging world.

They also felt comfortable speaking to him because he was one of them.

Occasionally the old man would invite the boy to join him for a meal, especially if Will had caught trout and he had not, and it was at one of these quite dinners that the lad dared to raise the issue that had been constantly asked of him by the servants - what was the relationship between Sir William, his wife, and the Admiral?

Rumours of the scandalous relationship had reached even their backwater, and they hoped the unique position Will enjoyed with Sir William might enable him to ask what no one else dared ask. If the worst eventuated and the lad was banished, well, they reasoned, he was expendable.

Will eased into the tricky conversation with all the guile a 12 year old boy possessed.

"M'Lord, how does it happen that Lord Nelson lives here with Lady Hamilton, and also with yourself?"

Minutes passed in silence as Sir William delicately dismembered the fine trout Will had caught that afternoon, seemingly oblivious to the question, sipping away first one goblet of wine and then pouring himself another.

"I suppose it would have been too much to ask that the malicious gossip would not reach out to his idyll," he said, not looking up from his fish.

The ensuring silence lasted a few more minutes, then, when he at last lifted his head to the boy, a great sadness seemed to have come over his face.

"Do you know of the Great Bard young man?" he asked, only to answer his own question; "no, of course not. How could you?"

"William Shakespeare once wrote: *'It's an odd thing, speaking to one so young at a time when I am approaching the end of a long life. When the age is in, the wit is out'*."

"So, near the end of a long life, is it worthwhile even talking? Trying to explain? Especially to one such as you?" he said, looking down at the boy, "but alone here in another man's house and sans my wife, who indeed is there left to talk to?'

"Life is nothing if not strange" he said before again turning quiet, concentrating intently on moving the bones of his fish around his plate. Five minutes later he resumed his monologue.

"Then again, fate creates strange and unforeseen circumstances.

"Do you know I grew up beside the King? It's true" he said, again not waiting for or wanting an answer. "We were even suckled by the same wet nurse, sharing the same tits at the beginning of life, and nearly later, but ... well, treated very differently by fate. I have lived my life in the company of Kings and Queens and the aristocratic, yet now, near the end of my life, I find myself sitting eating fish with a lowly born boy. It's true there is a gulf of years between my wife and I, but that is of no issue. I understood when we married that I should be superannuated when Emma would be in her full beauty and at the height of her not inconsiderable powers.

"So, as to my wife, I know not exactly where she be at this time, but boy let me assure ye of this" he said, pointing a long bony finger at Will, "if she be with my great and good friend Lord Nelson, then she is in good hands, for he is the bravest and best man I have ever met during all my time at dalliance with the royalty of Europe and, mark my words boy, I will not have a bad word said against him."

"He is first and foremost my friend," he said forcefully, mutely daring Will to say a word contrary to his, before lapsing once again into a long silence and pouring himself another goblet of wine."

Will sat dead still, afraid to stay but more afraid to leave.

"Yes my boy, fate takes many a strange turn and I have had my share of turns and then some. Let me leave you with just a few more words of wisdom to ponder, as the Bard put into the mouth of Henry the Eighth; "*Had I but served my God with half the zeal I served my King, he would not in mine age have left me naked to mine enemies'*.""

"So, my young fishing friend, let me give you some advice from one who has gained and lost so much - it all means little in the end. What is vital is to accept what fate offers, be it advance or adverse. Adversity will arrive, be assured, but it must be treated with contempt.

"The only way to beat adversity is to accept it with applause. Turn it on its head my boy and at all times endure and put on a brave face. Endure!"

With that the old man stood slowly, then gracefully turned and left the room. Will sat for a time afterwards, until the lone remaining maid poked her head around the corner to confirm the master was to bed, and quickly shuffle in to clear the dishes.

A week after that strange dinner conversation with Sir William, Lord Nelson and Lady Hamilton arrived at Merton - together.

Then, almost a week later, Reverend Nelson arrived.

A COGNOCENTI contemplating ye Beauties of ye Antique

8 Cartoon by James Gillray lampooning Sir William Hamilton as a cuckold over the scandalous relationship between his wife Emma and Admiral Nelson. Sir William was a noted volcanologist, historian and collector of antiques, so after the manner of the time, Gillray's drawing is littered with historical allusions which poke fun at the old man's predilections.

Will had still not been spoken to by either Emma or Lord Nelson in that time, in large part because Sir William had failed to mention the lad was there before he left on a fishing expedition.

When the Reverend politely enquired how young Will was getting on, both Emma and the Admiral expressed total ignorance of his presence. Servants were hurriedly despatched to find him, after which he was trotted out for inspection.

During his stay he had looked through the large glass doors into the house, but had not dared to step inside. Now standing in the foyer he could see that almost every square inch of every wall in the room and on the walls leading up the staircase were covered in paintings, mostly of Mrs Hamilton staring down at him in the most daring of costumes he quickly turned his eyes from, but also of Lord Nelson dressed in his uniform and scenes of sea battles and ships sailing wind-tossed oceans. He was so engrossed in the spectacle he failed to hear the three adults walk into the foyer.

"I said wake up boy" the Admiral's voice boomed, sending Will into such complete shock that he was struck dumb, unable to utter a word, standing looking down at his bare feet and twisting his hands. Reverend Nelson and Lady Hamilton were standing next to the Admiral, but neither said a word. Up close Lady Emma was a full-figured woman with a double chin and bright red cheeks and lips, dressed in a revealing gown and dripping with jewels.

Given to extravagant movements she was soon 'oohing' and 'aahing' at Will for the benefit of the men, before losing interest and drifting out of the room. The Admiral mumbled something and quickly followed. Left alone with the boy the Reverend looked heavenwards for a moment before placing his hand on Will's shoulder and smiling down at the boy, shook his head slowly.

Then he also turned away and followed his son into the house.

The adults had bigger things to discuss than a mute waif.

All in all the Reverend's long anticipated visit to his son did not go well. Several times during the Reverend's visit the Admiral was called away and during his absences Mrs Hamilton was coldly polite to the Reverend, their conversation stilted at best.

'After all' as she laughed with guests after the disastrous visit had ended, 'I have never had much in common with ministers of religion'.

When Sir William returned he was also not much of a host, at once aloof and disinterested in the presence of the Reverend. He also had absolutely nothing in common with ministers of religion and in other circumstances he would not have even deigned to speak to 'such people.' Soon the Reverend gave up and moved on to the warm waters near Bath, leaving Will with a vague promise that he was sure his busy son would 'no doubt' find a post for the boy as soon as he was able to do so. He left without a word beyond 'goodbye' to the Hamiltons, even more ill at ease with his son's decisions and his personal life than he had been before he had arrived.

In December, shortly after his visit the Reverend again wrote to his son, thanking him for his hospitality before then admonishing him: *"What you possess, my good son, take care of - what you may still want, consult your own good sense in what way it can be attained. Strive for honours and riches that will not fade, but will profit in time of need. Excuse my anxiety for what I esteem your real good."*

The message between the lines could not be clearer. There would be no acceptance of his son's relationship with Mrs and Mr Hamilton. Emma did not waste much time in turning on the boy as a way of getting back at what she saw as the disdain the Reverend had shown in the letter toward her, her lifestyle and her extravagant public displays of affection to his son.

Shortly afterward he left she wrote to the Reverend regarding the actions of the boy she archly noted he had 'left behind' in her charge and to her cost, without so much as a simple 'bye your leave'.

Will had been caught on a neighbouring farm setting snares and fishing in a prohibited pond and had been dragged before her Ladyship by an irate farmer. Sir William did not speak in his defence.

Such an opportunity to hit back could not go unaccepted. Lady Hamilton immediately dashed off a letter to the Reverend plainly expressing her disappointment at the behaviour of the boy he had left behind and asking what the Reverend intended doing about it.

Shortly before Christmas the Reverend wrote back *"... The intelligence you have troubled yourself to communicate to me, respecting the lad Cook, vexes me more than a little, as I am concerned that any act of mine should have given the least anxiety, or for a moment interrrupted the domestic quiet of my good son. The lad's mother must also be very much grieved, and his brother is greatly dissapointed by this rash act ..."*

Apart from that somewhat vague apology, if apology it was, it was clear that the Reverend had washed his hands of the problem.

When Admiral Nelson finally returned home early in 1802, Lady Emma was prepared, accusing the lad of having been planted by the Nelson family to spy on her and demanding he be sent on his way. Exasperated, Nelson sent for Will.

The confused boy was shovelled into the drawing room where the Admiral stood in full uniform, his empty right sleeve tucked into his coat, the other resting on a mantlepiece, his long grey hair hanging in wisps to his collar. To Will he looked like a hawk; his chin jutting forward, his brow furrowed above a narrow nose. Only when the male servant behind him pushed him forward did he realise that Lord Nelson was speaking to him.

"I said come here boy!"

Once again pushed forward, he managed to walk a few steps before coming to a halt. Lady Hamilton sat off to one side, looking at him with an intensity scarier than Lord Nelson's voice. A life spent on the seas dealing with boys such as Will meant Nelson recognised sheer terror when he saw it and his voice softened appropriately.

"Come here boy" he said, "no one is going to hurt you."

Will managed to walk a few more steps, but still stopped well short of the Admiral.

"How long have you been here?"

"I'm not sure my Lord, a few months or so. Maybe ..."

Again his voice failed.

"Call me Sir", Nelson said, once again the Admiral. "I'm sorry I have not been here to welcome you properly as I promised my father, or indeed to deal with you since first we met. It has been a busy time. Do you have a place to sleep? Have you been looked after?"

Will could only nod. Walking forward Nelson placed his hand on the lad's shoulder.

"Alright my boy, be assured I will look to your future in coming days as I have promised my sainted father" he said, looking around to Lady Hamilton as if to indicate he was talking for her benefit as much as Will's. "In the meantime try to stay out of trouble!"

Once again Will could only nod and he was still nodding when the servant guided him towards the door. As he walked he heard Lady Hamilton speak.

"I am sorry my Darling, but he simply cannot stay. There is no doubt he ..." The voice was cut off by the door closing.

Shortly later, in April 1802, the Reverend Nelson died.

Admiral Nelson was bereft with both sadness and guilt, however Lady Hamilton remained convinced the Nelson family was plotting against her and refused to attend the funeral, the sway she held over her lover made evident for the whole world to see when, at her insistence, Admiral Nelson stayed with her at Merton rather than attend the funeral in Norfolk. It was left to the Reverend's faithful servant Abraham Cook to travel to Bath to escort the body back to Burnham Thorpe and to take his son's place as a pall-bearer at the Reverend's funeral.

The Admiral's angst at not being present at his beloved father's funeral, and the increasingly scandalous gossip his absence generated, told on his state of mind and physical health, which had never been robust, while the occasional sight of the young Will, sometimes in the company of Sir William, only helped his guilt to fester.

Some weeks after his father's death the Admiral again summoned Will to the painting-strewn drawing room. The Admiral walked over to the salon window and spent a long time looking out over the lawn which sloped gently down to the imposing front gates. A tide of fear began to rise in Will that he was to be thrown out on the street. Finally the Admiral spoke.

"My good friend Mr Davison has contacted an old friend, Baron Ribblesdale, who has recently launched a merchantman, the *Enchantress*, which will be sailing from Bristol and Plymouth.

"He has promised you a berth on the vessel and I'm assured the captain keep a sea eye on you," Nelson said.

"I'm told it's a fine vessel and 'tis unlikely it will sail far from our shore. Nor will his Lordship need to push hard for profit, so 'tis a perfect first berth for a lad such as yourself."

He turned to look at the boy, silent and seemingly lost in thought for a few long moments, before carrying on.

"I myself was the same age you are now when I first went to sea, and a fine thing it has been. I am sorry that we have not been able to spend as much time together as I had hoped in order to speak with you about my father, but we live in complicated and restless times.

"Be that as it may, my father entrusted me with this task before he died, and I have been remiss in that regard. Seriously remiss. I apologise, but I will now strive to do all in my power to abide by his wishes. My father had good words to say of you, and especially of your mother, who he said had been of great assistance to him in his old age, and so too Abraham.

"I owe your family a debt, a debt of honour, which I here and now undertake in my father's name to pay in full. If, as my father wrote, you are a bright and willing lad, as my good friend Sir William also reports you to be, then all will be well.

"I now make another promise to you - on my father's grave. If in the future you find yourself in need of assistance you may come here, or find me where I may be, and I will do what I can to help you. If perchance I am no longer of this world, you should seek out my good friend Captain Hardy, in who I have confided this matter.

"Before he died my father also bid me to find a post for the most faithful Abraham, a good man who I know well and who has been placed in a difficult situation by my father's death. I promised my father to provide what assistance I could to both Abraham and yourself and I intend to keep that promise, but finding you a safe berth is the best I can do at this difficult time.

"My personal servant Tom Allen will accompany you to Bristol and see you safely aboard *Enchantress*, after that what you make of this opportunity will have to be up to you. I will try to keep abreast of your progress but, as I said, these are strange times."

Placing his hand on his Will's shoulder he said simply "good luck lad," and turned away. The next morning found the hulking Allen and the small boy, struggling under the weight of his bag, trudging the five miles past Poor Wood and Haywards Wood, then down Combe Lane to Kingston, a large village on the Thames from where they would catch a coach to Bristol.

Will had immediately warmed to Allen's thick Norfolk accent and was delighted to learn the two of them actually knew some of the same people who lived in Burnham Thorpe. He felt he might finally have found a friend he could talk to in this big new world he had been cast into, someone who could help him understand where he was going and what was expected of him, especially given Allen was a sailor who had fought beside Lord Nelson.

But he was wrong. Any thought the young boy might have envisioned of making friends with Allen were quickly slapped down when the taciturn, darkly brooding, self-opinionated brute quickly let the boy know that he was the personal servant of Lord Nelson, not a baby-sitter, and as such saw himself as several cuts above the homeless waif Lord Nelson had apparently taken under his wing.

"I'd no be wistin ya breath a tryin ta bring me to ya side youngster" he said after finding it impossible to ignore the lad. "I dout yew'll fit the life aboord ship," he said in his thick Norfolk accent. "If'n yew ax me, yew sholdna be gittin on ta ship, and sholdna be goan ta sea. Dast yew stay abord twil end badly methinks."

"Goan bick ta Burnam boy, there be nowt in ta worl as better as there, take my word." With that he pulled his cap over his eyes and slept, as much was sleep was possible in the springless coach as it rattled over endless ruts and holes toward Bristol. At the ship Allen took pleasure in seeing the look of surprise that came over Captain John Cole's face when he revealed who he was and, more importantly, who had sent him with the boy, before perfunctorily handing Will over and, without a word, turning on his heel and walking away. Cole, an old sea dog now nearing the end of his career, looked down at the boy with a raised eyebrow, but said nothing. He had already received puzzling instructions from the ship's owner Baron Ribblesdale indicating he had a personal interest in the boy, cryptically stressing that the lad should be kept safe but not mollycoddled. He wrote that Cole should teach the lad to be a sailor, adding that if the boy did well it would reflect very well on Cole - and hence him - but warning that should grief befall the boy, it would not do neither of their future lives any good. Cole now divined that it was Lord Nelson himself who had an interest in the very unremarkable looking boy who stood looking up at him.

After handing the lad over to the ships first mate with instructions to see him settled in, Cole stood staring across the water, deep in thought. That a clearly lowly born lad should have the interest of Lord Ribblesdale was intriguing enough, but for Lord Nelson himself - England's most renown hero and the greatest seaman in the world - to have an interest in the boy was beyond comprehension. Casting his eyes upward he slowly shook his head.

"Lord, what have I done to deserve this" he said softly to himself.

Merton May 3rd: 1802

My Dear Davison

I was so unwell yesterday that I forgot to mention a thing in which I want your assistance. I want the Chairman of the East India Compy: to give Abraham Cook my fathers faithful servant (out of livery) a place about their Warehouses of 50£ a year. He is a sober respectable man abt 40 years of age or 35 perhaps, writes an excellent hand and understands accounts. I have promised my Dear father to use all my interest with the Chairman to procure such a place, and to fullfill that promise sooner come upon me than I expected I must beg the interest of my friends. Will you see the Chairman and ask him if he will allow me to ask the favour of him. I am ever my Dear Davison

Yours Most Truly

Nelson & Bronte

My Dear Davison

Many thanks for your goodness abt: Abram & My Good Man Mr Thompson. I wished Lord Mulgrave & some more of the speakers at the Devil.   They know nothing of the Subject as far as Malta & the

9 Two letters written by Nelson written in May, 1802, shortly after his father's death, asking his friend and agent Alexander Davison for help in repaying his 'debt of honour' to the Cook(e) family. In the first, written on May 3rd, Nelson asks Davison to contact the Chairman of the powerful East India Company to find a position for Abraham Cook, his father's servant of long-standing. The power of the Nelson name is illustrated when just a week or so later Nelson was able to write and thank Davison for his success.
Nelson: The New Letters. Colin White.

Chapter Three

It took a few minutes for Haynes to finish writing his notes after Old Cookie had stopped speaking. As he waited for the journalist to finish his work, the old man grew more than a little concerned at the scribbles, wriggles, lines and question marks Haynes had scattered over his journal in between gulps of rum. To Cooke they didn't appear resemble anything like a true rendition of the story he had just told.

When Haynes finished, the first thing the journalist did was lift his hand to James for another two rums before turning to the old man with a bemused look on his face.

"Well, you most certainly have had your share of luck on your incredible journey it seems to me. It most certainly is a long way from Hampshire to Norfolk. And to end up at the parsonage of Nel ... I mean Lord Nelson's father, well it's incredible. Did you realise that you were literally treading in the footsteps of Britain's most famous hero as you wandered the fens around Burnham?"

Old Cookie pondered a moment before answering.

"Well, to tell the truth of it, I had never heard of Lord Nelson until it was time to leave Burnham, so while our different journeys would most certainly have crossed the same paths, there were many years between those crossings" the old man said, pausing at the end for a sip of rum. Looking across the table, Cookie noted an odd smile on Haynes' face.

"What!" he demanded.

"Well, I was just wondering what you got up to at Merton that led to your being packed off to sea" Haynes chuckled.

"I'll wager it was more of a lark than pocketing the fruit we used to pilfer from your farm."

Beneath his full beard Cookie had to smile.

"I don't wager" was all he offered in return.

"I must admit I am intrigued by your stay at Merton in the midst of the most famous love affair of the time. What was Lady Hamilton like?" He paused, considering his next question. *"Do you believe her husband knew of the liaison?"*

Cookie's cold stare was all Haynes received in reply, so he shrugged and moved on.

"So you actually spent time on another vessel before joining Victory."

"How did that come about?"

"Well, t'was actually a few ships. Like most of my life, the journey had many twists and turns" the old man replied testily. *"And at the end I hope that you can make sense of it from all those strange marks you are making in your journal."*

Enchantress
1802

The Enchantress was everything that Lord Nelson said it would be - clean, new and a safe haven for a young boy with no knowledge of the sea. A modest 80 footer of 175 tons built at Ringmore to ply the coastal trade along the south of England, it was the perfect berth for a lad to learn the ropes - literally - and give Cooke a taste for the sea.

Captain Cole's confusion about what to do with the lad grew when a few days after the lad's arrival he found the time to speak to Will, who had no knowledge of who the Baron was. However it took but a few questions to tease out the lad's connection to Admiral Nelson.

"So, you'll be saying that you grew up at the parsonage of the Reverend Nelson and that you have come 'ere straight from Admiral Nelson's 'ome at Merton?"

Will could only nod, again scared speechless. The brutal farewell of Allen had left him cowered, unsure what was expected of him and scared that if he was thrown off the ship he would be alone. He stood still, fighting back the tears that welled behind his closed eyes.

Cole, looking down on the clearly petrified lad, could only assume the boy was a pawn in a game neither he nor the lad knew anything about.

Perplexed but resigned, he put Will to work doing the same as the few other boys on board, which was whatever he was told by whoever told him to do it and wearing the clip about the ear that quickly came his way if he dared hesitate or complain.

Despite the inauspicious beginning to his life on the water, the serious lad soon won over the small crew with his sharp eye and quiet way. The words of the Reverend Nelson indelibly printed in his brain, Will applied himself to learning all he could about seamanship, but one aspect of the trade stood out - carpentry. In the age of wood and canvas the ship's carpenter was a man of particular importance, someone who would be called up to carry out everything from replacing masts or spars taken away in a storm to remodelling the captain's cabin.

The carpenter aboard *Enchantress* was Tom Hobbes, universally known as 'old Tom', and he had the job because he had been instrumental in the construction of the *Enchantress* at the small Ringmore shipyard.

At its launch, seeing his creation slip sweetly into the water, riding high and dead even, Tom decided on the spur of the moment he had had enough of a boring life in a small town and took on the job of ship's carpenter.

Hobbes had worked his way around the world, stopping off wherever he was wont, enticed ashore by a pretty face or the chance to learn more about his craft. As he was fond of saying; 'if there be anything I don't know about ships, I don't know it'.

He had become a skilled shipwright and Will was drawn to the old man and his enthralling tales like a moth to a flame, spending every spare moment in the alcove that passed for a carpenter's workshop.

Old Tom thrived on the adulation, normally there wasn't much of it going around, and Captain Cole was more than happy to allow the lad to spend his time in the carpenter's workshop.

It kept the boy out of his way, kept him safe, and provided a young back to help Old Tom.

Hobbes taught Will the tricks and tools of his trade, while the boy saved the old man's legs by running, fetching and carrying.

10 Enchantress at anchor in the River Dart shortly after being purchased by the Royal Navy. Original painting by Charles Martin.

Will might well have served his days out as a coastal seaman and gone on to become a ship's carpenter himself had not another event occurred that had major repercussions on his life.

"I had been aboard *Enchantress* a year or so when word went around that the ship had sailed its last voyage and was to be sold to the navy as a store ship" Will recalled to Haynes.

"My time on *Enchantress* was one of the best times of my life. Captain Cole was a good man who treated me, and all of the crew, very well.

"We moved cargo around the ports of the south of England and I learnt a lot about sailing, but the ship had also sat in port a lot, so I suppose it lost money for the owners and selling it to the navy made sense, but most of the crew were furious.

"Most said the last thing they wanted was to be on a navy ship that not only paid lower wages but also went nowhere.

"Old Tom, he said he'd had enough and was leaving. I didn't know what to do. His lordship had sent me there and I thought I shouldn't just leave without his word, but I didn't want to stay on a ship that just sat, doing nothing.

"I remember Old Tom sayin' to me that he had always followed the call of adventure and because I had my whole life in front of me I should get my adventuring done while I was still young, but that was easy for him to say.

"We were in Plymouth and just across the way a new navy frigate had just been launched and about to go on its first 'shakedown' voyage. Most of the crew just went across to the ship - the *Pallas* - and were signed on because the ship was having trouble meeting muster.

"There was no place for a boy like me, but my friend James Parker - the *Enchantress*' bo'sun - he liked me and managed to smuggle me aboard and hid me 'til the ship sailed.

"The Captain at that time, Lieutenant Laurence I recall he was, he was furious but there was nothing to be done and besides, his wife was aboard and she took pity on me and so I stayed aboard for that cruise, but as soon as we docked a new captain arrived, Cochrane his name was and he made no bones about it - he did not need me and so I was put ashore.

It was then the words of Admiral Nelson came back: 'If in the future you find yourself in distress, you may come back here and I will do what I can,' he had said.

"I was sure the Admiral had meant it when he said it, but it was a year later and so might have forgot? Still, the words were the only beacon I had."

Defiance 1803

Emerging from Merton's front doors in animated conversation with a knot of officers, the Admiral initially didn't see Will until the lad jumped to his feet, swiped off his cap and addressed his Lordship in a suitably nautical manner.

Nelson instantly recognised the lad but, if truth be told, was not pleased to see him.

He instantly divined that whatever had brought the lad to his door must certainly be related to the promise he had made the year before, but at this particular time the lad was a problem he did not need. Having not long returned to Merton after having been promoted Vice Admiral of the Blue, and informed privately that the war with France - on hold the past few months would inevitably soon re-ignite - he was engaged with issues far beyond whatever problems a young boy might have. Questioned brusquely, Will held his ground, a different lad from the tongue-tied one the Admiral had sent off to his fate over a year before.

He quickly told of the sale of *Enchantress* and of his short time on the *Pallas*. All the Admiral could do was sigh. Whatever his own concerns, the promise made to his father shortly before his death the previous year still hung across his shoulders like a dead weight, despite having managed to find a position for Abraham Cook. The Admiral's decision was, as usual, quickly made.

"I understand your position and, as I promised I will do what I can - when I can - but unfortunately that time is not now. For the moment you must stay here until I order otherwise. I have a growing list of lads to find places for and to do so will take time."

Turning to the housekeeper behind him he motioned her forward.

"See to it the lad is fed and has a place to stay, and see to it he is gainfully employed and not left to wander or get into mischief again. I will see to his future as soon as possible."

With that he swept into the waiting coach and was gone in a swirl of dust.

"Nice to see you again young Will" said the woman, whose face he remembered, though not her name.

"I'll be lookin' forward to hearing of your adventures" she smiled, "but for the moment let's get you settled and then I'll call the gardener and put you to work. Don't want you getting' up to mischief again."

Time dragged during Will's second stay at Merton. Confined to the estate and kept drearily busy in the garden, he felt like a prisoner after the freedom and adventure of life aboard *Enchantress*.

Admiral Nelson, pressed for time, quickly handed the problem of finding a berth for Will and a few other boys he had promised to help to his good friend and confidante Captain Thomas Masterman Hardy who in turn managed to secure Will a place on the *Defiance*.

When Captain Philip Durham received the short note from Hardy telling him of Admiral Nelson's 'interest' in Cooke and asking if he could help, he was more than happy to assist. He had only been given command the 74 gun ship of the line *Defiance* that April as it was undergoing a major refit at Portsmouth.

"Amphion, Portsmouth Harbour, January 20th, 1803.

"My Lord,

"The Amphion is to be paid off in a few days, and I shall be happy to take the youngsters your Lordship wrote to me about. Young Bulkeley continues to behave very well, and I have no doubt but he will make a very good officer. I have not the least idea what is to become of us, but shall always be proud to follow your Lordship, in whatever part of the world I may be in, should the country call for your Lordship's services again. I will trouble your Lordship to make my best compliments to Sir William, Lady Hamilton, and all friends at Merton. I have the honour to be, with the greatest respect,

"Your Lordship's obliged,
"very humble servant,
"T. M. HARDY."

11. Will Cooke arrived on Nelson's Merton doorstep looking for help early in 1803, giving Nelson another problem he did not need. The war with France was on hold and the newly promoted Vice Admiral Nelson was both shipless and landbound. Unable to help Cooke himself he did what Admirals do - he delegated - passing the problem on to his friend and colleague Captain Thomas Masterman Hardy. Having no doubt the Nelson name would open any door, Hardy immediately replied he would certainly help, while in the same note subtly reminding his influential friend he also needed a berth."
- Memoirs of the Life of Vice-Admiral Lord Viscount Nelson. Volume 2. Thomas Pettigrew. 1849.

Now, with war looming, he was struggling to fill her complement because so many tars had been prematurely dismissed when the armistice with France was signed just six months before - not that there was any leeway to refuse a request that originated from Nelson himself.

It had been August that Will was given some money and a letter from his Lordship addressed to Durham and sent on his way. In Portsmouth a sailor pointed out the massive ship, her decks swarming with men loading supplies and he stood for a long time watching the frenzied activity, Nelson's letter clutched in his hand and his few remaining coins jingling in his pocket. Finally, seeing a time when the bustle lessened, he gathered the courage to walk up and hand the creased letter to a guard - luckily one who could read - who immediately called an officer and Will had found his new home.

"Captain Durham was a Scot who did not suffer fools gladly" Old Cookie recalled. "In fact, I don't think he suffered anyone gladly. He ruled the ship with an iron hand, not sparing the lash."

After reading the letter Durham wasted no time dragging the story of his connection to Admiral Nelson and his life with the Reverend Nelson out of the boy - quickly understanding the boy's position and his own opportunity. Summoning the quartermaster Mr Brown, he ordered him to take Will under his direct charge, telling him privately the boy had the 'interest' of Admiral Nelson and to make sure that no harm whatsoever befell the lad. As an afterthought he told Brown to secure him a place to sleep next to the midshipman's mess where he could keep an eye on him.

"That was the start of two years aboard *Defiance*" Old Cookie explained. "Two years of hard work and boredom". In the next two years all *Defiance* did was sail up and down the channel. The letter from Lord Nelson had got me a berth, but it put me in a difficult position because no one knew quite what to do with me. The story of my connection to Lord Nelson had soon reached below decks, and I took a few poundings for it from the mids."

Seeing the puzzled look on the journalist's face the old man explained that the most difficult members to deal with on any Navy ship were the midshipmen, young men well above being a sailor but not yet an officer, a difficult situation made worse because many came from aristocratic families and were destined for bigger and better careers. Midshipmen could terrorise sailors who were required to treat them as the officers they would become, while officers were required to subject them to navy discipline - a discipline tempered by the knowledge that today's unruly young mid might well one day end up being their commanding officer.

Being neither sailor or mid, fish nor fowl, Will was largely to his own devices and so sought out the ship's carpenter, William Caught, telling him of the knowledge he had gained aboard *Enchantress* with 'Old Tom' Hobbes. As luck would have it, Will Caught knew Old Tom, as did most men in their small world, and he decided that if

Old Tom thought the youngster was alright, who was he to disagree, and put him to work.

Late one evening as Will slumped sleeplessly in a dark corner of the midshipman's mess he noticed someone sneak quietly to the hammock of Midshipman Dott, who was on watch. The shadowy figure rifled through the sea chest Dott had carelessly left unlocked, lifting what seemed to be the notebook that contained Dott's teachings. Midshipmen were required to undergo instruction in subjects such as navigation, mathematics and so on in order to pass tests to become full officers. The tests were not easy and were not taken lightly and so mids kept careful notes in notebooks. Competition for promotion was fierce and many of the officer candidates engaged in whatever tactics they could to seek preferment, especially among those who were not members of the aristocracy who - naturally - were promoted first.

The thief, who Will recognised as the aristocratic James Williamson, secreted the notebook beneath a locker where it might easily be argued it could have fallen, but where at the same time no one would easily find it. Will knew Dott as one of the older midshipmen, a flame-haired Scot with a muscular rangy build and a quick temper. None of the other 'mids' liked the rough-tongued Scot, but none dared advertise the fact. The next morning Dott, due for an examination later that day, was beside himself with anger and angst when he could not find the book vital for the final cram session.

As he raged around the midshipman's berth's everyone decided the safest cause of action was to leave the wild-eyed Scotsman well alone.

When Dott's rage subsided a little, Will carefully told him what he had seen and led him to the treasured notebook. Dott grabbed him by the collar and angrily demanded on threat of a good beating that he tell who had secreted the book. Will begged him not to force such an admission, pleading that for him to open implicate a Mid without proof would surely lead to his death, a fact Dott grudgingly accepted - provided Will told him privately who was responsible. Dott passed his test and Will won, if not a friend, then a potential protector.

12 Ship's Muster, HMS Defiance, 1803. The muster records William Cook of Bishops Waltham, age 15, joining the crew on September 3, 1803 - a late addition to the other boys who had joined months beforehand.

HMS Victory

By early September 1805 *Defiance* had seen two years of service in and around the channel blockading the French ports and transporting supplies, all while being battered by some of the world's worst seas - and it showed. *Defiance* and its crew were badly in need of rest and repair and the ship was ordered home for an extensive refit.

For Captain Durham the forced docking came at a significant time. His career had stalled; there was no prize money coming in to better his difficult financial position and it seemed as if the war with France was rushing to a final outcome sooner rather than later. With his ship in dry dock for what looked like an extended stay, he headed to the Admiralty to talk to the powers that be about what his future held - when fate unexpectedly brought him face-to-face with that future. As he passed time in the infamous Admiralty waiting room along with an odd collection of half-pay officers looking for posts and businessmen and grifters looking for preferment, a short, rather dapper officer wearing the uniform of a Rear Admiral emerged from the interior.

Even though the pair had exchanged letters, they had never met, however the missing right arm, the rather odd looking right eye and the dazzling array of medals on his chest immediately identified Lord Nelson. Without hesitation Durham stepped forward, careful not to offer his right hand.

"Your Lordship, Captain Phillip Durham of *Defiance* at your service."

His mind still on just completed conversations ringing in his head, it took a moment before the Admiral reacted, then he stepped forward, a smile on his face and his left hand extended.

"Of course, so good to meet you at last. How are you?"

Pleasantries over and done with, Durham immediately launched into the plea he had formulated the instant he had caught sight of Nelson.

"My Lord, good fate has contrived to put me before you this day. I hear that you are soon to sail to confront the French and I entreat you to allow *Defiance* to join your fleet."

The Admiral didn't hesitate.

"I would be honoured to have you Sir, but my understanding is that *Defiance* is scheduled for a refit and headed for drydock even as we speak. I am sorry your ship is not ready to sail, as I would have been very glad to have you."

Durham didn't hesitate.

"My Lord, ask Lord Barham to place me under your Lordship's orders and both ship and I will be ready, I assure you."

Admiral Nelson could only nod and smile - it was exactly the answer he would have given had he been in the same circumstance.

"Good man! Consider it done. I will arrange for the orders to be drawn up and delivered to you in Portsmouth. Whenever you manage to get your ship into the water, you will join me, and I hope it is in time for battle, if indeed the battle that that devil Napoleon has been avoiding for so long does take place."

As he turned to go, Nelson hesitated and turned.

"I recall that through the good offices of Captain Hardy, some time ago I burdened you with custody of a young lad named Cooke. I did not have time to reveal the reason for that burden at the time, but the fact of the matter is that I owe the lad a debt of honour for his family's service to my late father, a debt Reverend Nelson himself asked me to repay shortly before he died.

"I appreciate your help in the matter. Can I ask, how the lad is progressing, if indeed he is still aboard?"

"He is most certainly still aboard, and doing well I am informed" Durham responded after a brief seconds hesitation to gather his wits because he had long since forgotten about the boy and had no idea whether he was in fact still on *Defiance* or not. The Admiral nodded.

"As I said, it is a matter of honour so I would be pleased, if you do manage to join the fleet, that you would transfer the lad to *Victory* at your earliest convenience. Thank you again."

Two years of hard duty in the English Channel helping to blockade French and Spanish fleets had taken its toll on *Defiance,* but Durham flung himself into the task of refitting the ship with near maniacal fervour, doing whatever had to be done and paying whatever bribe had to be paid because, as he said to all and sundry 'there be no way I will miss this battle - no matter what'.

Within a day the mighty ship was literally swarmed by workers day and night, its three masts were replaced; her rigging repaired or replaced; deck and topsides caulked; guns removed from their carriages and any that needed it were repaired and refitted. Holds were emptied, cleaned and restocked with provisions and tons of powder and shot carefully loaded for the coming battle. In just two weeks a miracle had been wrought and the ship was back in the water, resplendent with a new paint job of black and pale ochre - matching that of the *Victory*.

Rendezvous
October 1805

Almost exactly a month later *Defiance* hove to within a short distance from *Victory* at the fleet's designated rendezvous over the horizon from Cadiz off southern Spain, and when Captain Durham was piped aboard *Victory,* Will was at the tail of the Captain's retinue.

On *Victory's* deck a dapper-looking gentleman dressed in a suit rather than a uniform signalled with a curt nod of his head for Will to come and stand behind him. Will assumed he was a gentleman because he was certainly not a sailor. Telling Will to wait, the suit turned to follow the officers, leaving Will alone to drink in the magnitude and magnificence of the ship which stretched more than 100 feet away from him in both directions. Looking up, the main mast soared up more than twice as high as that, stretching more than 200 feet into the heavens. Everything about the mighty ship was vastly bigger than anything Will could ever have imagined. He had been idle for several hours before Captain Durham emerged onto the quarter deck with a face of thunder, brushing silently past several officers to descend to his cutter. Not knowing what to do, Will did nothing, but shortly afterwards the suited gentleman emerged and signalled for Will to follow him, the pair coming to a halt on the upper gun deck at a double-door way painted light blue and decorated with pink filigree. Stretched out behind him the upper gun deck with its battery of 12-pounder guns stretched away, gleaming black and ominous against their blood-red carriages.

"Well, my young friend," he said, turning to the boy, "his Lordship has ordered me to take charge of you for ze moment. He 'as told me he wishes you be a part of 'ees personal retinue and that I am to be responsible for you, so" he paused, then grasped him by the shoulder, "my name is Chevaillier - William Chevaillier - you will call me Mister Chevallier. I am Admiral Nelson's personal servant and steward. Now, I want you to look at me and listen closely. You are a very lucky young man it seems to me. Maybe you 'ave no idea how lucky."

Will could only nod.

"Ze Admiral wishes to you to be near to him so you will make a place to sleep 'ere", he pointed to a corner of the gun deck near the last of the 12-pounders, jammed beneath a bench and hard up against the wall, "I will organise some bedding and proper clothing for you."

"My 'ammock is 'ere" he said, pointing at a comfortable looking bed slung over the gun.

"Be aware we are at the call of ze Admiral at all times. You understand"?

Again Will nodded.

"It seems as if you will be 'ere for some time. Captain Durham has been ordered to go back to England, so you will not be going back to *Defiance* perhaps."

"Why? What's he done?" asked Will, concerned for his own fate.

Chevaillier shrugged his shoulders.

"I don't know. It seems he has to return to London. Why? I don't know, but I know that the Captain Durham is a very unhappy man right now. He does not want to miss the big battle."

Will nodded his head.

"Zo, you 'av no tongue" the steward said, his blue eyes squinting as he smiled, "I understand. But - and listen carefully my little friend - theez is not a friendly place for you. Ze men who work for the Admiral are very, very, jealous of their places and will not 'elp you in any way - do you understand that?" Will nodded.

"Yes? You understand. Good. If you want anyzing, if you are worried about anyzing, if you hear anyzing you don't like, you will speak to me and me alone. You and I are to be ze Admiral's best friends, Yes? So, stay 'ere, do not go away and I will come back soon."

As Will was to learn, if anything Chevaillier had understated the situation when he said the tight-knitted knot of men who served Nelson were jealously protective of their role and not inclined to share the glory of their exulted posts. Initially there was almost open revolt at the news that a lowly born lad was to join them as part of the Admiral's personal retinue, but that was quickly quashed by the Admiral.

"Gentlemen, this is Will Cooke" Lord Nelson had addressed the members of his close retinue the day after Captain Durham had returned to *Defiance*.

"Before my father died, I promised him I would care for this lad to pay back a debt of honour to his family. It has not been possible for me to keep that promise in recent years, but circumstances have changed and I now intend to honour my word."

Placing his left hand on Will's shoulder – at well under five foot tall the lad was a head shorter than even the diminutive Admiral – Nelson gave it an affectionate shake.

"He knows his way about a ship of war I have been assured, but this role close to me is new to him, so I expect you ALL" he let the emphasis he had put on the work hang in the air to ensure that everyone fully understood his meaning – "especially yourself Mr Chevaillier – to help him as you would help me. That said, he will have work to do and he must do it."

Dismissing the men he turned to the boy, looking down at him with a stern gaze.

"My father said you were a good sound lad and that opinion has been supported by the captains of the ships you have served on, including my good friend Captain Durham.

"After this battle – should I live to see the other side of it – I will attend more to your education and hopefully you will fulfil my father's faith in you. For now, see to your duties with care and do as you are told."

That was the signal for his dismissal and with it Will was left to the none too tender mercies of Nelson's servants. Armed with Lord Nelson's protection he was not abused or harried in any way, but neither was he molly-coddled.

Later on Nelson found the time to introduce Cooke to his good friend and comrade-in-arms, the *Victory's* tall and imposing Captain, Thomas Masterman Hardy, telling him in detail how his debt of honour to the boy's family had been handed to him by his father in recompense for the care given to the Reverend by the boy's mother before his father's death. Hardy had known and admired Nelson's father, and he also knew the special affection his friend and commander had for those odd folk who came from the fens of Norfolk where Nelson had grown up, so the towering Captain also undertook to keep an eye on the lad. It was Hardy who ordered him to also serve as a powder monkey, tending the 12 pounders closest to the cabins of himself and the Admiral, when and if the English squadron should meet their combined Spanish and French enemies. The next morning Will was surprised to see *Defiance* once again range up close to the *Victory* and soon enough the ship's cutter set course for the flagship.

Aboard was Captain Durham, a much happier looking Captain Durham it must be said, than the one who had stormed off the Victory. It was left to Chevaillier to later reveal the cause of Durham's joy.

"Ah, the Captain has worked a ruse to stay and will not return to London," he said, "he 'as told ees Lordship that his orders do not *require* 'im to return, so 'he says 'he must volunteer to return!"

"That is crazy and he will stay to fight an' he is very 'appy, and the Admiral is 'appy, and so," he said, shrugging his shoulders

As unlikely as it may have seemed at the beginning, Chevaillier turned out to be Will's saviour. The man with the strange accent was a solitary individual. Not unfriendly, just self-contained, as if he had secrets he did not want to let slip by indulging in loose conversation.

Chevaillier came to regard the young boy with the intelligent expression and the quiet demeanour as someone he could talk to, whilst at the same time not confiding in; someone to share a joke with, without inviting closeness.

They had a shared interest in caring for the welfare of Admiral Nelson and that was enough for them to become friends with each other, so as not to have to become friends with others. Another reason for Chevaillier to foster friendly relations with Will was that just like Will, this was the first voyage for newly appointed steward. Chevallier fully understood the maxim 'the enemy of my enemy is my friend', which applied just as much among the Admiral's retinue as anywhere.

As always, exclusion bred confusion and eventually suspicion.

Some 'tars' whispered that the man with the French accent was a spy, sent to assassinate Lord Nelson, while others said he reported everything the Admiral said to his enemies back in England. In fact, as Chevaillier explained to Will, his accent originated not from France but from Canada. He had travelled to England many years earlier as a servant to Nelson's best friend, agent and financial wizard, Alexander Davison. Somewhere along his varied career path Davison had retained the services of the older Chevaillier.

The then ambitious young lieutenant Nelson and the aspiring young businessman had met during Nelson's tour of duty in Canada in 1782 and had quickly became firm friends - a bond later reinforced by their mutual membership of Freemasonry.

At a crucial time in his career when the Admiral confided he could no longer abide the insolence of the surly Tom Allen, Davison recommended that Chevaillier become Nelson's servant - a task at which he excelled. Chevaillier repaid Davison by keeping him informed on Nelson's business affairs and social circumstances insofar as they affected Davison's interests. It was inevitable that a relationship with so many twists and turns would be smelt out by men confined on a warship in extremely close circumstances, which - allied to his strange accent, appearance and manners, led to him being shunned by the other members of the Admiral's retinue. Just as Allen had been in charge of all of lord Nelson's personal effects, including his jewels, plate, telescopes and spy-glasses, uniforms, medals and other valuables, so Chevaillier now assumed that responsibility. He was also responsible for ensuring the Admiral's meals and other needs were prepared properly and timeously, so his day - and thus Will's - began early.

Breakfast was prepared very early, often in the dark. More often than not the gregarious Admiral had guests join him, after which the officers went about their daily duties while Lord Nelson set to writing an endless stream of letters, usually with secretary Scott and his team in attendance. A further two meals were prepared during the day; the main one in the late afternoon which also usually featured a long guest list, and then a smaller one before bed.

Chevaillier kept a close watch on the ordering and storage of all the Admiral's supplies, not only of food and drink, but also of all of his other personal needs.

Previously this had been the preserve of Chevaillier alone and it had been a more than full-time task. According to the Admiral, he did a superb job of it, to the point that Nelson suggested the man should consider running a fine restaurant! However once young Will appeared on the scene, it did not take long for the older man to take advantage of the situation. As Chevaillier's de facto assistant, Will quickly became familiar with the needs, wants and demands of the Admiral as only a servant can. Will's eagerness to help came in handy because even the smallest tasks could be difficult for the one-armed, one-eyed Admiral. Buttons needed to be done and undone; laces tied and untied; boots tugged on and pulled off; all manner of things fetched and carried; food needed to be cut in to bite-sized pieces; wine goblets filled, and with all of these small tasks Will's nimble fingers and quick eye proved invaluable. Will quickly learnt the layout of the Admiral's cabin and the officer's quarters and became indispensable for fetching things from within drawers or running off to summon whoever the Admiral might need for whatever reason.

Chevaillier's duties to an extent overlapped with, and sometimes clashed with, those of Lord Nelson's valet, whose task was to ensure that the Admiral was appropriately turned out for every occasion. That valet was a short, tattooed, dark-skinned and dark-visaged Sicilian by the name of Gaetano Spedillo, a man who had also only recently joined the Admiral's retinue and who, according to Chevaillier - who instantly despised him - was barely up to even the simple task of finding the right clothes to suit the occasion.

"He complains all the time. He wants to go 'ome. He misses 'ees family. I doubt he will survive in his position after this voyage." With arched eyebrows Chevaillier confided to Will, adding that the Sicilian had originally been the "close personal servant of Sir William ever since he was a young boy!"

"He was foisted on his Lordship by Lady Hamilton after Sir William's death because there was nowhere else to put him! And she had tired of him lounging around Merton. I will not talk to the man! He is an idiot!"

So Chevaillier ignored Spedillo, who in return ignored Chevaillier. The impasse meant Will largely took over the task of helping to dress the Admiral, being both more adept and easier to communicate with, an arrangement the indolent Spedillo - often nowhere to be found - soon readily accepted. While the Admiral might need many things done for him that a two armed man did not, he was far from being an invalid and discouraged anyone from treating him as such. Will also discovered - to his cost - the Admiral needed far less sleep than most men and at any time of the night might be found up and pacing the deck of *Victory* or poring over maps.

He might equally be found late at night sitting at his desk endlessly and awkwardly scratching out letters, to who Will did not know.

He did know that 'private' letters went into the Admiral's desk drawer, while the many others - Will mentally labelled them 'official' letters - were set aside to be copied and distributed or their post arranged by the Admiral's secretary, John Scott, who it seemed rarely slumbered and was always available, just outside the Admiral's door.

Although they did not discuss it, Will knew - as only a fellow servant could know - that his friend Chevaillier and Scott also disliked and distrusted each other, both rarely letting a chance go by to subtly denigrate the other to the Admiral. The thing that most impressed Will about the Admiral was that not only did he love to talk, but he had the remarkable ability of being able to talk to anyone - each at their own level and in their own words - be they highly or lowly born, be they the most junior crew member or senior officer. Unlike Captain Durham, who kept aloof from his crew and officers alike and invariably dined alone, Admiral Nelson loved company and whenever possible invited someone to dine with him, often over long dinners consumed with glasses of sweet port.

Midshipmen, the purser, the surgeon or even the ship's carpenter were as likely to be found at his table as were senior officers.

But the strangest thing Will discovered about England's greatest sailor was that he suffered from seasickness. He could be kept awake for days by his delicate stomach and at such times he was best avoided. He would take to his bed bemoaning the fact that he had no 'asses milk' - the thing that could best soothe what he called his 'colic' - and Will would be dispatched to the pens for goat's milk which was the only practical, alternative.

'Bosun' and 'Plank' were the Admiral's private goats. Despite their masculine names both were nanny goats and their main task was to supply soothing milk for the Admiral's stricken stomach.

As Will's workload increased and his hours of sleep declined, Chevaillier's workload decreased and his sleep time improved.

"You are young, it is fine for you, off you go," Chevaillier would say charmingly after a late night call from the Admiral's cabin for goat's milk.

But irksome the calls were not. Will quickly found he enjoyed the company of the Admiral during these late night calls, be they to the Admiral's great cabin, to the quarterdeck, the goat's pen, or to just to listen to the Admiral opine on any topic that he wished to.

Will quickly learnt the Admiral had a soft spot for fellow 'Norfickers', or North Anglians, as those from 'Norfick' are properly called, and had regularly recruited men from his home county and even from his home village of Burnham Thorpe, where the surly Tom Allen had been recruited from. The boy became a welcome addition to the Admiral's staff not only because of his Norfolk origins, but also because he had known Lord Nelson's father and because of the closeness between the Nelson family and the Cooke family. Better than any of the 1000 souls on board *Victory*, Will intimately knew the area where Lord Nelson had been born and raised.

His Lordship could speak precisely about the fens and shores of Norfolk and of his adventures growing up there without long explanation, because they were the very same adventures in the same places Will had enjoyed years later. He could even speak to Will about his father, whose wise and honest counsel the Admiral said he greatly missed, even as he had not always been able to follow it.

Perhaps most importantly, the Admiral understood the boy was a clean slate. He knew no one on board, be they the Admiral's friends or enemies, nor was he beholden to anyone the Admiral knew and so was not in a position to pass any of the Admiral's thoughts and musings on to ears that should not hear them. This unique position - at once at close quarters with the Admiral and at the same time distanced from the rest of his retinue and fellow officers - qualified him as the perfect mute sounding board. One evening as Will half dozed quietly in the Admiral's great cabin, his Lordship busy writing his interminable letters, the Admiral stopped writing and looked across at the boy, who instantly woke, awaiting a command.

"Tell me lad" he said, pausing for a long moment, "what was your mother's relationship with my good father?"

Will tensed, immediately grasping the possible import of the question.

"My Lord, your father was the kindest and wisest man. When we arrived at Burnham he gave us shelter and work to my good mother. She sometimes taught in the school. She and my sister cleaned the parsonage and worked in the glebe. She he did whatever had to be done and your good father was always full of praise for her work."

"I was supposed to work in the Glebe also, but in truth I did very little. I went to school, but most of the time I ran through the fens, huntin' and fishin', sometimes with the other children, but most often by meself".

He fell silent for a time, trying desperately to find something to say, his eyes brightening as a thought came to him.

"Later on my mother took on the Reverend's care, when he was ill, looking after him", he said, nodding as if to reaffirm his own words. Pointing to the Admiral's writing desk he carried on, "she even wrote his letters sometimes".

"And where is your mother now"?

"I'll not be knowing my Lord; After your good father passed away I did write once, but never had a reply, perhaps because I never had a real proper address for her to write back to. Maybe I missed her reply for I know she would have answered if she could."

He slowly nodded his head. "Writing is not an easy thing," he said, turning back to his letter. Finished writing, he stored the letter in his writing desk and turned to the boy again.

"It continues to astound that we have much in common young Cooke and I do wish we had been able to spend time together before now. I also lost my mother at an early age, a year or so younger than you I believe, and the loss has plagued and bedevilled, indeed beguiled me, ever since. I have often wondered what the lack of motherly love and guidance might have had on my own character. Not that I lacked love. My good and kind father gave me every possible care and consideration, but the fact is a father is not, and cannot be, a mother.

"Luckily I also had family who came to my rescue, in much the same way that my good father came to your rescue, but nothing can replace a mother's love. Perhaps only when one becomes a parent, can a man understand the full magnitude of what the loss of a parent might mean to a child.

"My boy, I undertake now that after this battle is won, and should fortune smile upon us both, I will reunite you with your mother, should it be possible. It is the least I can do."

Again the Admiral sat silent for a time, lost in his own thoughts.

"So be it. Now, tell me young Cooke, how are you finding life now? Are you treated well?"

Suddenly Will found himself in another quandary. He understood the Admiral was being friendly, but he did not want to confide to his Lordship that he and his friend Chevaillier both felt ostracised and unwelcome on the *Victory* by the Admiral's jealous retinue.

As always in tough moments, he thought of the advice given to him by the Rev. Nelson so long ago, to do as he was told and to do his best, so he chose his words carefully.

"Your Lordship, I am overwhelmed by the great honour bestowed upon me. Your father told me to always to do my best, so I ask only to be able to serve yourself and England to the best of my ability. All else does not matter."

Nelson nodded.

"Well said, well said indeed. My Father may well have read you correctly. To do one's duty to one's sovereign and one's country is the epitome of honour, but the sadness is that carrying out that honour often comes at personal cost."

There was a long silence before the Admiral continued, and when he did, he continued to look at the unfinished letter on his desk rather than at Will, the boy intuitively understanding that while the Admiral was seemingly talking to him, he was actually talking to himself.

"I have spent many years doing my duty, going far beyond the scope of my peers I believe. And I also believe I have paid a far greater cost than those who style themselves my better," he said, nodding to himself.

"I have paid the price asked for with my own body, giving an arm, and an eye, and more, all in the service of my country and my sovereign. My health has deteriorated to the point that many times I felt I would not survive. But unlike many of my brother officers, I have not contrived to serve in those areas where the danger is the least and the rewards the greatest.

"And what has been my reward?

"My reward has been that my own commander tried to purloin the lion's share of those prizes I did capture! I had to take the unimaginable action of turning to the law for redress! Indeed! It's true! I have had to take my own commander to the courts of law to retrieve prize money that was rightfully mine. My own commander! That I should have to resort to such action should be unthinkable, but I had no choice!"

Will sat very still, not knowing how to respond, as the Admiral stared silently at the letter he had been writing. Finally he continued.

"And yet do I continue to labour for the common good because it is the right thing to do."

Turning to Will, he looked at the boy for some time before speaking.

"I understand that some lessor men may mock you for your lowly birth my boy, just as some mock me for mine. I know they mock my accent, behind my back of course, but there are no secrets kept from a commander on a ship at sea, I can assure you.

"And my father was right. The best answer to such fools lies in doing your duty and doing it well. I believe that this war, or at least my time in it, is coming to an end. I hope to survive to live a long life with my beloved Emma, but that outcome is not in my power. I might have at this very time been at home with my loved one's if those scoundrels at the Admiralty had not conspired to steal my rightful prize money at every turn and divide it among their most aristocratic selves."

Again he slipped into a long reverie before continuing.

"When, if, a great battle is fought, all England can ask is that each and every man trusts in the Lord and does his duty to the best of his ability."

The unexpected bonding between Will and the Admiral was cemented in the midst of a suspenseful lull in the war as the English fleet played cat and mouse with the combined French and Spanish fleet holed up in the port of Cadiz, just outside the straits of Gibraltar. "It's but a game," he once explained to his receptive young student, calling him over to look at a map of the area they were in to make it clearer.

"The enemy's combined fleet is at this time hiding in the port of Cadiz, here!" he said, stabbing a finger on the map, "they are sitting and waiting for an opportunity to escape without having to fight if they can."

"I believe their ultimate aim is to sneak up the English Channel to support that devil Napoleon in his planned invasion of England."

"If that proves impossible - and I intend to make it so - their backup plan is to sail back through the straits into the Mediterranean where they have both safe bases and easy targets aplenty. Only Nelson stands between them and their plans" the Admiral mused, speaking to himself at the same time as he turned back to his writing.

"I have been playing this game for over two years now and the truth is I have become heartily tired of it," the Admiral finally said.

"At the time you arrived back into my life, I had thought perhaps the time had come that I might be able to leave this game behind me, but alas, I fear it may never cease."

Again he returned to his writing for several minutes before pausing and calling Will over to massage his cramped left hand, carrying on speaking more to himself than to Will as the boy set to work on the cramped fingers as he had taught to do by Chevaillier.

"The French are holed up just over the horizon over there" the Admiral said, pointing his chin through the cabin windows to the west.

"Given half a chance they mean to move northwards up the Channel. Look at the map boy, not at me! That low-bred Corsican schemer wants to invade England. By all I know, the scoundrel desperately wants to have us under his heel as he does the rest of Europe and if so then he needs a dominant fleet to enable and protect his landing.

"Without control of the Channel he cannot invade. Without defeating me he cannot control the Channel. I have bloodied their nose before and they know I can do it again, but a bloody nose is not enough now. I am tired. I need to destroy them. Annihilate them and have done with it once and for all!

"To do that I need to provoke them to fight. To do that I need somehow to lure them out of port, either to head north to the

Channel or south to the Mediterranean. Either direction matters not, but they must leave port and to do that they need to think I am not here.

"So young Cooke, here we sit, hiding over the horizon far enough for them not to find me, but not too far so that if they do decide to move, I cannot find them!

"It is a fag and a deadly jig I am being forced to dance."

Once again he bent to his writing. Will's attention wavered and his head slowly began wobbling on his neck as he tried desperately stave off sleep, only to be snapped awake as the Admiral once more shouted to no one but himself.

"I must have more frigates! More of those like the *Pallas* you served on" he said, turning to look at Will.

"They are the eyes I need in this game! But my self-interested Lords refuse to give me what I need. They want me to win, but at the same time I believe they don't care if I lose! And each day out here my ships suffer. Each day I suffer. We need to buy more supplies if we are stay out here, but those Portuguese devils cheat and lie to me without honour or fear of God. By the Lord I will have them by the ear one day."

After the outburst the Admiral again turned to look the lad squarely with what Will thought was a softening in his Lordship's one good eye. Most of the time Will could not read the Admiral's face because - well, he dreaded to even think the words - because his lordship's 'dead' eye acted to deaden his face, making his mood very difficult to gauge.

Once again the boy found refuge in staying mute, understanding the Admiral did not expect a reply. He also vaguely perceived that the great man had opened a window to his inner self that few people had ever had the privilege of looking through.

As he turned back to the laborious task of writing with his 'wrong' hand, Nelson pondered the fact he had come to enjoy the company of the boy over the short time he had been aboard.

His mind even drifting to that terrible place he dared not visit often - his pain at not having a son of his own, perhaps one not too different from the boy who sat before him.

He was eager to learn, was quiet until spoken to, was deferential without being obsequious, and perfectly understood the nuances of the Norfolk accent the Admiral was won't to use when fully at ease. Perhaps just as importantly, the boy had begun to anticipate the Admiral's needs before they were articulated, just as a son might.

Will sat in what had become his usual position, huddled in the corner of the Admiral's great cabin as his Lordship worked. Out of the corner of his eye he saw the Admiral cast a stern look around and rise to his feet. The boy also rose slowly in anticipation.

"Ah, lad. I'll not be feeling well. Be off and fetch me some goat's milk, and bother Chevailier for a small glass of wine to wash it down.

"Away with ye!"

After drinking the still warm milk and taking a sip of the wine, the Admiral finished the letter he had been working on and then stood and struggled into his coat to take his customary afternoon walk on deck. Will stood quietly, ready to help with the buttons should he be required to do so but knowing not step forward unless asked. As the Admiral moved through the doorway he asked Will to bring his telescope. Turning to where the Admiral kept his 'glasses', hanging one beside the other on the wall behind his writing desk, he hesitated, not knowing which one he wanted.

"Sorry sir, which one sir" he said.

Smiling, the Admiral walked over and selected one housed in a fine leather carrying case. Gripping the case between his knees and flipping up the case cover, he pulled the instrument out and handed it to Will to hold while he placed the case back in its place.

"This one sees further by far than any of my other glasses. It was created especially for me by the best instrument maker in Britain, Mr Ramsden, and by heaven he certainly made me wait for it. He took so long in the making of it that he died before it was finished!

"I had given up on ever receiving it, despite having paid for the damn thing in advance mind you, when suddenly it arrived! What is it with these infernal instrument makers? Are they all so lost in thinking up new ideas that they don't have the time to actually build anything?"

Will ran his fingers along the shining brass and fine leather grip of what he would come to know as the 'long' telescope.

In the days ahead he learnt it was the one which the Admiral usually called for to use on those rare clear days where he could scan the distant horizon for any sign of a signal from the small string of frigates patrolling the Spanish coast.

On those days, without needing to be asked, he would take the instrument in hand and follow the Admiral up to the poop deck, taking a position behind his Lordship, patiently waiting. The Admiral would stand quietly as the breeze began to ease into its afternoon lull, peering into the distance for an enemy he could not find but who he knew was lurking. When the Admiral grew a little restless and looked around for Will, the boy knew what order was coming and would take the telescope from its leather case, extend all three draws and hand the instrument to the Admiral, leather grip first, while at the same time discreetly signalling the nearest midshipmen to come and stand before the one-armed Admiral. This was a standard task carried out by whatever midshipman was on watch, their shoulder a convenient resting place for the telescope. For his trouble Will was usually given a dismissive snarl from the midshipman, who nevertheless moved forward as indicated. Chevaillier was correct, the boy's closeness to the Admiral was not winning him any friends.

As the days slipped one into the other with no sign of the enemy, Will in turn quickly slipped into a routine. During the day the Admiral would spend much of his time in his great cabin, furiously writing letters and speaking to the endless line of officers who arrived seeking his advice or direction on anything and everything, and during much of this time Will was free to catch up on sleep or, more often, take the time to watch how the great ship worked.

Although he spent most of his time in his cabin, the Admiral seemed to know everything that was happening on the *Victory*. Apart from officers, he would often summon what he called the ships 'professionals' such as the surgeon, Mr Beatty, but also the carpenter, the purser, the chief gunner, the armourer and so on, at all times engaging in conversation with them, so intent on what they had to say so that when they left the great man's company they felt they had been listened to rather than just ordered. In turn, while not saying much, the Admiral gained invaluable insight to what was happening in each man's area of expertise and on the ship as a whole, information he then used to his advantage in discussions with his officers.

Will learnt that only in Captain Hardy did Lord Nelson confide his deeper thoughts and concerns, often speaking of his fears for the future of his 'beloved Emma' and his distress that, should he fall in battle, no one would care for she and her daughter.

"My good friend, you know Emma as well as anyone" he said to Hardy late one evening after a few cups, not noticing Will in the corner, "she is a little, ah, profligate. With funds."

Captain Hardy coughed politely to signal he understood the Admiral's playful understatement.

"Yes, quite. But one must know about her upbringing and how much she has achieved despite her birthright. Other women I have known have never moved an inch from the position they were born to and have remained little more than ornaments their entire lives.

"Mrs Hamilton has achieved more than all of them combined and deserves to be recognised for that. She has a fine hand and has learnt several languages, all without the benefit of school. Despite her lowly beginnings and lack of mentors in high places, she has made friends of Kings and Queens and engaged in diplomacy of the highest level on behalf of her country, and what has she received for that?

"Nothing! I warrant you my friend, I will see that changed should I live through what is approaching us, mark my words.

"If, however, I should not survive the battle, I mean to provide for her to the best of my ability, but you know as well as I that that may not be enough. That nest of incestuous blackguards at the Admiralty have done their best to rig the prize system in order to keep to themselves the just rewards of my victories, to my great cost.

"Thank the Lord my God for my good friend Mr Davison" he said, turning to face Hardy, "and of course your own good self, my friend. What would I do without my good friends, because as God is my judge, a simple sailor like meself must know that inevitably the high and mighty Lords of the Admiralty are there to look after their own interest first and foremost, not those such as us who actually win the battles."

Toward Trafalgar

The sea in the Gulf of Cadiz had been unusually calm since Will joined the *Victory*, light breezes barely ruffling the deep blue to the north of the soaring pillars which guarded the mouth of the Mediterranean.

The kind weather meant that while the British fleet patiently patrolled back and forth over the horizon from Cadiz, the Admiral was able to regularly entertain guests from his fleet, refining his plans and ingraining into each Captain what would be required of them if - hopefully when - battle was joined. But as day followed day, night followed night and watch followed watch, the Admiral's mood darkened and it began to seem as if his Lordship's worst prediction - that the French and their Spanish allies would bide their time in Cadiz until he had to abandon his vigil - might come to be true.

The weather became the Admiral's main preoccupation. While the weather had been kind since his arrival off Cadiz, he fully understood that the fool's summer he was experiencing could not last. Indeed for the past few days the wind had been freshening, mixed with squalls, no doubt a precursor of things to come. The arrival of winter weather would soon turn the Gulf into a hell on water and the Admiral perfectly understood that from the French perspective it made tactical sense to wait for the foul Atlantic to do their work for them rather than come out and fight a battle both sides knew they could not win, but that did not mean he liked the tactic. Both sides knew as surely as Autumn falls into Winter, that month upon month in torturous conditions would take a terrible toll on Nelson's ships and eventually force him to break his headlock on the southern end of the Channel and either head back to England to refit and repair his fleet, or send all or a good part of it into the more docile Mediterranean.

Either option would allow the French and their Spanish allies to slip Nelson's noose. Early one morning, about two weeks after Will had joined *Victory*, he was busying himself polishing some of the cabin's silverware and furniture when the Admiral, who had been poring over his charts after having spent his first waking hours reading reports from his captains, suddenly stood erect, putting Will instantly on alert.

"Well young Cooke, I believe we may be in luck," he said as he sat back at his desk. Will by now knew no answer was required by him, so he merely stood and looked at the Admiral with what he hoped was a quizzical, interested look on his face - this was not the first time he had heard these words or words similar from his Lordship.

"For weeks the wind has been blowing from the north and west, but today I sense it blows from the east and south."

"Those cowardly rascals in Cadiz will not have finer weather to set sail, if set sail they ever mean to do."

The words were prophetic for the very next morning the Admiral received a signal that sent a surge of energy pulsing through the ship - the enemy had been spied preparing to leave port. That was followed two days later with the news that the ships had indeed left Cadiz and had been spotted heading south-east. Toulon!

"Ha, their nerve broke my boy! There will be a battle after all," the Admiral shouted when he got the news, immediately charging out of his cabin and up to the quarter deck. Shortly afterwards Will felt the giant ship shudder as more sail was hoisted and *Victory* swung to windward on a course south-east to head off the enemy before they could gain a head start on their run back home through the straits.

The game of cat and mouse was over, now it was a game of big cat versus scared cat. For most of the next day and night Will saw very little of the Admiral as he issued orders to his captains to bring the British fleet into one powerful force, which then moved first to cut off the combined enemy fleet from entering the Mediterranean, then moved northward toward Cadiz to prevent the enemy from scuttling back to port. That night Nelson was in an ebullient mood, hosting an anticipated 'victory' dinner with his good friend Captain Hardy and ordering Chevaillier to bring out the best wines he had and to prepare the best meal possible.

"This is my chance to end this once and for all. End it in a way that will justify my retiring to Merton to enjoy the fruits of my years of labour" he said. "I admit to an ill-feeling as the hour approaches, my friend, but I put my faith in my maker and leave all final decisions to him."

"It has been a long and demanding trial I have faced, but one way or the other I have no doubt it is coming to an end. So let us celebrate! You more than anyone have served me the best Hardy, and the longest."

"I will tomorrow ask you to serve me just a little while more and carry out some instructions I leave should I not be here to execute them myself" he said, lifting a hand to stifle the Captain's protest, "the die is cast. It is as it will be."

Despite the importance of the occasion, the celebration did not extend to any late hour, for not only did the morrow portend a momentous battle, but a battle his Lordship had long said would determine the fate of Britain. That night as the great ship slipped silently through the water, quietly and privately each man's mind turned to thoughts - not only of his own fate, which now hung in the balance - but also those of his loved ones, wives and children, family and friends, whose fates would also be irrevocably changed forever by the outcome of tomorrow's battle.

Few got much sleep.

Chevaillier, wide awake in his comfortable hammock, looked down at Will lying wide-eyed on his blanket, dwarfed by the brooding black presence of the cannon beside him. The valet had never experienced battle and he, like many, found sleep impossible.

"Mon ami" he said to the boy, "are you scared? 'Ave you ever been in a battle before?" Will could almost touch the fear in the man's voice.

"I have been in battle" Will replied after a little while, "but none such as the morrow brings. Those battles…well, they were not battles really, just little fights more like. But I have faith. Faith in his Lordship who has never lost a battle, and faith in the Lord. What will be, will be."

"Merde" replied valet replied angrily, pulling his blanket over his head.

As the first rays of light broke through the bank of early morning clouds the next day the deck of *Victory* was thronged with men and officers alike, all eyes desperately searching the horizon - but seeing not a thing. After a quick breakfast *Victory* hove to and a council of war was quickly convened of the captains of all the ships that could be contacted.

"I believe the enemy is still to the north of us" the Admiral intoned, "we will thus head north-west and hope to find them. The fleet will remain into two columns, which, as we have discussed previously will be our battle formation, so should we happen upon the enemy we may immediately attack."

"Thank you gentlemen. You have your orders. May God be with us."

The mood was solemn as the captains went back to their ships.

Speaking among themselves, most of the crew of the *Victory* thought the French and Spanish had evaded them and retreated back to the safety of Cadiz, an action that would surely signal the end of the British fleet continuing to maintain its present station, with most ships forced to head back to the home ports to refit, repair, and hopefully fight another day.

Throughout that day the desultory breeze strengthened and swung to the southeast, then swung to the southwest, then prevaricated, bringing rain squalls - all perfect conditions for the enemy to first hide and then to make a run for it. Throughout the fleet in captain's staterooms and sailors hammocks alike, gone was the expectation and elation of the night before, replaced with a dread that once again the 'Corsican Conjurer' had contrived to whisk his fleet away from sure destruction. Then, late in the afternoon, elation.

Signals officer Lieutenant John Pasco, sweeping the ocean with Nelson's Ramsden telescope from his lookout in the crosstrees spied a dot on the horizon. Squinting through the rain he managed to make out the frigate Euryalus, under full sail and heading for the *Victory*. Sometime afterwards the ship had moved close enough for him to decipher a telegraph message the frigate was sending repeatedly; 'enemy spotted, heading west'!

The news ran like wildfire through the ship, bringing forth a cheer and celebration from the officers on the quarter deck to the sailors deep in the bowels of the mighty vessel. There might still be a fight! The Admiral immediately signalled the fleet to turn west so the enemy ships could not pass him to seaward and sneak past him and into the Mediterranean.

"That will not happen" raged Nelson to no one and everyone.

He ordered Lieutenant Pasco to signal the *Euryalus* to hasten back toward the enemy fleet and for it to contact all the other frigates and brigs out spying on the enemy. As usual he was relying on them to be his 'eyes and ears' in these critical hours, ordering that they must keep the enemy fleet in sight through the night and to do whatever they had to do to achieve that.

That night Nelson did not sleep a wink that Will was aware of, instead by turn poring over maps and stamping up to the poop deck to talk to the officer of the watch, then down again to confer with Captain Hardy, then back to the officers of the watch. Will was his shadow, his eyes following his Lordship's every move, alert to the tiniest sign that the Admiral might be in need of anything, but for Nelson the rest of the world beyond the enemy had ceased to exist. His entire focus was on the French/Spanish fleet, willing it to be directly in front of the twin lances of his squadron.

From the lowest deck to the lookouts, from the huddled midshipmen on watch on the poop deck to the cooks preparing the morning meal, from the officers mess to the tars gathered around the guns they hoped to be firing in the morning, there was only one topic of discussion - would tomorrow be the day? Most of the men had spent years training and straining, sweating in the Mediterranean and Caribbean heat and shivering in the Atlantic cold, waiting for the moment they would get to look along the barrels of in their guns and see the hated French.

"I'll wager a month of grog there'll be nought but mist and water in front of us in the morning" said Ebbs, running his eye over his gun crew sat around their dinner table, "those French scoundrels and their Spanish lap dogs is far too clever to fight Lord Nelson. His Nibs has the measure of them and they know it. Right at this minute they are high-tailing it out into the black hole of the Atlantic and that will be the last of them this voyage.

"No lads, its back to jolly ole England for us and I'll not be the worse for it.

"I've no desire to spend another winter endlessly sailing these waters while the enemy piss it up in port, warm and merry and laughing out us waiting just over the horizon for a party wot ain't gonna happen."

His crew knew better than to argue with Ebbs, so they nodded into their grog and kept their tongues. High above Ebbs on the poop deck, officers of the watch Lieutenants John Yule and Andrew King were huddled together with midshipmen John Lyon and James Pond discussing the same topic. Yule had been on *Victory* for almost two years, all of which had been spent, as he said, 'chasing Napoleon's shadow' and he had also had enough. He had a young wife and a very young son he had hardly seen waiting from him at his father's estate outside London, and for some time he had regretted not taking his father's advice about taking up the offer to join *Victory* and its scandal-ridden Admiral who, according to his father, more resembled a pimp in his outrageous attire than an English officer.

"I must say I think we are on a bit of a fool's errand dashing about in the darkness like this on the vague premise that we will just happen upon their fleet sitting and waiting for us. I'll take a penny to a pound the Frenchies are back in Cadiz quaffing that terrible Spanish wine and laughing at us. Wot say you Mr Pond?" he said to his second.

Mr Pond, a relatively new-comer to the French adventure wasn't so sure, but wasn't about to disagree with the senior officer on the watch.

Not publicly anyway.

"Yes, well I have no doubt that if anyone can find the scoundrels it is Lord Nelson. He is after all a genius, don't you agree?"

Yule looked at the newly promoted Lieutenant with disdain.

"I think the French will already have our position well and truly noted from the glitter of our leader's jewels and medals shining out on the water on this moonlit night and have taken the appropriate evasive action," he scoffed, eliciting the reaction he wanted from the two midshipmen who laughed into the sleeves of their jackets.

"Let's be genuine shall we Pond.

"The fact is our glorious leader has been rather lucky to date, but I fear his luck may have run out and I for one am ready for a more traditional approach to throttling the French. Off with you gentlemen, you have work to do even should it come to nought."

As the men queried and quarrelled and Nelson's parallel lines of ships surged forward in the black night, far over the horizon fortune was beginning to shine on British.

Lookouts on the rearmost ships of the combined enemy fleet had spotted the trailing British frigates and the news that the French officers had dreaded, that the feared British Navy was near, and possibly in force, quickly spread pandemonium and discord.

At a hastily convened meeting of captains, the thought foremost in many minds was the disastrous defeat at the hand of Nelson at the Battle of the Nile just seven years previously. Officers who had fought at that battle argued that the defeat had come about after the unpredictable madman Nelson had attacked the impregnable French position in an unheard of night-time attack. Caught unawares by Nelson's attack, the French fleet had been destroyed.

The French commander of the combined Franco-Spanish fleet, Admiral de Villeneuve - already under threat of dismissal and possible execution - panicked at the mere thought of another defeat on the scale of that of the Nile disaster and immediately ordered the fleet to line up in battle formation. The only way to transmit such an order at night was by signals, so the British lookouts on the trailing frigates straining their eyes to maintain sight of the French were suddenly treated to the sight of the almost invisible enemy ships letting off flares and rockets as commanders ordered the fleet to cease their individual headlong rush out into the Atlantic and instead form the traditional line astern formation. In the early hours of the morning Will was startled to hear the Admiral cheering to himself, a cheer that echoed throughout the *Victory* when word arrived that the enemy had been spotted and was being followed.

Not only had the enemy been found, but according to reports from the trailing frigates it appeared that beyond all expectation and common sense they were lined up to awaiting the British and were preparing to fight! Nelson immediately ordered his squadron to reef sails to slow its approach. The last thing he wanted was for the French to lose heart and commence to run if it saw the full British fleet appear over the horizon during the night. Once again, before first light the next morning every British sailor who could find any reason to do so contrived to be on the upper decks of his ship, peering into the darkness for any shape of a sail. Again there was nothing to see, but then, almost as if by a magician's sleight of hand, as the morning mist lifted the entire enemy fleet magically appeared on the horizon, strung in a long arc directly in front of the two British columns aiming straight at their heart. The time had indeed come to fight. After ordering the fleet to immediately haul all available sail aloft to catch the slight breeze which was coming from almost directly behind the British, Nelson returned to his cabin and recommenced writing letters. Even as sailors dismantled his cabin walls and stowed the Admiral's furniture in preparation for battle, the Admiral worked furiously at his laborious left-handed letter writing rather than call his secretary Scott.

Will believed he was writing to 'his Emma'.

The progress of *Victory* was aided by the long slow swells running up to the ship's stern, but nothing seemed to be moving quick enough and Will wondered if perhaps the enemy might not escape over the horizon. Skipping back down towards what remained of the Admiral's cabin, he had barely put a foot on the chequered floor when he was brought up short, almost running into the Admiral who was deep in conversation with Captain Hardy and Captain Blackwood of the Euryalus.

Ducking aside, he flattened himself against the wall as the three men walked past, deep in conversation.

"My friends I want to thank you for your confidences in witnessing the codicil to my will, a will which Captain Hardy is already familiar with, so I need not explain.

"It has long been vexing my mind that my Emma needs to be cared for should I, as I half expect, not survive this encounter.

"No," he said, raising his hand to silence the objections that almost made it out of the mouths of the two captains, "I realise nothing in this world is preordained, but I have a very strong feeling that my day may have arrived.

"Captain Hardy I hesitate to charge you with another duty on this day of extreme adherence to duty, but I do ask you to make every effort to ensure that the conditions of my will, especially as it pertains to Lady Hamilton, are adhered to by the King and his government.

"I have never asked for much in return for my sacrifice to my sovereign and my country, and even now I ask nothing for myself, only for a remarkable woman who has served her country in ways that may never be fully realised.

"I hope to see you both on the other side of this battle. God speed."

As the two men walked away, resuming their huddled conversation, the Admiral spotted Will pressed up against the wall.

"Ah young Cooke, you certainly have a gift for appearing at the most inopportune moments." He stood looking at the boy for a few seconds.

"This is a glorious day and you are privileged to be a part of it, albeit through the most convoluted set of circumstances. We may not see each other again and if that is so, I will now say I regret not having fulfilled my father's last wishes regarding you, but fate has a way of turning life on its head. If I do not survive this battle, I would like you to have something of mine to remember me by. Can you think of anything you would like to have?"

Tears sprung to the boy's eyes and he stood, unable to speak.

"Come boy, the enemy awaits. Speak now and be off with you."

"I would have your far-seeing telescope my Lord, to remember the times I have held it for you and for the times you have let me look through it as you explained what I was looking at; things I never thought I might see, so that each time I look through it I would see the world through your eyes."

The Admiral looked at him, clearly perplexed, but not unpleased.

"As so often you have, you confound me with your clear speech.

"The telescope shall be yours and I will speak to Hardy of it, for I have promised him my glasses. Now be off to your duty."

Chapter Four

Haynes slowly realised that Cooke had stopped speaking. In fact the old man had been silent for some time before Haynes, pencil poised but completely caught up in the adventure which had been played out before him, realised the yarn had come to a halt.

"My good Lord, what a life you have led" Haynes blurted out. Then, seeing Cookie's reaction to the unintentional blasphemy, he quickly put up his hands in supplication.

"I'm sorry. I apologise. But never have I heard such a story. It is incredible that here, in musty old Morpeth, such a tale has stayed hidden all this time. I declare this eccentric little town continues to amaze. It has the most fascinating stories in all of Australia!"

Turning to his neglected notebook, he quickly flipped back to the beginning of the notes he had long since stopped taking down.

"I wonder if I can just clarify a few points," he asked, signalling to the barman for another rum, giving Cooke a querying look as to whether he would like another drink and receiving a frowning refusal in reply.

"So what happened to you after the battle? I assume you came back to England on the Victory with Nelson's body. Wasn't the body placed in a barrel of rum and strapped to a mast? That must have been a surreal experience, walking on the deck of the Victory knowing that Admiral Nelson was slowly marinating in a barrel of rum nearby?

"Did you attend the funeral? I believe that was the biggest funeral London had ever seen, so it must have been quite a show. Did you ever actually get the telescope?

"And what was it that brought you across the world to Australia?"

Cooke looked hard at the young journalist as the young man sipped his rum and turned the page on his journal, pencil poised.

The old man did not like the way his story was being received and recorded, but was at a loss about what to do about it. Leaning back in his chair, Cooke closed his eyes, grimacing at the effort of casting his mind back to far into his past.

"After the battle a huge storm blew up. It lasted all night and through the whole of the next day and that storm nearly did for us what the Frenchies could not!

"I thought I would die there and then. I've never seen the like, the wind howling like old King Neptune himself was furious with what we had delivered to him.

"At the top of the storm Victory lost all sail and everyone was convinced we were bound to reach an unhappy landing on the shores of Spain. All around us were ships being driven by the waves, their sails and rigging shot to pieces. We had picked up a lot of the enemy from the water during the battle, but after the fighting ended every man Jack of us were no longer friend or foe, we were all just sailors - English, French, Spanish - it didn't matter, we all just worked to survive. Those men we picked up ended up working like demons to save us, and that just after we were all trying to kill each other!

"We was at the mercy of the sea, but the Angel of Mercy took pity on us. The Neptune arrived and even though it was just a frigate, it managed to take us in tow, otherwise I don't think we would have made it and I wouldn't be here to tell this story. It still took us a week to make it safe to Gibraltar and a lot of other ships only got to port the week after that.

"After a few days Captain Hardy called for me. He was sitting at Lord Nelson's desk. He was short with me he was, though to be fair he had a lot to do. He said Lord Nelson had spoken to him and said I was to have his Lordship's telescope if he did not survive the battle, so he was offering it to me. He wasn't happy. He said Lord Nelson had left all his other sea-glasses and telescopes to him and asked me if I really wanted it and offered me five pounds for it."

Cooke dropped into silence again, his mind caught in history's web.

"I was angry that he should think he could buy what Lord Nelson himself had given me, but held my tongue. I said as Lord Nelson *had told me he wanted me to have it, I should have it, 'but thank you for your kindness Sir' I said.*

"Oh, he was not happy, but sitting there at Admiral Nelson's very own desk, still warm from his Lordship's presence, but he could not deny the Admiral's request. 'So be it' he said.

"I remember his exact words. 'I will honour M'Lord's request, however I warn you that you have a valuable instrument in your possession that men would kill for. I will write you a note authorising your ownership, but I warn you that you should be wise not to show the glass to anyone lest you become an object of criminal envy."

Haynes thought he detected a sob caught in the old man's throat as he carried on speaking.

"To this day no one outside my family knows about that telescope" he said, realising he had said more than he had wished and regretting his loose tongue.

"So the answer is yes, I was given the telescope and indeed I still have it. I would ask you not to mention that I have it in my possession still, for Captain Hardy was right to say that if thieves thought I had such a thing they would think nothing of taking my life to get it."

Haynes reluctantly nodded his agreement as Cooke continued his tale, sighing as another key part of his story slipped away from him.

"Captain Hardy said that because of all the confusion and disruption following the battle, he thought it best I return to the Defiance because it would be too complicated to transfer to the Victory at this time with so many of the crew dead or wounded or still missing and the final tallies still being made. He said it would be easier just to row me across the bay to Defiance. Truth be told, with his Lordship gone, I didn't want to stay on the Victory either. I went and found Mr Chevaillier to tell him I was leaving, but he was not in the least concerned. I returned to Defiance and truth to tell, didn't get much of a welcome there either.

"Below decks the first person I saw was Dott. I recall he laughed when I dropped my kit. 'Well, well, well, if it isn't Nelson's Boy, returned from the war, minus his Admiral though.'

"I said nothing, just looked around to see where my abuser Williamson might be. Dott, I had to hand it to him, he was as quick with his wit as he was with his fists and his tongue.

He saw my eyes covering the mess and guessed my object. 'If you be looking for your friend Mr Williamson you can stop looking. Unfortunately the poor lad met with a terrible accident. No one knows how, do they boys', he said, glaring defiantly around the room at the mids, daring them to say anything.

"That was when I decided to leave the Navy."

Throughout the involved account of this ship and that ship, Haynes had been waiting for a pause and when it came, he pounced, cutting to the section of the story concerning Nelson.

"If I remember correctly, Admiral Nelson's body was put in a barrel of rum to preserve it, and the rum from that barrel became to be known as Nelson's blood. Can that be right?

"I assume you never actually saw the body."

Cooke closed his eyes, dragging his mind back to the shadowy darkness of Victory and peering around a stanchion at his Lordship's body.

"Yes. Yes I did see his body. Later was placed in a leaguer - a big barrel" he said, answering the journalist querying look - "the doctor ordered it filled with brandy, but there wasn't enough brandy so it had to be topped up with rum. I heard later that as the body swelled ..."

The old man stopped for a moment, overcome with the horror of the scene described to him later by a tar who had been there.

"Sorry. As the body swelled the top was forced and liquid escaped. The mixture was collected by the tars - we're a superstitious lot - and 'tis that which is properly called Nelson's blood."

While Cooke spoke Haynes had finished his rum and turned to signal for another, only to find the bar had closed and the two were alone. The journalist quickly charged on, asking the question that had been nagging at the back of his mind for some time.

"Mr Cooke, Sir, how is it that this remarkable story has remained hidden for so long? Have you not told anyone of your adventures? Surely it is time this incredible story must appear. You could even write a book - provided, of course, that all this is true."

Cooke kept silent, but Haynes could see that he was struggling with something, something he perhaps needed to say but did not know how to say.

"I need to tell you something" Cooke said finally.

'Here we go' was the journalist's first thought, closing his eyes and shaking his head slowly, waiting for the flood of excuses and qualifications he had no doubt were coming.

"While everything I have told you is true" the old man said carefully.

"I have not told you the whole truth."

Suddenly Haynes had the feeling his marvellous story was slipping through his fingers like beach sand.

"This world that you live in Mr Haynes, is not the only world that exists around us. You are young and impatient. I know that. You have always been the same - the first over the orchard fence and the last to leave," he smiled, triggering a rueful smile in response from Haynes.

"So let me tell you, young Johnny Haynes, I am not of your world and there are things that, if they are revealed, could bring my world tumbling down around me."

Intrigued, but still suspecting to hear more lies or excuses, Haynes kept his tongue.

"Yes, John Haynes, I have not been entirely truthful with you, but" he added quickly, lifting a finger to stop the journalists response, "though not in the way you may believe. The question I have for you, Mr Haynes, is whether I can trust you not to reveal the whole truth if I ask you not to."

Surprised, Haynes sat back in his chair, pondering what Cooke meant.

"Are you saying that you want to tell me something off the record?" he asked, using a journalistic term that Cooke obviously did not understand.

"You want to tell me something, but at the same time you would like me not to write about, or put into my - your - story what you tell me?"

The journalist quizzically raised his eyebrows and pursed his lips in the universal language that said he was considering the option.

"OK. We have come so far and so, yes, I can agree to that."

Cooke nodded. *"I am about to trust you with my life's work. Perhaps even my children's. I hope you will not betray my trust because if you do, my world - and my children's world- could fall around my ears.*

"As I said at the beginning, this is a long story with many twists and turns. I beg your indulgence if it takes me some time to search deep into an old man's memory, so please do not interrupt me. But if you linger a while, I think it will be worth your time."

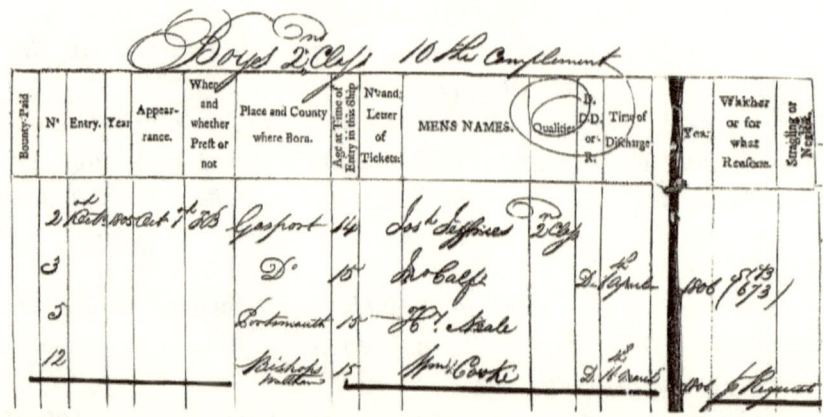

13 Extract from Defiance Muster 1806. Cooke - spelt with an 'e' as opposed to his enlistment in 1803 - but retaining the same individual muster number of 12 he had been assigned when he joined the vessel - is recorded as leaving Defiance 'per request' on March 16, 1806.

Bristol 1810

After *Enchantress* was sold Old Tom Hobbes left the ship, told in no uncertain terms by his wife that his time 'gallivantin' round the world was over. For a short time he worked as a shipwright before finally retiring and was living as a superannuated pensioner on the outskirts of the bustling seaport of Bristol when Will chanced upon him some time after signing off from *Defiance*. The young man and his elderly mentor immediately recognised each other and set about renewing their friendship over an ale. Hearing Will had no lodgings, old Tom offered to have him stay a while with him and his Portuguese-born wife Maria until he found lodgings. The couple lived in a small cottage on the banks of the River Severn on the outskirts of

Bristol, 'so's I can see the ships coming and going' Hobbes said. That first night Tom and Maria slowly teased his story out of the melancholy youth.

"After *Defiance* arrived back in England I stayed aboard but a short while," said Will, "but the truth was my heart had gone out of being in the navy.

"I stayed long enough to see his Lordship's funeral, and the most wonderous and enormous funeral it was.

"I remember it like it were yesterday. It seemed to me like every soldier and every sailor in the world was there, and every Lord and every Lady, even the King himself.

"After that, well, I've done nothin' but just waste time."

He recalled he tramped north to Burnham Thorpe where he learnt his mother had died not long after Rev. Nelson. The rest of his family had moved away, no one knew where. He worked for a while on local farms but soon understood that the prospect of farming for the rest of his life was intolerable. Then there was a time working on small fishing ships in the area, but that also paled. Restless, he drifted south, even visiting Lord Nelson's home at Merton, where none knew him and he was quickly shown the road. Along the way he recalled the longing he had once had of becoming a ship's carpenter and, with a sudden burst of certainty and enthusiasm, headed for Bristol to find a position as a carpenter's mate, the first step to becoming a ship's carpenter.

"And here I am," he smiled to Tom and Maria.

"And I have been here for over a month and have found nothing, nor the glimmer of anything, but so be it. I am not daunted. After my time with Lord Nelson and after living through the most famous naval battle in all of history, nothing will ever daunt me again. God alone knows my future and I have no fear of what will or will not be."

While Will may have seen himself as a young man with the whole world his to command, Tom and Maria saw him as lost and bewildered boy. It was but a small step for the childless couple to welcome that boy into their home, but on the non-negotiable condition that he give up all plans to go to sea. With one eye on his fearsome wife, Old Tom told him why.

"Tis no life for a man with no wealth or skills to be always away at sea" he said, casting a glance at his wife, "do let yourself first become a carpenter if you so wish, and then go to sea, if you still want to. You are young, but listen to the words of an old man; time rushes by without let. One day you will awake to a different world because you have become old without realising it and from then on you look backward, not forward, and hope sometimes dies - which is even worse than death."

The old man gave his wife another sharp look. In turn she gave a non-committal nod Tom knew promised they would soon have words.

"If you choose to stay here in Bristol, Maria and I would be honoured to have you stay with us. Not for nought mind! You will pay, be it by coin or the strength of your back, but pay you will and I promise you will be the better for it. In return I will help find you a position."

In truth Will did not take much persuading, not only because of the high regard he had for the old man, but because his plan made perfect sense. And besides, his own plans did not appear to be working well at all! Thomas Hobbes was well-known in the worlds of shipping and carpentry. Being an officer-bearer in both the Worshipful Company of Shipwrights and the Worshipful Company of Carpenters, he soon found the lad an apprenticeship as a cabinetmaker with local builder Henry Browne. Over the following years life slowly became mundane for the young man. Recalling again the words of the Reverend Nelson, he applied himself and worked steadily at his trade, becoming first a carpenter, then cabinet maker, and saving a little money, he bought himself out of his apprenticeship. His was an ordinary, even mundane life, and his future seemed set for him to become a solid citizen and member of the middle level of society and he was content with his lot - until Elizabeth Browne decided to enter his life.

Bristol 1818

Headstrong, wilful, a spoiled only child who saw herself as the woman of the house after the death of her mother a year earlier,

'Lizzie - as she preferred to be called - decided Will was to be her first love, no matter what Will or anyone else thought differently. As much as Will protested, the more set and determined Lizzie became. It is a rare young man indeed who can long resist the charms and wiles of a determined and willing young woman, so it was not long before the pair were stealing a kiss and a warm embrace in those moments when no one was watching - or so they thought.

Before long whispers of the pair's trysts reached Browne's ears. At first he was not too concerned. Lizzie was just 14 and he respected young Will and to an extent even sympathised with the lad for Lizzie was a formidable force when set upon an outcome.

'I'll speak to her and put an end to it' he thought. When he finally summoned the courage to do so, the girl launched into a tirade against her father that literally left him speechless, accusing him of both hating her and trying to both run and ruin her life.

Aghast, he immediately went to speak to Will, initially more to warn the lad than to accuse. Will was stunned into silence, not knowing where to look or what to say, his face blushing bright red beneath his blond locks. Browne took his silence as an admission of guilt and a tide of panic rose in his gut. The idea of his only daughter making a match with a mere mechanic - no matter how fine a young man he might be - was something the socially ambitious builder could not countenance and he let Lizzie know the same in no uncertain words. But the more he bellowed the more determined the young woman became. Unable to dissuade her, and at his wits end over how to stop his only daughter ruining not only her life, but also his legacy, not to mention his carefully husbanded fortune, he confided his dilemma to his good friend Thomas Price, a businessman who Will was doing some work for.

Over an ale or two too many the pair hatched a plan to have Will arrested for a minor theft and put on probation to Price.

It seemed like a good idea at the time.

The aim was to discredit Will in Elizabeth's eyes, and possibly even have him detained for a short time, just long enough to let his daughter's passions settle and to give Browne time to find his wilful daughter a suitable match.

The plan suited Price because he wanted to hold on to Will, who was a good worker. It suited Browne because while he had nothing against Will, indeed he liked the young man, he was totally dedicated to his daughter being happy, an outcome he truly believed she could only be when settled into a match of his design. Three nights later they triggered the plot.

Browne left a message for Will to meet him at a quiet spot on the outskirts of the city and then watched from a hiding place as two hired men and the local parish watchman grabbed the bewildered youth and marched him off to the nearby Lawford's Gate 'Bridewell' - a common term for a local lock-up. There, as was the law, he was held until a grand jury, comprised of leading business and civic leaders, could be convened. Browne had no doubt he could cajole any grand jury - for the most part being friends and acquaintances of he and Price - into giving him the sentence he wanted and went home content with his day's work. The next day he was not so sure.

'What if he is gaoled' he thought, 'how could I live with myself'?'

Once again he confided in his friend over some ale and once again the pair came up with an infallible plan. They decided to take the precaution of approaching an influential friend of theirs, Stephen Cave, the powerful Bristol city banker and councillor - a post which automatically made him a magistrate - asking him to take his magisterial seat when Cooke appeared. They asked him to be lenient and give the young man a warning, presenting as fair and reasonable men prepared to forgive a youthful indiscretion and not wanting to destroy a young man's life for a 'misdemeanour.'

The plan instantly collapsed when Cave proved to be less forgiving.

"A crime is a crime and must be punished" he intoned. "It is intolerable that these miscreants believe they can get away with theft! What will happen if all of the lower classes think they can steal with impunity? Why, our very civilisation will collapse. You are good men and your forgiving stance is noted, but I deal with his type every day and believe me, I know their kind far better than your good selves. Fear not gentlemen, justice will be done!"

The two men were aghast, but once the charge had been laid there was no turning back - the matter had slipped from their control.

Will spent the weeks after his 'arrest' in the damp, dark, cold cells at Lawford's Gate, his time behind the stone walls made bearable not only because of his unshakable belief that he would be found innocent and released, but also by visits from Old Tom. When word had reached him that Will had been arrested, Old Tom had tracked him down to Lawford's Gate, bringing food and clothing and a little money to make his incarceration as comfortable as was possible, a trip he then repeated every few days.

"Don't worry Sir" Will had said, trying in turn to ease the angst etched all too obviously on the old man's face.

"They say Mr Price and Mr Browne allege I stole some lead, but the men are my friends and so there must have been a misunderstanding."

"Once they give their evidence it will be settled and I shall be set free with an apology to boot! I have done nothing wrong! There is no evidence! They could not even produce the lead they say I stole! Tell mother Maria I would love some of her special Portuguese wine to celebrate with" he laughed."

It was a belief he held right up until his appearance in the court.

Bristol Court of Petty Sessions
April 1819

"Hey me matie, what they got yer fer?"
Will looked up at the man. He was taller and a bit heavier than Will, looked a lot older, and even a novice could tell this was not the man's first time in the dock. The old lag carried on, not waiting for an answer. "They got me for some wool wot was given me! Bloody 'ell. The one time I's ain't dunnit, and I's nicked. I might get a free trip to the colonies I reckon. Wot you say they gotcha for?"

Will didn't feel like talking, but he felt even less like antagonising the toothless ruffian, after all, they were chained together and this was not the time to make an enemy.

"I'm accused of stealing some lead" he said at length, "but I didn't".

"Yeah, a course not. Me name is Nate. Nate Lusty. Lusty by name and lusty by nature - geddit" he laughed. "Say, 'ow old are you? You're a littleun and don't look all that old. An' this your first time ain't it."

	Prisoners' Age, Names, Cause of Commitment, &c.	Rec. 1819.

Guilty Sentenced to be — 1 **Thomas Hall**, aged 14, committed April, 21, 1819, by Henry Burgh, Esq. charged upon the oath of Richard Eldridge, with feloniously stealing, taking, and carrying away from a barge called the Commerce, on Saturday night last, in the parish of Stroud, four bundles of ropes, the property of Mr. John Brewin, of Cirencester. 10

Guilty Sentenced to be — 2 *Thomas Webb*, alias Orchard, aged 25, committed April 29, 1819, by Wm. M. Adey, Esq. charged on the oath of Daniel Plomer the younger, of Wotton-Underedge, brazier and tinman, with suspicion of feloniously stealing, on the 22d day of April instant, at the parish of Wotton-Underedge aforesaid, a copper pipe, weighing about twenty-one pounds, the property of the said Daniel Plomer. 19

Guilty. Sentenced to be Transported for seven years. — 3 *William Cooke*, aged 20, committed April 30, 1819, by Stephen Cave, Esq. charged on the oath of Thomas Price, of the parish of St George, smith, with having feloniously stolen, taken, and carried away from the gig-house and stable of Mr. Henry Browne, of the parish of St. James, a quantity of lead, of the value of 20s. the property of the said Henry Browne. 21

Remanded to the Assizes — **Nathaniel Lusty**, aged 34, committed April 30, 1819, by Henry Burgh, Esq. charged on the oaths of Nathaniel Lloyd, of the parish of Uley, clothier, and others, on suspicion of feloniously receiving, on the 3d day of April instant, at the parish of Minchinhampton, a quantity of wool, the property of the said Nathaniel Lloyd and Daniel Lloyd his co-partner, he the said Nathaniel Lusty, at the time of receiving the same, well knowing the said wool to have been feloniously stolen from, and to be the property of, the said Nathaniel Lloyd and Daniel Lloyd, his said co-partner. 22

Remanded to the Assizes — 5 *George Pinnegar*, aged 20, committed April 30, 1819, by Henry Burgh, Esq. charged on the oaths of Nathaniel Lloyd, of the parish of Uley, and others, on suspicion of feloniously receiving, on the 3d day of April instant, at the 23

14 *The official court record of Cooke's first court appearance at Bristol Court of Petty Sessions, April 1819, immediately prior to the appearance of the man who would become his firm friend, Nathaniel Lusty. Will's surname is correctly spelt with an 'e', and his age is given as 20 computing to a (false) birth date of 1799. The hand-written comments regarding his sentence would have been added to the court records later when the records were being updated.*

Will nodded. "I'm almost 30."
"Umm, bad age" said Nate, "If you're young they take pity on ya, and if you're old they go easy. But anywhere in the middle and you're in trouble. "How much was it?"
Will looked up at him again. "I don't understand."
"How much lead? How much they say was it worth?"
"I never stole any lead, or anything else. They say it was worth 20 shillings and it's nonsense," he added. "I'll be acquitted."
At that Lusty broke out in a long low cackle.
"Ain't no one gets 'A'- quitted" he said, mockingly, "but for 20 shillin' and your first time frontin' the beak, you might be alright. Anything over two quid will definitely get you a free ticket to the colonies. Under that and you usually end up at Gloucester nick for a bit. Not a bad place that nick is. Bin there once or twice meself. If yur outta luck here you'll prob'ly get kicked up to the Assizes. There's a chance of walkin' from there, but it's a chance you don't want to take if you can help it, 'cause you might also find yourself dancin' 'pon nuthin'."

Will looked at the man as if he had no idea what he was talking about, which he hadn't.

"Dancin' pon nuthin" Lusty persisted, shaking his head, "swingin' like a dope on a rope. Hung by the neck 'til you're well and truly bloody dead. You really are new aren't you. You a mechanic?"

"Yes, a cabinet maker" Will replied.

"Good lad, gotta be somethin' or you're nothin'. I'm a weaver this time, but I reckon you really are a bloody cabinet maker aren't ya?"

"Yes. I finished my apprenticeship two years ago and I'm almost finished paying off my master."

"That's him in the long velvet coat at the end."

"Orl right, got it. And your master now says you stole don't he. Bloody masters, they want you payin' off that 'prenticeship for ever an' a day 'cause they aren't partial to payin' you more, or you opening up a business in opposition to them.

"Look, you're a little fella so if you get a chance, tell 'em you're 19 or 20. You might get away with it as'n you being so small 'n all. That way they might let you stay in lovely ole England. If not, you might be joining me in a free trip to the colonies me matie."

The two men were part of a group standing in a cordoned area at the back of a small room at the rear of the Bristol Council House in Corn Street, Bristol, which made do as a temporary dock when the Magistrate's Court of Petty Sessions was in session. Will, Lusty, and three other men were chained together, the five book-ended by two large local lads, both temporary 'special constables' attached to the local county lock-up. Jostling for room around a large circular table in front of the men were a motley collection of civilian accusers, a lawyer or two, a few council employees and other assorted hangers-on.

At the table sat Henry Browne, talking to Thomas Price.

Will tried to catch their eye, but they did not look his way.

Their conversation was cut short as the magistrate strolled into the courtroom. Stephen Cave was rotund, his bald head festooned with a few wisps of hair and a set of jowls which hung over the collar of his shirt and high jacket. Will thought he managed to look both serious and disinterested at the same time as he plodded to the high-backed magistrate's chair and sat down, immediately looking down at some papers on the bench in front of him without bothering to look at anyone else in the crowded room.

To Cave's left sat the clerk of the court, an equally disinterested reed of a man who didn't look up when the magistrate entered, instead continuing to scribble in a large ledger spread open in front of him. Immediately Cave sat down both Browne and Price rose and walked across to stand behind the councillor-cum-magistrate, deferentially waiting from him to acknowledge their presence.

Lusty pulled Will's sleeve, nodding his head toward the group.

"That don't look good matie" he whispered.

"It's alright, they are my friends and I have no doubt they are defending me to the magistrate" Will replied, buoyed when Cave stood and shook each man's hand warmly in turn. Browne and Cave then sat and, leaning in towards each other, began talking earnestly.

"See", Will smiled at the old lag, "it will soon be sorted out. I told you."

Lusty merely pursed his lips and shrugged. "Well me lad, I've come across this Cave fella before.

"One of his brothers is the sheriff. He's Quaker, and a politician and a banker he is. And rich. Very rich! Not very often he bothers to come 'ere. Not like other councillors who are here because they can't afford to pay their way out of doing it, or those what are 'ere all the time 'cause they needs the money. P'haps your 'friends' asked Cave to sit as a special favour just for you."

Getting no response to his scarcasm, Lusty shrugged and carried on.

"You from Bristol then?"

The man's mutterings had begun to inject fear into Will's mind. Try as he might, he couldn't order his thoughts as the old lag talked on and on, refusing to shup up.

"Not born here, but I have lodgings here. Tom Price is a merchant and Henry Browne, my master, is a friend of his. Henry sent me a message to meet him, but before he arrived some men and a watchman grabbed me and took me to the lock-up saying I was a thief."

The old lag looked at him and slowly shook his head, smiling from ear to ear.

"Oh my Lordy Lord. My boy, you were well and truly stitched up seems to me."

As Will stared, Browne sunk his face into his hands and appeared to weep. Price leaned back and looked up to the heavens, despair written on his face. A wave of nausea swept Will.

"Why are they doing that?" Will asked, closing his eyes closed as fear gripped him. Lusty scowled and shook his head. Will was dragged back to the present by the constable tugging his sleeve. The clerk of the court was standing in front of him, his broad ledger balanced across his left arm, pen poised in his right hand, eyes focussed entirely on his book.

"I said, are you William Cook? C-O-O-K" he spelt out as Will looked everywhere but at the man, suddenly unsure of how to answer or what to say. He looked at Lusty, who nodded. A sharp jab in the ribs from the constable beside him quickly triggered a response.

"Yes" he said. "But it's Cooke, with an 'e'" he added quickly.

The clerk looked him in the eye for a long moment before writing the word down, with an 'e'.

"Age?" Will looked at Lusty, who nodded.

"Twenty" he answered. The clerk wrote it down, then slid across to stand in front of Lusty.

"Nice to see you again Nate, it's been a while. How old are you today?"

"Twenty" the lag replied quickly.

The clerk looked up from his ledger, a smirk spreading across his face.

"Must I go back to the records Nate? If I have to waste my time it will not go well with you."

"Twenty six?" Lusty said quizzically. Again the clerk looked up, but merely shook his head and wrote down 34. It was no skin of his nose how old the lag said he was, provided it was vaguely believable. Besides, this group were just the first of many more in what promised to be a long and tiring day. With a barely perceptible shake of the head moved on down the line.

"Are you Thomas Webb?"

"Yes"

"Age?"

"Eighteen." At that the clerk again looked at the man, pen poised. With a sigh he wrote 25.

"Are you George Pinnegar?"

"Yes"

"Age?"

"Twenty". The clerk wrote it down, already tired of the game.

"Are you Thomas Hall" he asked the last prisoner.

"Yes Sir" came the halting reply.

"Age?"

"I'm not sure Sir." At that the clerk looked up to see a thin waif who looked like a child. 'Not another one' he thought to himself, hesitating an instant before writing down 14 then returned to the table and placing the ledger down before proclaiming in a loud voice; "Hear Ye. Hear Ye. Hear Ye. All prisoners present, this session of the Court of Petty Sessions of the City of Bristol before the most honourable Stephan Cave is now in session."

Turning to Will, the first prisoner in line, he read from the ledger.

"William Cooke. You have been charged on the oath of Thomas Price of the Parish of St George Smith with having feloniously stolen, taken and carried away from the Gig House and Stable of Mr Henry Brown of the Parish of St James a quantity of lead of the value of twenty shillings, the property of him the said Henry Brown.

"How do you plead?"

Will closed his eyes and visibly swayed, his world crashing down around him. He looked desperately at Henry Browne, but the man would not raise his head.

Despite what he had just heard, Will could not believe his master, a man he had trusted totally and a man he had worked with and considered a friend, had sworn under oath he was a thief.

'Why? Why would they do that?' he asked himself. 'What reason could they have?' But even as he asked himself the question, he knew the answer.

"It has to be Lizzie" Will said aloud, finding his voice, leaning forward on the balustrade for support, his knees threatening to collapse beneath him as the terrible truth of betrayal dawned. 'Oh God, Lizzie, what have you done.'

"How do you plead," the clerk asked again.

Looking up, Will at last found his voice. "I plead not guilty! I would ..."

His desperate attempt to explain his plea was quickly cut off by the clerk.

"This is not the place. You will keep quiet."

"But I ..." He was cut short by a hard elbow in the ribs from the constable beside him, who also pulled viciously on his chained wrist, hissing "shut it."

Will was about to protest but the clerk was already reading the charges against Lusty. When he had finished, the old lag quickly pleaded not guilty, as did the remaining three prisoners. Immediately the last plea had been voiced Will watched in horror as Browne and Price stood and, sidling around the table, bent over to once again begin a whispered conversation with the magistrate. For a few seconds as the magistrate seemed to ponder, then he dismissed the two with a wave of his hand and loudly voiced his verdict.

"All these prisoners are committed to stand trial at the next session of the Court of Assizes." Instantly the clerk was on his feet. "Next" he shouted, then sat to await the next group as the warders turned and, tugging on the chain, dragged the group out a side door and onto the laneway beside the building.

"Wot's that all about then" asked Lusty as soon as they were out of the dock, "I thought you said it was sorted? And who's this Lizzie then?"

Will couldn't answer, his mind swirling. How could it be? Even if Lizzie had betrayed him, out of some revenge, why would her father turn against him? And how did Tom Price come to be involved? Again he was jolted by an elbow to the ribs. He looked up at Lusty.

"I said, who's this Lizzie then" he asked, his eyes shining and a leer spreading across his face.

"Elizabeth Browne. She is determined to be mine. I have told her it is not possible. She's a member of the Browne family! I'm just a poor carpenter, but she won't be dissuaded."

Lusty immediately broke into a loud cackle.

"Oh my good lord, I should have known. There's always sure to be a woman somewhere in the story of a good man bought down to his knees. Is it Browne's wife, or his daughter?"

Will's look of indignation told Lusty all he needed to know.

"It's the daughter" he almost howled, slapping his knee.

"That's worsen the wife!" he shrieked.

Will could only close his eyes, lost in despair. Back in the courtroom Browne and Price were dumbfounded. This was the very last thing they had wanted. Browne looked at Price and was about to turn and approach the magistrate when Price grabbed him by the jacket.

"Say nothing more" he hissed, "or it is not Will but you and I will be leaving here in chains."

They sat silent as the court proceedings carried on around them, a profound melancholy gripping their hearts as the realisation dawned that they had unwittingly delivered a good young man into the vice-like grip of a legal system which had unfettered power - power that could relentlessly and remorselessly grind away the life of any man. Only the knowledge they also sat on the precipice of that bottomless pit bound their tongues.

'What just happened?' Will thought as he stumbled along, head bowed.

"How is that justice?" he asked Lusty walking beside him.

"Not to worry matie. Old Cave has just kicked the matter up to the Assizes. Called the quarterly court 'cause it sits four times a year don't it. For some reason Cave didn't want to take the decision himself, so you still gotta a chance, just not a very big one" he said, again breaking out in a cackle, pleased at his own wit.

"I reckon the rest of us just got kicked up to Gloucester with you!"

"What happens now?" Will asked, his head spinning from the speed with which events were unfolding, totally unable to comprehend what he had heard.

"Well, it's back to the Bridewell for us for now. Then later it'll be on to Gloucester Prison."

Outside the Council building the two constables sat the prisoners down on a low wall and set to devouring a corked jug of ale along with a loaf of bread and lump of cheese one of them had produced.

"Now that looks good me hearties" joshed Lusty, "where's mine then?"

The joke raised the expected laugh from the country boys.

"I'm thinking you better get used to drinking sea water and eating wild animals where you're gonna end up, 'less a course you end up dancing at the end of a rope" the older one retorted, reducing both the bumpkins to tears of laughter. Before too long Will's group of prisoners had been joined by another group, and then shortly after that by another and then another as the court sped through its duty with little ceremony and no argument, unhindered by bothersome evidence or testimony.

As dull-witted as the constables seemed, they knew their job and as quickly as one group emerged from the court they were shackled to the last group, while at the same time a new group was shackled to other constables and hustled into the court in quick rotation.

Only two men, both represented by the same lawyer, had been found 'not guilty' and released. At the end of proceedings the bumkin constables quickly shackled all those prisoners ordered to be returned to the lock-up into pairs, shoved them into two rough lines abreast and began shepherding their charges back to Lawford's Gate House of Correction, a short walk away past the town marketplace and the ruins of the once mighty Bristol Castle.

It seemed all the good citizens of Bristol they passed had a word to say to the prisoners, be it a good-natured jest or a sneering gibe, the prisoners giving back as good as they received in a foul-mouthed and ribald a manner. Through it all Will remained silent, deaf and blind to all but his own gut-wrenching horror at what the injustice of what had just befallen him.

The trudge back to Lawford's Gate took just ten minutes, but it might as well have been a lifetime for Will, for by the end of the walk all hope had drained from him, leaving him empty of any feeling but utter despair, his eyes closed to all but the feet of the prisoner in front of him. His mind flew back to the words of Reverend Nelson that in all things in life he should do only his best and trust in God.

'I have done nothing but my best' he thought, on the verge of shedding the tears of a boy despite now being a man. 'I have followed the law of man and God and yet this is what I am come to. How can this be? My most dear Reverend Nelson, please, please tell me: why has God forsaken me?'

But there was no answer.

The House of Correction was not designed to hold long-term prisoners, so once through its doors the group was quickly divided into those who had been referred to a higher Court and those who had been given short sentences. Those lucky few given short sentences were immediately reunited with family and friends who brought them food and money, the later in reality destined for the pockets of the keeper to ensure good treatment in the short time they would stay, or if great enough, to buy their way out immediately.

Those who were to face further trial in Gloucester were led by the constables through a narrow stone walkway to a line of four cells. Two of the cells had straw mattress' and were reserved for prisoners who had money to buy such a luxury.

The other two had a blanket on a bare stone floor.

If being a sailor had taught Will anything, it was to be prepared for a sudden change of the weather - or fortune - so he always secreted some coins in reserve. One of them was now exchanged for a bedded cell rather than a cold floor, as well as a pile of firewood to warm the dank hole. Since he and Lusty were shackled together, Will's good fortune became Lusty's.

Once their shackles had been removed the pair were shoved forward into a 'double' cell, about 20 feet by 16, with only a small barred, glassless window for light and air.

In one corner of the cell was a fire-blackened circle of stones.

As soon as they were bedded down in their cell the old lag recommenced his permanent and continual jabber, giving his expert opinion on what the pair might expect in Gloucester and beyond and extending to what they would need to do to survive should they end up aboard a ship bound for the colonies. In Lusty's mind the two were already friends and partners in crime, but Will, sitting silently on his straw mattress, his head sunk into his bent knees, barely heard a word. In his mind he was already as good as dead.

"Come on Cook wif an 'e" Lusty laughed, "no use being melancholy. Fings could be an awful lot worse, believe you me. Pretty soon we'll be heading up to Gloucester and the prison there is new. More like a fancy boarding establishment it is. And besides, I've heard that the New South Wales colony is like a paradise. Plenty of food and land for whoever wants, not that I wants to farm, wouldn't know a plough from a sheep and the ..."

Will lifted his head, suddenly realising how Lusty had addressed him.

"My name is William Cooke" he said defiantly.

"Not no more it ain't me ole mate, now you just Cook, wiff or wiffout an 'e', and you better get used to it or you are not gonna last in 'ere. You had better get that because if you don't, life will become very hard for you."

Will had no idea how long the old lag droned on for after that, but at some time during the night the jabber finally dulled him into sleep. His new 'friend' shook him awake early the next morning and soon both men were standing before the small fire Lusty had coaxed into life, shivering, hunger gnawing at their innards.

Prisoners at a House of Correction were by law allocated two pence a day by the parish to buy bread and whatever else that could be afforded, possibly meat, usually vegetables, to supplement the thin potato soup they were also due. The 'keeper' of a Bridewell was not paid a salary, it being expected he would earn money from charging prisoners or the families for anything 'extra' they wanted and could afford to buy.

When prisoners such as Will were only being kept for just one night before being moved on, the Keeper would usually pocket the two pennies and send the men off hungry. Unless they could come up with another penny or two that is. Will did have a few more pennies sewn tightly into his jacket and trousers, but guessing he might need them on the walk to Gloucester, he decided to keep them hid. Besides, he had no wish to continue feeding Lusty who had begun to talk the instant his eyes opened that morning and who showed no signs of stopping even though Will barely answered. He had often done the 30 mile walk from Bristol to Gloucester easily in one day when walking alone, but he estimated it would take a group of men shackled together two or three days. If so, he might well need those few pennies.

As it was the next morning the keeper did provide the 18 men earmarked for the walk with a little bread to send them on their way. Most ate the crusts immediately, though Will and a few others, including Lusty, tucked some precious food away just in case none other was forthcoming. Shackled together in two groups, the men were guarded by four local special constables, young men in from the farms to make a few extra pennies.

The group set off early the next morning, immediately after receiving their rations and, stopping only to drink from local fountains, walked steadily 'til they reached the small village of Iron Acton where a simple lunchtime meal had been prepared. Then they walked on to an overnight stop at the cross-roads village of Wotton-under-Edge where, after a basic meal served up by a local inn, the two groups were shackled chained together and to the sturdy posts of the stable behind the Inn and settled down for the night.

Lusty as usual was full of prittle-prattle, talking endlessly to the guards or the prisoners or anyone else he thought might listen.

"Excuse me young man" he said to the big country lad chosen to stand the first watch, "do you think I could slip these chains for a short while? You see, I live just up the road at Kings Stanley and I thought I would just stroll home and say hello to the wife, if you catch my drift", the suggestion triggering a laugh from both guard and prisoners alike.

"I'm thinking the only 'wife' you have is the one on your leg," the guard retorted, making a pun of the word that was commonly used for both wife and a shackle.

"And I'm thinking the only stroll you'll be takin' anytime soon is a walk down the plank, but thanks for the suggestion and I'll be sure to drop by Kings Stanley on the way back and give your best, I mean my best, to your wife, seeing as she may not be seeing yourself for quite some time."

This brought forth an even bigger roar of laughter from the prisoners and Lusty, seeing himself bested for once, retreated into silence. An early start on an empty stomach saw the gaggle of prisoners reach Gloucester the next afternoon.

The group entered the city through the southern gate, turned left towards the River Severn and were then marched directly into the massive stone edifice of what used to be Gloucester Castle, but which was now Gloucester Prison.

Prisoner of Mother England
Gloucester. July 1819

Compared to the squalor and decay of Lawford's Gate lock-up, Gloucester Prison was, as Lusty had said over and over, a veritable mansion. Recently rebuilt, with several new sections added to the main building which was now three stories high. It was divided into three sections; a County Gaol for short-term prisoners on one side; a Penitentiary House for longer term prisoners and those ear-marked for transportation on the other side - both with separate sub-sections for women. The middle section was a strongly-built entrance gatehouse which boasted a chapel and an infirmary. It also featured an imposing arched gate wide enough to admit a horse and carriage, along with side doors that led to a porter's lodge, a reception room, a messenger's room and even a keeper's room. There was a fumigating room and a bathroom for new prisoners to be deloused and given clean clothing, after which they were examined and their defining features such as height, eye and hair colour, scars and other body marks were again meticulously recorded - a description which would follow the prisoner through the rest of his life in the prison system. The gatehouse also featured a flat roof on which executions took place.

When a hanging was imminent a bell would be rung to alert the citizenry should they want to come and watch the entertainment. After their induction prisoners were assigned to their differing areas. True to Lusty's word he along with Will and the other prisoners still to be tried at the Assizes were separated from the rest of the prisoners and shown to a different section from that reserved for the convicted felons.

"Just been rebuilt she has" said Lusty, slapping the brick wall. He knew the gaol so well he all but took control of the process of being entered on the gaol's books.

"Stick with me and we'll be gettin' some first class accommodation, built special for those of us who are presumed innocent until found guilty, which we will be" he cackled.

Each of the awaiting trial prisoners had their own cell, measuring eight foot by six foot, and such was Lusty's familiarity with the system that he virtually picked out his own cell before showing Will into his, conveniently next door. It was to be Will's home for ten weeks. Every bed had an iron bedstead, a straw mattress, a rug, a blanket and a coarse sheet, as well as a water bucket and a waste bucket. Every morning prisoners were woken by a bell which was a signal for them to wash their hands and face, and make their bed.

After prayer in the chapel there was a breakfast of gruel and bread before they went to their assigned places of work, the worst of which was a two hour stretch walking a small treadmill which pumped water up into a storage tank. Other jobs included weaving and sewing items such as socks and purses for sale to the public. In addition to oatmeal gruel and bread for breakfast, awaiting trial prisoners were given vegetables with either meat or cheese in the evening.

"Luxury, that's what it is" crowed Lusty, "bloody luxury."

The biggest imposition was a rule which in theory prevented prisoners from talking to each other.

This didn't bother the solitary Cooke at all, but it would have been easier to prevent Lusty from breathing than talking.

Will had been behind bars for almost a month when he was told he had a visitor. Escorted down to a special room, he was told to stand behind a large iron grate set into the wall while his visitor was produced at the other side of the gate and Will was struck speechless when he saw Old Tom Hobbes.

Both men blinked back tears.

Unable to touch, the men stood close to the grate and said nothing for several moments, a constable standing beside them to stop any goods being passed.

Will knew how much it must have taken for Old Tom to make the trip from Bristol and was at once grateful beyond words, while at the same time concerned for his well-being.

"Tom" he eventually got out, the words almost cut by the sobs the word triggered, "my dear friend, I thought I would never see you again. Are you alright? How is Mother Maria? How did you get here? Oh my dear Lord, I am so glad to see you my heart is near to burst."

Tom put his hand to the grate, but the constable moved immediately and pulled it away.

"I am well my son, how are you? Are you being treated well?"

Overcome, Cooke was unable to utter a word, so Tom continued.

"Please, tell me what is happening? Are you bound for trial or …" his voice petered out. Finally Will recovered enough to talk.

"I'm due to appear in the Trinity Sessions next month and to tell you the truth, it doesn't look good. If all the men in here are right, and most of them have been here before, hardly anyone gets let off, especially with good citizens like Browne and Price against them. They reckon I'll be transported to the New South Wales colony."

The men again lapsed into a silence, which Tom finally broke.

"I don't know what to do or what to say. I know you didn't steal anything. I'd put my life on it, but I just don't know what to do. What can I do?"

Will's silence was the most eloquent answer, but eventually he spoke.

"There is nothing to be done my good friend. Long ago Lord Nelson's father told me to put my faith in God and all would be well. It's taken a month for me to arrive at the conclusion that all I can do is trust in God. Can I ask you to still store my things? My tools and a few other things that are precious to me, my 'scope especially, are in my tool chest. You know where the key is. Everything else, my clothes and the other things, you can sell because if what everyone says will come to pass does so, I will not have the need for them.

"I will do whatever it takes to either get that chest myself or send someone for it, but Father Tom, my friend, I have no idea of when that will be."

The old man bowed his head to hide his tears, nodding slowly before speaking again.

"I have a good friend who lives here in Gloucester, Bill Caught, who you know was carpenter on Defiance. He also remembers you and wants to help, so I am able to stay here until you are acquitted, and you will be acquitted, fear not. I will be there for your trial so please, do not worry. For as long as I live I will guard what is yours and if that is not possible, I will send your chest to you, wherever that may be.

"My son, I know this is of little succour, but you must trust in God. It is all any man can do."

Gloucestershire Court of Assizes
Gloucester Shire Hall

The morning of his trial Will woke early and quickly ate breakfast before once again having to go through the process of being chained to the others scheduled to appear in court that day, all taking the short walk from the gaol to the courts in the newly built and imposing Gloucester Shire Hall building.

Once again he and Lusty were 'partners', but for once Will was heartened by having a familiar face and voice for company as he went to meet his fate.

The walk took just a few minutes to reach the impressive Shire Hall which featured a wide portico supported by four tall Ionic columns in the classical Greek style. Lusty, an endless font of knowledge on everything to do with the prison system, explained that the two doors inside the portico led to different parts of the building.

"That door over there," he pointed to the western door, "that leads to the seats of the judges and prosecuting lawyers.

"The other door - over there - that doesn't" he said, cackling at his own joke, "it goes to offices.

"These big doors open to separate half-circle court rooms, so two cases can go on at the same time and that means more people can go to New South Wales quicker. There's holding cells below each dock, but the real treat is that each court has public galleries that can each hold 200 bloody spectators.

"It's a bleedin' circus it is, and we're the main attraction."

He explained that at the front of the building was a room reserved for the Grand Jury. Cases the jury merited continuing were labelled 'true bills' and went to trial, while those they considered without merit were labelled 'ignoramus' and summarily dismissed.

"The fing is" intoned Lusty when informed that his and Will's trials would go ahead despite the fact that neither had been questioned by the Grand Jury or given the chance to address it, "that if you been fingered by good citizens, like you have by Browne and Price, then you're gonna go to trial. No question. Those rich businessmen on the grand jury aren't gonna go against one of their own are they?"

Once inside the building the prisoners sat in order of appearance and once again Will and Lusty were included in the first quartet to appear. As they walked up stairs to the dock, they could hear what sounded like a mob baying for blood - their blood. The noise increased with each step he took higher and higher until they found themselves looking out at a scene of total madness as the full scale of the noise hit the prisoners like a wall of sound. Standing silent and stock still at the centre of the cavernous room, Will's head slowly swung back and forth in amazement as he tried to take in the enormity of the commotion that surrounded him. Beside him stood Lusty, two other prisoners and two special constables, all jammed into the small dock. Directly in front of him a few lawyers and their clients - both in effect prosecutors - sat squashed together around a long table. There were no defence lawyers, each prisoner having only himself to depend upon in an unequal fight for freedom. The prosecutors joked and chatted casually as if gathered for a friendly get-together, some of the men eating from plates, others drinking beer or wine and lounging back in their chairs in a way that sent the unmistakable signal that they were the men in control here. On the table were stacked books, sheets of writing paper, ink wells and quills, tools of the trade for the men of the legal profession. On the other side of the table, looking down on the legal gathering, was a raised dais surrounded by an ornate balustrade behind which was a high desk and a number of empty chairs, the realm where judges sat and weighed people's lives.

Sitting in judgement on the scene was a public gallery that ran around the whole length of the room and was packed with the good citizens of Gloucester. Hawkers walked through the gallery bantering with the crowd and each other as they held up their wares - trinkets, souvenirs, nuts, fruits, cakes, boiled sweets - anything and everything a person watching a public humiliation might need or want. Sellers and buyers shouted at each other across the heads of people talking to each other, the hawkers praising their wares and abusing those who refused them. In turn the audience abused the hawkers, the two sides going back and forth in a good-natured bantering contest. Court day in Gloucester was the best entertainment the people of the town had on offer, a veritable feast of fun unveiling all of the scandal and drama of the town for the people to relish and later rehash endlessly.

The legal circus opened a window on to the private lives of friends and neighbours rarely glimpsed and, if the crowd was lucky, through which the peccadillo's of the town's elite might be revealed, to be laughed at without fear of retribution.

The process even allowed audience participation, with the mob all too willing to join in the deliberations, unafraid to voice their disagreement with the decisions of the judges, loudly demanding sterner punishment for obvious villains let off lightly and quick to berate the same judges if they felt excessive punishment had been meted out to ordinary men and women perceived to have been unfortunately and unfairly caught up in affairs beyond their control.

It was all good fun for the good citizens of Gloucester.

The learned Sir William Hamilton had often spoken to Will about the history of the Greeks and Romans, and the story which had grabbed the lad's attention the most had been the one about a Roman Emperor who had built a huge arena, 'bigger than a village' Sir William had said, called the Colosseum. Will had been spellbound by tales of warriors called gladiators who fought each other and even wild animals, purely for the entertainment of the people. Sometimes the Emperor would signal for warriors to die, Sir William said, and to Will the court looked and sounded like he had imagined the Colosseum to be, he and the other prisoners playing the role of gladiators, beaten and awaiting the final death sign from the Emperor, in this case a disinterested judge.

As the judge entered, the gallery eagerly turned as one to watch the show. Will scanned the gallery, picking out the face of Tom Hobbes. The old man sat quietly, his head in his hands amid the maddening chatter and laughter surrounding him.

As he sat he heard his name mentioned in the din and turning, eager to put his case, could not believe what he heard: "William Thomas Cooke you are hereby sentenced to seven years transportation to the colony of New South Wales. Next!"

And as quickly as that it was over. Dragged back down to the holding cell, he stood dead still in the centre of the small cage, in a world completely different to the one he had been in just minutes ago.

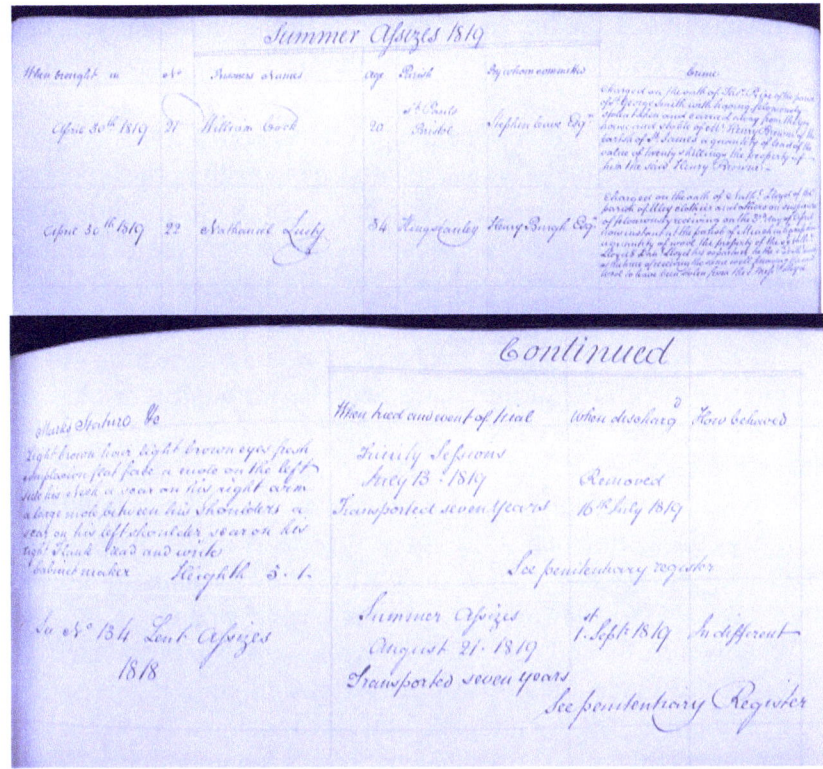

15 Gloucester Court of Assizes, 1819. Original court documents recording Cooke sentenced to seven years transportation. It is worth noting that while Cooke was spelt with an 'e' in the Bristol Court documents, in Gloucester he was listed as Cook without the 'e', underlining the vagaries of spelling in the era of manual copying of documents or recording of verbal answers.
All other details regarding the charges are exactly the same as those recorded in the Court of Petty Sessions.

'How could this have happened?' he asked himself softly. 'I didn't even get a chance to say anything. I need to explain'.

He and everyone in his group had been convicted and sentenced to transportation to Australia; most like himself for seven years, a few to fourteen years. According to Lusty, only rarely were other sentences ever handed down.

"Why only seven and fourteen years?" he asked. Lusty shrugged.

That night, laying on his straw bed, Will hit the very rock bottom of despair. The walls of his cell seemed to close down on him, pressing the very life out of him. When the sounds of the gaol finally died down, he stood at the tiny window, holding the bars tightly, spending the hours until daylight staring at the stars, sure he would never see them again.

He thought back to those seminal turning points in his life, moments when he had had a choice to choose one path or the other, and to the many times when the choice had been made for him. What would his life have been like if he had never left the Reverend's protective wing he wondered? What would have become of him? Would he have married a Norfolk farm girl? He thought of his time aboard *Enchantress*, perhaps the happiest of his life, learning to use the tools of his trade during many hours spent talking to old Tom Hobbes, the man who had become his adopted father. He had planned to take care of old Tom and Maria in their dotage.

Now what would happen to them? He wondered if he should have been less the gentleman with young Lizzie Browne, perhaps she could well have made a good match for him? Perhaps by now he might be the son-in-law of a prosperous businessmen?

Wherever he looked it seemed the wrong turn had been taken, the wrong choice made, the tide of life ever pushing him to this nadir.

'I truly am in hell' he thought, 'things cannot get any worse'.

But he was wrong again. The day after his conviction Will was taken from his relatively cosy cell and marched to the penitentiary section of the prison and to a much meaner life. Whereas before he had been a prisoner awaiting trial, theoretically innocent and entitled to certain rights under the law, now he was convicted, at the stroke of a pen reduced from free man to felon, at the mercy of a massive bureaucratic machine mindlessly controlling his every movement, every minute of every day, for seven years. As Lusty had said, he was no longer Will, he was just Cooke, 'wif an 'e' or wifout an 'e'.

And the changes began immediately. Once in the penitentiary section he was stripped, deloused in cold water and dressed in the prison uniform, a blue and yellow patchwork jacket, trousers and cap. Then his head was shaved and an iron collar rivetted around his neck so he could be easily shackled during transportation.

That final move, he was told, by other felons, could happen within days, or weeks, or months, or maybe even years.

"You better get used to not knowing what's gonna 'appen to you" one lag snarled when he asked when he would be shipped off, "you ain't human no more, you're a felon and you do what you're told, when you're told."

A rule of silence was stringently enforced in the penitentiary and strangely it was that more than anything else took him to the edge of denying the faith the Rev. Nelson had instilled in him.

The silence reinforced the fact he had been reduced to a nothing, a non-being existing in a dark, silent world. In that still darkness he understood how it was possible for a man to be reduced to the level of a mindless brute, stripped of all humanity and dignity, an animal kept alive merely to work.

Which is what was in store for him the very next morning.

His days of lying in his cell had ended and now he was required to do hard labour, the most taxing being forced to walk nowhere endlessly on a treadmill, no better than a mule or an ox, grinding grain or pumping water. His final despair was the realisation that no one might ever know of his fate. In the gaol section of the prison, inmates had been entitled to receive visitors, even if a small bribe for the guard was required. In the penitentiary visits required permission in writing from a magistrate, effectively ending all visits.

Will would never get to say goodbye to Old Tom and Maria. Time inches along in a prison when there is no goal to aim for, no end in sight. Cooke existed in just such a timeless maze for several weeks after his conviction, going through the motions of working and eating without conscious thought, resigned to being a citizen of the land of the living dead.

Oddly enough, Lusty was his saviour.

One day he had just finished a stint on the water-tread when he was called over by Lusty.

The old lag was at his babbling best, jesting and jousting with wardens and prisoners alike as if nothing had changed in his life. He and a group of about a dozen other prisoners who had all been sentenced to transportation were gathered in a close knot earnestly discussing something, 'discussing' in effect meaning being talked at by Lusty.

"Ah Cooke me lad. Well, the waiting is over, we're off!" he said, waiting expectantly for the obvious question which never came.

"Come on me ole son, snap out of it!" he said, slapping him on the shoulder.

"You can't go on like a lost soul forever. What's done is done and life goes on and we jus' gotta go on as well. The big news is, we're going this week!"

According to Lusty those earmarked for transportation were to be transferred to the prison hulk *Retribution*, anchored off the Sheerness at the mouth of the River Medway. Even the irrepressible Lusty spoke with trepidation about life on the battle scarred warships that had been turned into floating hells, staging posts where convicts from all over England were sent to spend their last days in England before being shipped to the bottom of the world.

"Mark my words" Lusty said to the audience who always congregated when he spoke, "the only job of those mindless morons on the hulks is to make sure we don't bloody want to return to England. I 'eard from one sharp lad who spent a bit o' time on one of those wooden monsters, might 'ave even been *Retribution* herself come to think of it, that a lot of men just can't stand it and jump into the river to escape. Escape from life that is" he laughed.

"He said *Retribution's* the worst of the worst of the hulks and those overseers wot work on 'em are the scum of the earth. Fact is, no one cares what 'appens on 'em because the only souls on 'em are lost souls. The walking dead, like Cooke 'ere," he laughed again.

But no one else laughed.

"Bad food, no sun and endless work in the mud. But the worst is ..." he paused for effect, "once you disappear down below those decks, ain't no one can rescue you. It's the law of the jungle on a hulk, so listen up lads. When go down, we need to go down together, in uvver words, we 'ave to stick up for each other. Mark my words, when we get to that hulk two-legged rats will be swarming all over us and if we don't stick together, we go down separately."

The next day the official word followed Lusty's. A group of 19 men, all sentenced to transportation, were told to be prepared to leave early the next morning, adding nothing about where and how they were to travel. The lack of even that little information was a calculated humiliation, though it failed because Lusty already had the details.

"We're off on a little sea voyage me hearties. We get on to an empty coal trow tomorrow for a dirty little cruise down to Bristol, better'n walkin' I reckon, and there we join a London-bound packet for the trip to Sheerness and from there it is but a hop, skip and a jump onto his majesty's prison hulk *Retribution*. Let's hope it's just a short visit."

Sheerness
September 1819

The journey from Gloucester to Sheerness passed in a blur for Cooke, lost in such deep depression that even the light of day barely made an impact on the darkness shrouding him. Shackled at wrist and ankle, and linked at the neck into manageable groups of half a dozen, the newly found felons were fed only intermittently on the four day journey, all of which was spent in the holds of ships not designed for human cargo.

Late on the afternoon of the fourth day they were disgorged onto the docks of Blue Town, the port just below the town of Sheerness, then immediately marched to ruins of a burnt out and largely roofless old customs shed in which dozens of other convicts, gathered from all over Britain, already sat chained together. Numbering 111 in total, all were due to be transferred to the hulk the next morning, but overnight a ferocious storm swept in so powerfully that the boatmen refused to face the sleet driven waves to row out to the hulk anchored in the channel. For the next two days gale-force winds drove endless sheets of rain over the exposed grey mass of convicts who, dressed only in light slops, huddled tightly together in the cavernous shed. With little food and not even blankets to shelter them, tempers flared and several times the civilian guards, bolstered by a handful of soldiers, were forced to wade through the heaving mass with batons or knotted ropes to break up fights, the flickering light from storm lanterns sending grotesque reflections of the men's hell dancing across the walls.

On the second night of their ordeal, there arose from the men a howl of anger and anguish that threatened to drown out the noise of the storm. The few troops guarding them nervously cocked their weapons, but the men's cry was not a call to violence, but of a vast upwelling of helplessness and despair.

On the morning of the third day the storm eased enough for the transfer to the hulk, the sight of which across the grey waters of the

Medway was another vision of hell. What had once been a proud battleship now squatted forlornly, its fighting deck defaced with shabby canvas shelters, its once threatening gun hatches screwed shut to keep its denizens in, its masts removed. Only the bow sprite remained, looking like the giant stinger on a mythological sea creature. Cooke, filled with dread, closed his eyes and tried to pray, but no words came. Many of the convicts had at one time or another served in the British navy and knew the story behind *Retribution*. Once HMS *Edgar,* a 74-gun ship of the line with a proud record of rendering long and honourable service to Britain, the ship had fought under Admiral Nelson at the Battle of Copenhagen where it had led the Admiral's line and was the first to open fire. A tear came to Cooke's eye as he saw what the ship had been reduced to. Turning to Lusty, to who it seemed he was destined to be forever shackled, as well as the dozen or so men in his chain gang, he lifted his head and spoke with such conviction that the beaten down, despondent men were shocked.

"Alright, you God-forsaken bunch of lowly-bred bastards, let's get out there and get this damned operation under way. The sooner we get it over and done with, the sooner we all get out of this miserable bloody rain and cold and head off to sunny New South Wales!"

Lusty was inevitably the first to pick up the note and run with it.

"By God yes, let's get the hell outta here and into the hell over there, because I can't get any bloody colder or I'll die right here and I for one ain't ready to die just yet. I've got too many ladies to meet and too many drinks to have!"

That brought a bedraggled cheer from the gang, a cheer that for some reason quickly spread to the rest of the men now lined up on the rainswept dock.

That cheer scared the guards more than their anguished cries of the previous night had, because there was no reason for it.

Gripping their weapons tighter they exchanged surprised looks.

"They've all gone mad" said one, "had to 'appen, and it's as good it 'appens sooner as later."

Retribution

Cooke had stood on the deck of a man-o-war many times in his relatively short life, but nothing he had experienced had prepared him for his first steps upon the deck of *Retribution*.

First up was the usual roll call and head count, carried out by a mix of civilian overseers, soldiers and sailors, to a constant chorus of coarse language and liberal use of knotted ropes laid on arms and legs to force the men into a resemblance of order.

They were then led to the canvas-covered quarter deck where they had their 'prison' shackles and 'prison' clothes were removed and they were made to wash in two large tubs of cold sea water, a process designed not just to de-louse the prisoners, but to continue their systematic degradation and humiliation, not to mention providing a bit of comic relief for the guards.

Each man was then issued a new set of coarse 'slops' before being re-shackled in 'convict' fetters at the ankle and waist and again chained together.

According to law, convicts were to be given a quality linen shirt, a brown jacket and a pair of breeches, but in fact the slops consisted of cheap lightweight grey shirt and pants - those in charge pocketing the difference.

Once through the washing, clothing and fettering procedure, another roll call was taken and then they were forced into a lines and addressed by the head overseer.

His message was brief and to the point.

"The captain of *Retribution* has asked me to address you. You have been found guilty by his majesty's court and will be transported to the colony of New South Wales, but until that 'appens, you will be under my command on this vessel.

"I have no doubt you have heard of this vessel as being a very 'ard place. It is a well-deserved reputation.

"You are not here to be rehabilitated, whatever that means, you are here to be punished.

"During your time here you will strictly obey all orders given to you or you will be punished.

"You will at all times show proper respect to the members of the crew, the soldiers and the civilian wardens, or you will be punished.

"If you attack, injure, or steal from any of his majesty's convicts you will be punished.

"These punishments may include being shackled in a pit, or receiving a taste of the lash.

"The Reverend Price here beside me is available to talk to you about saving your mortal soul should you wish, but in the meantime you belong to me body and soul and I strongly advise you to heed my warnings.

"If you do, time will pass quickly and you will leave in good health. If you do not, your life will be a living hell."\

"Good day."

With that the overseers set about moving the men toward the stairs to the lower decks. As the first prisoners began the descent into the portal there rose from below deck a sound like nothing Cooke had ever heard before; a rumbling noise somewhere between a growl and a howl. The hairs on his neck rose stiffly. With each step he took into the darkness the foul smell which rose to meet him deepened.

The upper deck of the old warhorse was partly lit by natural light through the hatchways, but as the guards herded the shackled men down to the lower decks, his eyes struggled to accustom to the deepening dimness. As he stepped foot on the middle deck a cacophony of caterwauling broke out from the cells, assaulting his ears with such intensity he almost lost his footing. Closed cells stretched out along on both sides of the deck, but having to focus closely on the step directly in front of him so as not to fall, he envisioned rather than saw the contorted faces mocking and calling from the shadows, arms stretched out to snatch and grab whatever they could reach.

"Ow's it goin' me darlin' shouted one animal, "nice of you to come on down here after your bath. I'm waiting for ya."

"Fresh meat tonight maties. Get yer coin ready me darlin's, you're gonna be needin' it if you want to wake up tomorrow."

Cooke looked around to Lusty, as ever close behind him.

"What on earth …"

16 Prison Hulk Retribution. Sheerness. September 1819. Original by John Grieve. National Maritime Museum.

"I tol ya," hissed Lusty sharply, "I heard from those wot know that this 'ere is like nothin' on earth. Listen up me hearties" he said, turning to the rest of the group, "I warn you now, we need to stick together or we will be destroyed. Follow my lead, support me and we survive."

Huddling even closer together, the gang was shoved down the hatchway to the lowest deck where the whole group spontaneously stopped, desperately trying to adjust to the dim yellow light thrown by a few purser's glims, fearful and on guard against whatever might be lurking.

Once his eyes had adjusted Cooke could see that the first two thirds of the deck had been divided into tiny compartments, separated from each other by bulkheads and from the gangway down the centre by iron bars, giving the space the appearance of a zoo - a human zoo. Behind the bars human animals screeched and cackled abuse at them.

The last third of the deck was fitted with tables and benches where the convicts ate and could spend what time they might have out of their cell, if any. Cooke's gang was halted while a guard went ahead to unlock a cell next to the eating area and he had time to take in just a little of the scene around him. Each cell, originally designed to hold between five to eight convicts, now held 16 or more. He saw that some of the cells had built-in bunks, designed initially to sleep a single convict, but now two men were forced to sleep in the same space of about two foot by five foot. To solve the space problem most cells used hammocks which, navy style, were rolled up and tied to the walls during the day.

As Cooke and his group waited, he could see most of the convicts who were heckling and shouting abuse and making lewd comments were fettered at the ankle and locked into their cells, however a number of big men were out of the cells, lounging against the bars and intently watching the new group. He assumed they were convict warders, men who he already knew from his own experience were the worse of the worst, far more brutal and callous than the civilian overseers or army guards. After a few minutes his group was squeezed into the cell opened for them, the guards then left, presumably to fetch new groups, but immediately the guards disappeared one of the big men who had been loitering sauntered into the cell and, grabbing Cooke from behind by the collar of his slops, shook him violently.

"Where's your stash then shorty," he barked. Cooke tried to swing a punch to meet the challenge, but was powerless in the thug's steel grip. He was saved when Lusty suddenly stepped up behind them and smashed his fist into the thug's face, sending him staggering and falling sidewards, dragging Cooke with him. Tossing Cooke aside the giant let loose a roar and swinging wildly charged at Lusty, who ducked expertly but was swept forward and onto the cell floor by the weight of the charging thug.

Cooke could see that Lusty would be no match for the brute and struggled to his feet to help, but before he could do anything the rest of his group rushed to the attack. The thug was smothered in fists and knees as all the men in the cell waded in with blows and kicks, felling the big man and quickly bashing him unconscious.

It happened so quickly that other thugs in the area were dumfounded.

For a few moments there was a stand-off.

After a minute a few of the other big men stepped forward to intervene, but stopped upon seeing the phalanx in front of them. Lusty stepped up to end the impasse. Standing over the beaten and bleeding thug he pointed a bloodied fist at the men who were slowly coalescing into a group to reignite the fight.

"You lot! Mess with anyone of us and you mess with us all and don't expect to get off as light as 'im. Next bloke will end up going for a swim! And anyone as opens their gob to the guards can expect to go for a swim as well. You got it!"

It was not a question. None of the men gathered around looked intimidated, they were all far beyond fear of anything for that, but the downed man was a man of mark who had ruled the area by fist and head and teeth since he had arrived, so no one was prepared to challenge the cell that had put him down, in part because no one cared. Accepting the status quo with a shrug, they drifted away, preferring the easier pickings no doubt on their way down.

Cooke was dumbstruck. He remembered Lusty had spoken about what would happen on the hulk and what needed to happen, but at the time he had dismissed it as mere talk, because Lusty talked a lot. He now understood that not only had his friend been right, but that he had had the presence of mind to act in exactly the right way at the right time.

'In the jungle, the law of the jungle prevails' he thought, 'and I need to know this is the way it will be.'

It didn't take long for the new men to become acquainted with an ordinary day on the *Retribution*. The cooks started the day 3am, getting breakfast ready for the 450 convicts who were rousted from their cells at 5.30am to be mustered onto the deck for rollcall fifteen minutes later. Breakfast, usually bread and boiled oatmeal, was eaten in strict silence, as were all meals. Breaking the rule of silence resulted in rations being cut for every man on that table, which might prove to have been a fatal mistake for the speaker. Lunch was the same, but the evening meal consisted of meat, either boiled or made into soup. Two days a week the meat was replaced by oatmeal and cheese.

Another variation was soup of salted split yellow peas served with bread or biscuit, both usually mouldy.

Each prisoner was entitled to two pints of beer four days a week, depending on their behaviour and the attitude of the head overseer, with just plain water on the other days. At 9pm every night the overseer would give the order for silence throughout the ship.

All boats would be secured and accounted for and all fires extinguished. Locks were examined by the Officer on Watch who took possession of the keys. The night watch, consisting of two guards, were relieved every three and a half hours. Every half hour during the night the officer of the watch struck a bell and his cry of 'all's well' was replied to by all guards until the time for morning rollcall.

Below decks were supposed to be patrolled at night by one guard while another guarded the hatchway, but rarely were either soldiers or overseers brave enough to venture into the murderous anarchy that regularly erupted in the dark, evil-smelling purgatory that prevailed once cells were 'locked' at 9.30pm.

If mayhem or riot demanded action, regulations decreed that the sergeant of the watch had to be called to make a decision, but it would have to be a serious matter to risk raising the non-commissioned officer from his slumbers. As soon as breakfast was finished, on rotation one of the three decks on the ship would be sluiced down with river water - cold and salty. This was supposed to keep the ship clean but instead merely help create a damp and fetid environment which bred disease.

The officers in charge of this caricature of a naval vessel had quarters at the stern in cabins once occupied by real navy officers, but they were rarely to be found on board because in reality there was little for them to do. The role of guarding the convicts was relegated to the civilian overseers and a few soldiers who, like the sailors on board, resented the lowly position they found themselves in and took out their resentment and frustration on those who they saw as being responsible for it - the convicts. Because *Retribution* was in theory a navy ship there was a navy surgeon on board, but sick convicts were given little medical attention because the surgeon, like the officers, spent most of the day and into the night visiting local inns or local ladies.

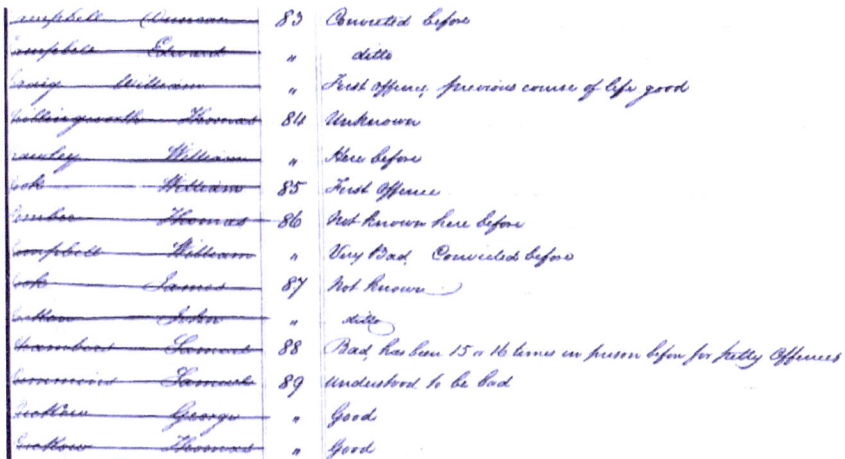

*17 UK Prison Hulk Registers and Letter Books, 1802 - 1849.
A telling record of how gaolers saw hulk prisoners, rating them from 'good' to 'bad' or even 'has been 15 or 16 times in prison...' to 'very bad. Convicted before'. Cooke is recorded simply as 'first offense'.*

Over the next few days Cooke and the new arrivals learnt just why the *Retribution* was so hated and feared. Convicts were kept fettered below decks at all times, mostly in their cells, let out only for the thin, tasteless meals which seemed to have been deliberately designed to weaken convicts and keep them docile. Everyone was constantly hungry.

Cooke soon realised that the practice of locking cells at night was a largely pointless operation on a ship containing a concentrated collection of professional lock-picks and house-breakers. It also soon became obvious that there was some form of nefarious agreement between the roving convict stand-over merchants and the guards, who would leave some cells unlocked, no doubt to secure a share whatever loot resulted.

Cooke's cell was untouched, not only because of the thrashing his fellow inmates had given the first thug, but because his mess had set up a system of round-the-clock watches to warn of other roving thugs. In addition they managed to secure the cell door at night with a length of brass wire Lusty had contrived to 'find'. The wire would not stop a determined invasion, but it would give the defenders time to prepare to repel the attackers.

The last man on watch had the job of hiding the wire because if found, it would have meant a taste of the lash for everyone in the cell. In those cells where no defence system was devised, chaos and mayhem were regular visitors. The sound of men being beaten and of young juveniles who shared cells with the men crying and howling as they were attacked and oft-times abused was night-time's constant lament.

Despite the constant threat of being beaten by either the overseers or their convict enforcers, and despite all of the men being constantly alert to the slightest possibility of robbing their cellmates - or being robbed by them - or of being informed upon or informing on their cellmates, there were at times an uplifting of the common man's indominable spirit; a coming together of men of the same ilk and breed - almost of the same tribe - who at the end of the day had pain, suffering and profound loss in common.

The irrepressible humour of the British working man, for that is what most of the convicts had been and would still be if they had the chance, meant that there was always a funny observation to be made or a witty remark that could lighten a dark day. Unlike other prisoners on other hulks, who spent ten hours a day toiling in the muddy warrens of Woolwich or elsewhere, there was little hard labour to be done near where *Retribution* was anchored.

In the hour between the last meal and 'lights out', and often for long periods afterwards, men would gather in knots to play draughts, cards or dominos, but mostly to talk of the life they once knew and speculate on their life to come. There was talk of wives and children left behind who might never be seen again, of sweethearts most certain to find someone else, of elderly parents bereft at the loss of a son sure never to be seen again. There was also a fathomless anger at having been misjudged and misused and for being forever stained with the mark of Cain merely because their accusers and judges were of a different class, and dark talk of revenge to be meted out should ever a chance be presented. There was sometimes talk of escape, though no one knew of any successful escape from the hulk, anchored as it was midstream in freezing cold water swept by deep and deadly currents.

"I've left behind a lovely woman I 'ave" admitted Lusty, "an' I'm sorry to say I did not treat her well. She was a good woman, none too bright mind" he added to catcalls from the dark, "but there's nothing I wouldn't give to be back wrapped in her generous bosom right now."

"Me too" came the call from at least half a dozen voices.

"Oy, watch it you bastards" he shouted, with lightness in his voice.

"I've heard that New South Wales is a strange land full of unknown creatures" said Ed Sheppard, the oldest man in the cell.

"If'n they be unknown, 'ow come you 'erd of 'em then" someone piped up, triggering another burst of laughter.

"No, seriously. I 'erd tell of monstrous rats, big as men, wot hop faster than a horse can run and wot can jump over the tallest trees; an' of snakes whose bite can kill a man in seconds."

"There's said to be black men wot throw sticks that come straight back to them wot frew 'em. That is dark magic that is," he said to an outbreak of incredulous laughter.

After the laughter died down a silent moment of reflection fell on the cell, each man again lost in his own world of angst and regret.

"How long you reckon we gonna stay on this hell ship then Lusty" asked young Tom Hall. At just 15 he was one of the youngest on board and already had seen and heard enough about what could happen to him that he walked about with constant fear clearly visible in his bloodshot eyes, "you seem to know everyfing".

"I know better'n to guess" Lusty shot back, "but I know this, it can't come too soon. From everything I've been told it seems we've 'ad it pretty good so far. No pestilence, no murders, almost food enough. Bad as it is, mark my words, the good times can't last."

Prophetic words they turned out to be.

That night the strong winds that had buffeted the ship for more than a week finally eased and the next day stopped altogether, leaving a deadly calm in its place. As annoying as the wind had been, only when it stopped did the men realise the bitter wind had been a blessing in disguise as it forced fresh air into all the dark corners of the ship. Over the next few days as the sun shone down, the temperature steadily rose, especially in the dark and overcrowded lower decks where the river water used to sluice down the cells sank into corners and crevices, only to well back up again filled with pestilence.

Four days after the wind died the coughing began.

The first to go down with gaol fever in Cooke's cell was old Ed. During the night he began calling for water and his fellow convicts found him bathed in sweat and burning with fever. They called for the night guard, who simply shouted down the gangway for them to shut up and wait for morning. Shortly before morning the old man died, the first of many to do so in the days ahead. Soon dry barking coughs and urgent cries for water had replaced that of men shouting and fighting and swearing as the sound of the night.

Everyone quickly recognised the symptoms. The raw coughing was followed by a swelling in the neck, said to be a sure sign of consumption, the dreaded 'white plague' for which there was no cure. Soon after beginning to cough those afflicted began to suffer raging fevers, even as their hands and feet were ice cold and they had shivers that rattled their bones. Constant coughing delivered nothing except blood as lungs were torn apart.

Once one man went down ill, usually the rest of his cell followed soon afterwards. Many cells lost up to a quarter of their number in the few weeks the scourge raged, with survivors having to spend nights cooped up with corpses until overseers unlocked cells in the morning. The speed and power of the epidemic as it swept through the ship meant that there was no hope of isolating sick men, even though they had all been unshackled, in part because the guards would not touch the dead. Once the tell-tale swellings appeared those afflicted were simply dragged out of the cells by their 'mates' in a futile attempt to at least keep them away from everyone else.

Victims soon lost control of their bowels and very quickly the entire ship smelt so foul that the guards refused to down below decks, instead leaving cells open all day so the dead could be dragged up on deck by their cellmates.

The ship's surgeon quickly gave up the unequal fight and relocated to shore, boarding the ship only to give orders to overseers and soldiers, and then not daring to venture below decks into the writhing mass of contagion. In less than three weeks almost 100 convicts died, as did several overseers and a lone sailor. Cooke was one of those spared, as were most of the younger convicts, so he ended up being placed in charge of one of the work details man-handling the dead onto boats to be taken ashore for burial, though not to the town's cemetery because the reverend refused to accept the bodies of the accursed. Instead the ship's cutter constantly ferried the corpses across the gunmetal grey width of the Medway to a small swampy spit of land which quickly came known as Deadman's Island, to be buried in shallow graves or, if time was short, to be left on the shore for the wild dogs, the high tide and the fish to do their work.

Being part of the burial gang became one of the most prized work details on the ship and each cell vied for the job of running it. The gang's job was to wrap the bodies in canvas before ferrying them across to Deadman's Island.

Once on the island the hardened old lags would unwrap the body to steal the dead man's clothes and any coins they contained, often slicing up the body to look for any other hidden money.

After the epidemic burnt itself out, the daily procedure of 'normal' life returned to the hulks, which meant that the visitors returned. One of the few perks convicts on the hulks enjoyed was that friends or family members were able to visit them on a virtually unlimited basis and to bring them things that might help them, on the understanding that the guards were to receive a gratuity for allowing the visits. A less welcome visit was the regular post-church Sunday outing for the fashionable youths of the area, especially young girls, who thought it amusing to be punted across to the hulk and, keeping to a cautious distance with perfumed cloths to nose and mouth to stifle the smell, circle the stricken colossus so that the guide might point out the convicts who were paraded by the overseers for show. It was several weeks after the plague had ended that Cooke was told he had a visitor.

Bewildered and excited, while at the same time telling himself that it was surely a mistake and that he would soon be back in his cell, he was escorted to the top deck and at once recognised the gnarled and bent figure of Old Tom Hobbes standing beside the gangway.

He was leaning on a walking stick, a new accoutrement, and was with difficulty carrying a duffle bag. The old man waved and began to hobble forward while Cooke, constrained by his fetters, did the same, the pair embracing for a few moments until an overseer stepped forward to break the clinch. Tables and benches were provided on the covered quarter deck for these visits and the pair sat silently, each unwilling to break the silence lest they dissolve into tears.

"How has it been my boy" old Tom said at last.

"Are you being treated well?"

Cooke nodded, unable to speak. The old man nodded slowly in reply.

"Are you well? How is mother Maria?" asked Cooke.

Old Tom nodded again.

"We are both fine. Fine. Don't worry about us. Maria sends her love and she has made a cake, which I have here, and some warm clothes and a good pocket-knife."

"Ah, and some medicine she wants you to take. OK?"

Cooke smiled and nodded.

"How did you find me here? In Gloucester I didn't know where I was being taken. I wrote you a letter from here. Did you get it?"

"No, no letter" said Tom, "but I have been travelling and not at home for a while, so maybe it will be there when I get home."

Then, looking around to see that no guards were nearby, he leaned in to whisper to the only son he had ever known.

"I have some news. I have been making some inquiries. The Shipwrights Company knows everything and it seems you are to be put on a ship called *Mangles,* under a Captain Coghill, sometime in March. No one knows Coghill, so ... " he trailed off.

"But I have some good news also. I have a friend here, another old shipwright, and I am staying with him. And Bill Caught from *Defiance* is also here, come to support me and help if'n he can. I have brought your tool chest and it is there, but I don't want to risk bringing it aboard this stinking tub. We need to make a plan for you to get it aboard the *Mangles*. You have a right to keep it there because the *Mangles* is controlled by Navy regulations, so it will be fine. Here it would be stolen in a day."

Cooke said nothing, his head bowed, tears welling in his eyes.

"My boy, I know how really bad this is, but you must hold your head high. There is no other way and you must survive. I know seven years seems forever to you now, but you are young and you will survive it. I am old so I know how short seven years is."

As he finished speaking a local overseer walked over.

"Mr Hobbes isn't it?" he asked, almost politely.

Both men looked at him in shock.

"I am told you are a friend of Mr Wainwright here in Sheerness, who is my father. My father says you are ex-Navy, as is he."

"That's correct" the old man replied, breathing a sigh of relief, "as is my son here. I was told Wainwright's boy was on board and I'm thankful you have made yourself known. I have a few things for my boy," he said, lifting up the bag, "and a little something for yourself" he added, deftly slipping something into the man's hand. "I will make sure more reaches you through your father."

The overseer nodded.

"Time is up, so you must go, but of course you may come again. Anytime."

Cooke and the old man stood and again embraced.

"Father, for indeed you are my only father, thank you from the bottom of my heart."

The old man gave him a final hug, whispering, "be strong."

"You can do it."

Back in his cell that evening Cooke carefully divided the cake among his cellmates, all savouring each and every crumb. He slipped the pocket-knife inside his jacket and stowed his new gifts in his rolled up hammock, the eyes of each man following his movements.

"I trust each of you" Cooke said simply, not bothering to turn around, "if anyone needs anything of mine, you have only to ask."

Each week for the next two weeks old Tom arrived with gifts, including more cake - a gift beyond value to the convicts and which bought tears to many hardened eyes. Each time old Tom visited the overseer made sure he was nearby, confident in the knowledge his 'gifts' had been passed to his father, who in turn had bade him treat the old carpenter well, for he was well-known and loved in naval circles. On the third week, after handing over a few more gifts, Old Tom leaned in and, speaking softly, gave Cooke the news he had been desperate to hear, but was now dreading.

"*Mangles* arrives in about three days and will leave as soon as it loads, though that can often take some time I'm told. I have not been able to find out anything about the captain so the only thing I can think to do is to bring your chest down to the dock and, as you board, I will try to somehow arrange for it to be loaded on your behalf, perhaps with the help of that fine young man" he said with a nod to the overseer.

"You have a right to it as it's your property, but that may count for nothing, depending on the Captain. I have been told that having a chest or other things delivered to convicts being transported is often done. Our friend the overseer will be on hand to help if he can, but the problem is that he may be on the hulk and cannot control what happens on the dock.

"Be strong my boy, and all will be well."

Three days later on the 15th of March, the *Mangles* sailed into the Medway, tying up at the Blue Town docks. News of the arrival of the ship that would take them to the other side of the world swept through the *Retribution* within minutes, fermenting a sense of agitation and fear among the convicts that was quickly transmitted to the guards, who quickly locked prisoners into their cells early that afternoon. The next morning Lusty was on kitchen duty and by the time the breakfast muster was over and the men returned to their cells, he was able to let his cellmates know what fate held for them.

"Well, the first thing is, not everyone on the hulk is gonna fit on *Mangles,* it's too small and I hear there are to be lags from other hulks to be put on board as well. I got a look at the ship and it looks fast. But only about 200 will get on board and I don't know how they're gonna pick and choose, but if we can we must stay together" he said.

Mangles
March 1820

The next morning Cooke and those inmates selected for transfer to *Mangles* were mustered on their respective decks before being herded piecemeal on to the top deck to be ferried over to the docks. On deck there was yet another muster and roll call. Any possessions held in storage for the transportees were handed over to the officer designated as the Receiver of Prisoner Property for *Mangles* and signed for. The men were then again stripped and issued yet another set of slops, fettered in new irons and herded onto a cutter to be ferried ashore to *Mangles*. Looking across the Medway, Cooke's sailor's eyes lit up as he looked across at the shiny black hull and rakish lines of a three-masted schooner of about 600 tons.

He had already learnt from Lusty that the ship had been built in Calcutta in 1802, from Indian teak, and even boasted a copper sheathed hull to repel wood boring worms.

To the inexperienced eye it looked sleek and fast and anything but a convict carrier. A more experienced eye would have noted the small, barred hatches, high bulwarks and barricaded exercise area midships. The ship had had her two decks above the lower cargo hold converted to fit about 200 convicts, squashing the officer's quarters up as a consequence. Already on board were a detachment of 30 soldiers of the 48th Regiment of Foot, ten of them accompanied by their wives and children, under the command of Lt. Matthews of the 1st battalion, 59th Regiment of Foot, along with Royal navy Surgeon Matthew Anderson, an experienced naval doctor on his second voyage to New South Wales.

As he shuffled slowly forward Cooke looked around for Lusty, concerned his one-time nuisance become trusted friend was not at his side. Turning to a knot of overseers, he asked if they knew where Lusty might be.

"Missin' your sweetheart already then are ye?" came a chorus of ribald comments. "Don't you be frettin', maybe you'll get together over in the wilds of New South Wales, but it won't be on this trip. He's been restricted to kitchen duties for insubordination."

Cooke was devastated. The two men had not only become good friends, they depended on each other, their different talents and abilities blending perfectly.

Closing his eyes he involuntarily uttered a rare obscenity, raging impotently against the arbitrary system which controlled all aspects of his life without any regard to consequence and which had once again, without malice or even purpose, had torn from him yet another thing he had come to hold dear, but as usual there was nothing to be done.

As he shuffled toward the gangway and off the hated hulk he looked around one last time, but Lusty was not be seen and Cooke never saw him again.

'He'll be fine' he thought, 'he'll land on his feet wherever he goes. Probably be better off without me', but inside his guts were churning with the dread of once again being alone. From where he stood he could see clumps of family and friends who had found their way to Sheerness over the past weeks and months, ferrying out to the hulk almost every day to support sons, brothers, and even fathers. Now they had come to wave a final farewell.

Among them he made out Old Tom, standing with two other men, Cooke's tool chest at their feet. They were all being kept away from the convicts by a few armed soldiers, so there was no chance to speak to the old man. Once again his heart sank. Only now did he realise how desperate he had been to once again touch some link to his past freedom, even something as simple as his tools, his instruments and his treasured telescope. Now it seemed that even those last few things he could call his own were to be ripped from him.

As he walked up the gangplank of *Mangles* he saw Old Tom and Bill Caught in an animated, agitated conversation with a knot of sailors and an officer from the ship and he guessed that the men were doing all that could be done to get his precious chest on board. His head sank to his chest, his spirit again crushed at the capricious way fate had turned her face against him. Recalling the many times he had spoken to the Reverend Nelson, he raised his eyes heavenwards. 'My Lord', he said softly, 'why hath thou forsaken me?'

Then, once again, he was standing on the deck of a functioning ship of sail. At any other time his heart would have been lifted, but now he stood stooped and beaten. The convicts had been shepherded together on what would have been the quarter deck but which was now set up as a pen. Both port and starboard bulwarks had been built up higher than was normal on a merchantman - designed to dissuade anyone from clambering overboard. Instead of the usual largely ornamental balustrade, the poop deck and forecastle featured sturdy barricades, each with slits for rifles, backed up by swivel cannons mounted fore and aft which could command the closed-in quarter deck. Any attempt by the convicts to storm the ship would find them beneath the guns of the soldiers and crew and they would be slaughtered in the killing field of the quarter deck.

Deep in the background he heard someone addressing the convicts.

"... remember what I have said. If you obey the rules, if you obey the officers and crew, if you show the right attitude, you will be treated fairly on this ship.

"Whatever your crimes, you have been sent to the other side of the world to atone for them and that is your punishment. It is not my aim to add to that.

"Nor is my aim to reform you or to improve you. I dinna care about you. My contract is to transport you to New South Wales and I will do my best to get you there in as good a condition as possible because I am being paid to do so, and for nought other reason.

"On board is navy surgeon-superintendent Matthew Anderson, who will also do his best to see you are delivered to Sydney town in good health.

"During the voyage here will also be opportunities for you to improve your education. Those of you who have possessions or money you wish to hand over for safe-keeping will, after I finish speaking, stand to the port side where those goods will be handed to the second officer of the ship, Mr Atherden, acting Receiver of Convict Property.

"Your goods will be recorded and secured to be handed back to you at the end of the voyage.

"Once we are at sea your fetters may be removed, but know they can be replaced in an instant if needs be.

"Now listen carefully. I warn you, be aware any infringement of the rules, any action of disobedience or revolt may result in all privileges for all prisoners being revoked. I have authority to use whatever means necessary to ensure discipline and I will have no hesitation in doing so. You will be treated well if you behave well, it is a simple as that.

"Good day."

As the words seeped into Cooke's brain, somewhere deep inside a memory stirred. A link reconnected. Looking up he saw a tall, strong-looking man beneath a shock of red hair.

Dott! He almost shouted the name out loud. Standing there in the guise of captain was none other than James Dott, his former shipmate from *Defiance*. Older, bigger, but the same confident, self-assured and commanding figure of James Dott. Instantly he knew he had to talk to the man. If he could somehow get Dott's ear perhaps his fortunes might yet change for the better, the question was how?

'Where is Lusty when I need him' he thought.

Dott had finished speaking and sometime after that the overseers from *Retribution* left the ship, having handed the convicts over to the crew and the soldiers. The mass of men waited as those who had possessions lined up to hand them over and but when a sailor walked past he took his chance.

"Sir, excuse me." The man stopped.

"Would it be possible to speak to Captain Dott?"

"Who?"

"The Captain. Captain Dott."

The sailor looked at him as if he were crazy.

"There be no Captain Dott on this ship, you loon", he said, "there be a Captain Coghill, who just finished speaking to you."

With that the man moved on, shaking his head. Cooke thought he might actually be crazy. Turning to look at the man who was still standing on the poop deck speaking to the Captain of the hulk, he looked carefully at the man. He was bigger than he remembered, but in his mind there was no doubt the captain of *Mangles* was the man he knew to be James Dott. Even the man's Scottish accent was the same as he remembered.

As the convicts were shuffled below decks, Cooke's mind was racing. Why was Dott calling himself Coghill? He knew that probably only half the men on board on any naval ship were using the name they had been born with, each for his own reasons, but whatever Dott's reason, he knew he had to speak to him.

The question was how, and, more importantly, what would he say if he did get the chance to speak?

He knew that even if Dott remembered him, there was nothing the man could do to change Cooke's plight and a convict he would remain.

'But perhaps' he thought, 'just perhaps, I may well be able to get him to allow me my chest'.

As a first step in the new direction promised by the captain, the chains linking the convicts together were struck off, albeit while the armed soldiers kept a close watch, leaving them still fettered at the ankles. The convicts were then escorted below decks, every man noticing at once the lack of shouting and beating they were accustomed to.

Each man was issued with a pair of shoes, three shirts, two pairs of trousers, a jacket, a bowl, a plate, a wooden spoon, a cup and a water jug. Below deck the prison-like iron bars of the hulk were gone, and instead both sides of the two decks above the cargo deck were divided into two rows of sleeping berths, each berth holding three-tiered bunks one above the other, along on each side of the between-decks of the convict ship.

Each bunk was a regulation five foot six inches by eighteen inches and came with its own blanket and pillow. Lining the side of the deck were scuttle-holes that could be opened and closed according to need which provided both ventilation and light, though they were barred to prevent even a small lad trying an escape. Access to the 'tween decks' was by means of ladders which were pulled on deck at night, with the final hatch closed and guarded by an armed sentry. On the upper deck was a 'hospital' space beneath the forecastle, a strong bulk-head separating it from the accommodation of the soldiers and the married quarters, with two doors strongly bolted - on the inside with locks to keep out intruders. The aft section of the convict's decks included tables for eating, teaching classes, religious instruction and even occasional plays, with bibles, prayer-books and psalters distributed among the messes. In the brief moment while the convicts stood in awe and the guards prepared for the next step of dividing the men into messes of nine, Cooke acted. Quickly gathering as many as he could of those around him who had shared the same cell on the hulk, he whispered that once the guards had signalled for them to step out, they should all crowd into the one berth.

Less than a minute later when the guards gave the order to fall out, the group acted as one, surging into the nearest berth and in the process knocking aside two men who were not of their group.

In seconds each sat on their own bunk, in their own space, grinning at each other, a small victory won. In truth they need not have bothered, the other convicts from hulks in London and Portsmouth had not yet arrived and would not do so for weeks, so there was plenty of room. Unlike the perpetual deep shadows of the *Retribution*, on *Mangles* there was enough light for the men to see each other clearly, the afternoon sunlight streaming in from the scuttle-holes. Not every berth had a scuttle-hole, but Cooke's did and the light and air raised the spirits of the men.

As the men sat and talked, grinning inanely, Cooke's mind was spinning. He had to find a way to speak to the captain, but how. Normally the very idea of a convict asking to speak to the captain of a convict ship would be ludicrous.

Casting his mind back to his days on *Defiance* after he had saved Dott from failing his midshipman's exam by pointing him to his precious notebook, Dott had not only acted as his protector, but had admitted he owed Cooke a debt, a debt Cooke had never collected. He fully understood now was the time to call in the debt, very carefully to be sure, but most certainly called none the less. As he wracked his brain for a ploy to speak up he became aware of a prisoner rasping the dry and hacking hulk cough which been a permanent background noise on the hulk, unremarkable and unremarked upon, but now the noise stood out and several of the men commented on it, pondering aloud if the man should ask to see the doctor.

Instantly Will saw the way forward. Without uttering a word he walked to the hatchway where two guards stood.

"Excuse me Sir," he said, perhaps overdoing the servility, "would it be possible to see the doctor? I have a bad cough and I'm struggling to breathe."

The one guard looked to the other and then at Will.

"You seem alright to me," he said, not moving.

"I have the catarrh and I don't want to spread it through this fine ship like it went through the *Retribution*. We lost over a hundred dead" he replied, adding a cough to underline his plea.

Both the soldiers unconsciously stepped away.

"Wait here" said the older one, "I'll find out if the doctor will see you."

Ten minutes later Cooke was standing in the cramped and airless room that passed as a doctor's surgery on *Mangles*. The Surgeon looked too young to be a doctor Cooke thought, but sat quietly while the 'sawbones' wrote some notes into what seemed to be a diary.

"Alright, ah, Cooke, what is it? Come on, speak up," he said as Will hesitated.

"Sir, I just want to say first up that I was once in the service. In fact Sir, I was at Trafalgar, on the *Victory* for a while, but mainly on *Defiance*."

Anderson looked anew at the man before him. He certainly had the look of a sailor he thought, and had the scars to prove it. His blonde hair was short-cropped above deep-set blue eyes that did not waver - a good sign. The man was a bit on the short side, about five foot Anderson thought, but well-built and he carried himself well. Importantly he knew how to address an officer, unlike most of the trash on board.

"Yes, well that must have been quite an adventure and well done. But what is wrong with you now?" Again Will hesitated.

"Well, you see Sir, I believe I know Captain … uh, Captain Coghill who I think also fought at Trafalgar Sir, and I was hoping that you might allow me the chance to very briefly renew my acquaintance with the Captain, Sir."

Seeing the instant look of disbelief that crossed the doctor's face, he quickly rushed on.

"It's just that, well Sir, I believe I have some information that may be of use to the Captain Sir. It's not that want to misuse my position of once having served Sir, but I do believe I can be of service once again."

To Cooke's relief, Anderson now at least looked intrigued.

"You say you think you knew Coghill? At Trafalgar? Well, that's more than anyone else on this ship knows about the man I warrant you." For a long moment he looked at Cooke, who thought that the surgeon must have seen right through his ruse and he would shortly not only be thrown out of the surgery, but into the ship's black hole. Then the surgeon sat back in his chair, consternation narrowing his eyebrows.

"Come with me" he said, suddenly standing and walking off briskly.

A moment later he was at the captain's cabin and, motioning Cooke to stay where he was, knocked on the captain's door. An armed sentry stood on the other side of the door.

"Come" came the bark. Anderson entered and closed the door behind him. Standing rigid, partly from fear, partly scared and elated, much like he had felt on that fateful day as *Victory* sailed into action all guns blazing. And just as he had on that remarkable day, he felt fate was taking control again and that life might never be the same for him. That feeling was strengthened when soon the murmurings coming from behind the door escalated into what seemed like angry words. He literally stopped breathing when the door opened and a white-faced Anderson pushed past him and stalked down the corridor, not saying a word. A moment later the Captain appeared at the door and stared intently at him.

"Who are you?" he demanded.

"Sir" Will responded, instantly dragged back into navy style, "William Thomas Cooke, Sir. I was a cabin boy on *Defiance* before going onto *Victory* at Trafalgar, Sir."

The red-headed giant - he stood at least a head over Cooke - stood rock still for a moment, before turning back into his cabin. "Come inside" he said, "and close the door" a deep frown crunching his forehead.

Just as he had when he was a midshipmen on *Defiance*, Cooke could feel the latent menace of the man hovering near the surface. Violence seemed permanently coiled within him, ready to be unleashed by the slightest provocation. But while the physical threat inherent in the man remained, Cooke felt something else had changed. He well remembered that Dott, or Coghill, if that was indeed his name, had always been more than ready to fight over any real or imagined slight, but it also seemed that back then there had been deep inside the man a touch of humanity that had stopped the violence becoming meanness. Cooke intuitively felt that touch was gone.

The face was harder. Deep lines ran from his nose to a mouth pressed tight. A scar sliced through his left eyebrow down to his ear and another cleft his chin, but it was the eyes that frightened Will. The light that had once danced there was now gone, replaced by a darkness that spilt out onto the surrounding skin.

The captain was leaning back on a small desk, hands spread back in support, and he stood like that for almost a minute. Fear that began to spread up from Cooke's gut.

'This man may kill me right here and now' he thought, 'and not give the slightest damn'.

18 Captain John Coghill, circa 1820.
By unknown artist - Wikimedia Commons. Public domain.

But then Coghill's frown faded, to be replaced by a snarl Cooke would learn was as close to a smile as the man could ever achieve.

"Well, well, well. If it isn't Nelson's boy," he said at last, "you've grown up since last we met. T'was on *Defiance* just after the funeral of Lord Nelson if memory serves me correctly. A strange time it was, and now fate has thrown you into my world at another strange time."

Walking around the desk he bent to look out of his window, bumping his head as he did so and cursing aloud in response. He stood looking out at the dock for several minutes, evidently deep in thought, leaving Cooke standing uncomfortably to attention, before walking around to sit behind the desk.

"I admit to being bit surprised to see you here among these rogues and fools Cooke. I recall you were always the well-behaved one. What have you done to warrant being amongst this sorry lot?"

"Sir, I swear on the honour of Lord Nelson, whose honour I hold above all else, that I did nothing but reject the advances of a young girl. Her father accused me of larceny in stealing some lead, of which I assure you I did not, but my pleas were of no avail.

"I am here not guilty of any crime, but I can do nothing about it."

Coghill nodded, perhaps in agreement, perhaps not, but saying nothing.

"Yes, well, not only you but no doubt every other felon on board has such a story" he said.

"I can believe your tale, but as you say, that is as it is and there is nought to be done about it."

"I also recall you helping me at an important moment in my life and I assume that that is why you are standing before me now, am I correct?"

The long silence Coghill had used to gather his thoughts had also given Cooke time to recover his own and to restore his determination to follow to the end the dangerous course of action he had set himself upon. In truth the knew there was no alternative. He understood that the man standing before him, whatever his name was, literally held his life in his hands and he now remembered the fatal end that had befallen midshipman Williamson, his tormenter on *Defiance*. He also remembered this very man relating Williamson's fate and implying he may well have been the messenger of that fate. He had no doubt that if the man in front of him felt threatened by his presence in any way, he would with no compunction treat him as he had treated Williamson.

"Sir, I would never be so bold as to presume anything. I recall the incident, but at that time I did only what I believed was the right thing to do and I do not in any way wish to profit for having done so."

Coghill sat looking askance, clearly not believing a word.

Forced to continue, Cooke rushed on.

"Sir, I would plead for just one thing. On the dock right now stands my father who guards a chest of mine. An old friend you may recall, William Caught, who was the *Defiance* carpenter, is also here in support. If I could only get that chest I would be very grateful. That chest may be the difference between life and death for me in the land I am being sent to."

Coghill looked at him sharply.

"I remember Caught. I never liked him, nor he I. What's in the chest that you want it so badly and that these men would be here to help you have it?"

"Sir, both my father and old Bill are shipwrights and carpenters as am I now, as well as a cabinet-maker, and in the chest are my tools. If I were to have those tools I may yet be able to rebuild my life in the colony."

Once again Coghill said nothing. Getting to his feet he again walked to the window, again bumping his head, and in that instant Will perceived that his plea was about to be rejected. In desperation he looked around the tiny, ill-designed cabin and a sudden idea arose in his mind.

"Sir, I could even use those tools to rework your cabin. I can see that it does not befit a man of your position, or indeed of your stature, Sir."

Coghill looked around and shook his head.

"I recall Captain Durham said Lord Nelson called you a bad penny that kept on turning up, t'was not an insult I gathered at the time. And yes, you are right. I have only recently bought into his vessel and this" he spread his hands "does not suit me at all.

"This is my first voyage to the colony of New South Wales and while I intend to complete it in record time, it is a long voyage and already I can see this cabin and my sleeping quarters will be a fag. So you may well be of assistance to me."

He turned to look out at the dock, obviously debating with himself.

"All right Nelson's boy, you shall have your tools. And indeed it is a fine idea that you should remake this humble abode into something more fitting, but I will have something in return. You will speak to no one about knowing me at any time in the past, nor of my time on *Defiance.* Most importantly you will not, on pain of death, ever mention to anyone under any circumstances the name of James Dott.

"Is that clear?"

Will nodded. "Of course Sir, but I fear I may have already made a slip of the tongue to the good doctor Anderson. I am so sorry."

Squeezing behind his desk to sit down, Coghill dismissed the issue with a shake of the head.

"Anderson will nay be any problem, I'll see to that. But from here on Captain John Coghill is the only name you will use, no matter who questions you. Is that clear?

Will again nodded, not trusting his voice to speak.

"You have taken a big chance contriving to come here, just as you long ago took a chance to help me, risking the ire of the mid's deck. I could have you clapped in irons and see to it you did'na survive to speak to anyone, but given your past service, that would do dishonour to me and my family.

"So take this chance Nelson's boy, but do not fail me, I warn you. I accept I owe you something for being brave enough to help me when I needed help and I will not forget that, but it carries just so much weight and none more.

"Alright, you may fetch your tool chest and you will indeed spend your voyage remaking this hovel into a proper Captain's cabin. And there may be other reconstructions needed as well. And another thing, if I need you to, I expect you to be my ears below decks."

Standing up he called for the sentry. "Soldier, this man has a tool chest on the dock that needs to be brought aboard. See to it that two men accompany him to fetch it, and if he tries to escape, you have my permission to shoot to kill."

Back on the dock Old Tom was alone, sitting forlorn and distraught at the turn of events, when he heard what he first thought must have been a voice from deep within his own soul.

"Father," came the voice, "despair not, all will be well".

Looking up he saw his son standing before him at the head of a group of three soldiers and two convicts. Climbing unsteadily to his feet, he almost fell into his son's arms, clinging to him until the corporal stepped forward.

"Orlright, orlright. Nuff's enough, we don't 'ave orl bloody day. Ere, you two" he said, pointing at the convicts, "carry that chest to the Captain's cabin. Smith, Thompson, you escort them" he said to the two other soldiers. After they left he turned to the two men still locked in their embrace, and, softening his voice added, "you two have just a minute. Sorry."

Taking the old man by his shoulders, Cooke held him at arm's length.

"Sir. Dear Tom. You have been the only father I have known. You have taught me so much. So much about love and caring and duty. It does not come to many to be able to say goodbye beforehand, but the truth is we will not see each other again. I love you as only a son can love a father. Please tell mother Maria I love her."

With that he hugged the old man one more time then turned and walked away without looking back, the soldier following in his wake. It took another two weeks before Mangles was ready to sail, time for Cooke to compile a list of the timber and fittings he would need to carry out the modifications Coghill desired. Finally, in the first week of April, 1820, *Mangles* slipped her moorings and headed out into the English Channel.

The Voyage Begins
April 1820

Captain Coghill quickly proved to be as good as his word. Two days out of Sheerness the fetters were struck from the convicts and they were released onto the secured quarter deck to watch as mother England slipped slowly away from them.

In spite of the freezing cold and wet conditions, not a single man opted to remain below as the ship bucked slowly down the Channel, Cooke spending every second he could in the wind and rain, facing out over the white-topped grey, sea eyes closed and nose in the air like a dog sniffing out the way home, his spirits soaring.

For the first time since he had been grabbed by Price's men that fateful night in Bristol almost a year ago, he felt clean and at peace. The stiff sou'westerly sliced his face and cut through his thin coat to chill his very bones, but his legs were free of fetters for the first time in longer than he could remember. He was standing on the deck of a ship at sea and his mind was beginning to clear. As mother England drifted in and out of sight in the misty rain, he leaned into the wind and prayed softly.

'I will survive and prosper,' he promised himself, 'for my dear mother and the good Reverend, for precious Tom and Maria, for Lord Nelson himself. I will not let this be the end of me. I will not bow down or be bowed down ever again.' A week later *Mangles* coasted into the protected waters of Falmouth to pick up a paying passenger who turned out to be the unprepossessing Charles Throsby junior, nephew of noted New South Wales settler and explorer Charles Throsby.

The very next day, April 11, 1820, in brilliant sunshine, *Mangles* set sail to Australia. Although this was Coghill's first voyage in charge of a convict ship, it soon became clear to those attuned to such things that the man had a very clear understanding not only of how to captain a ship, but also how to command men, be they convicts or whatever. Within days of leaving Falmouth he showed he could also be both as good and as bad as needed.

A fight between cellmates resulted in the guard being called. The two men were hauled before the captain, who took the opportunity to display both his indifference to and understanding of the nature of men. From his cabin he produced a unique instrument of torture, a length of wood forked at each end, both ends closed by a length of chain. Both men were locked into the device at the neck, the length of the wood allowing each just enough room to strike weak blows. At the same time neither could sit, stand or move freely in any direction without the consent and aid of the other.

The two were then ordered to remain on deck, day and night, until they had become friends. For several hours the men abused and beat each other, to the huge amusement of both convicts and crew, but soon they were battered, bruised, exhausted and almost hysterical with pain and anger. They admitted defeat, apologised and said they were friends, but Coghill was indifferent to their sudden conversion, and for another day the men were paraded around deck until they were on the verge of insanity and not even their fellow convicts were able to poke fun at them. Only then were they brought before the assembled convicts and made to apologise.

That was the last incident of violence on the voyage.

After the gory spectacle came to a close, Coghill addressed the assembled convicts, stressing that while he wanted to deliver his human cargo in good health to Sydney town, which was why he had struck them from their chains and why they had good food and conditions, he would not tolerate fighting, disobedience or insubordination.

"Let me assure you, I take no pleasure in such action, but equally let me assure you that disciple and obedience to the rules of this ship will be maintained, no matter what the cost.

"These fools sought to test me and have paid the price. Let their punishment be a lesson to you all. For the moment I will allow you to remain free of fetters, but if there are further infringements, that will change. I urge you to instruct your fellow felons to obey the rules for the good of you all."

It was a graphic and telling application of the dictum of holding rewards in one hand, and punishment in the other and a chilling omen of the calculated callousness with which Coghill would go about controlling his ship. It was at this time that Coghill choose to institute a secondary system of control to complement that of the soldiers, appointing a number of carefully selected convicts as 'wardens' of the lower deck, tasked with enforcing rules and regulations 'tween decks', especially at night when the few soldiers on guard naturally hesitated to enter the dark pit, even in pairs.

These 'wardens' were bigger, older, more experienced convicts who knew the system and were prepared to work it in order to have it work for them. They were given the power to enforce Coghill's rules upon their fellow convicts and they immediately set about doing just that, sure in the knowledge they had the full support of the Captain.

One warden was appointed to maintain order in a group of five mess cells, each 'mess' consisting of nine convicts, and the warden alone was made directly responsible for the orderly conduct of that group. He was tasked with ensuring the area was kept clean, that rations were distributed correctly and that two individuals were employed on filling the water buckets every day.

If the mess was disorderly, the warden would be flogged. The wardens were paid in kind for their work as both enforcers and informers, each allowed a double allowance of wine every day it was served, as well as a glass of rum during the other days of the week. Two pounds of tobacco was supplied for their use on the voyage and they were given their choice of clothes. Finally a blind eye was turned to any minor depredations they made on other convicts.

Just as Coghill had demonstrated the power of the whip to control men, so he showed he understood the value of food. Unlike the meagre poor quality food provided on the hulks, rations aboard *Mangles* were plentiful and of good quality. The bread ration was three-quarters of a pound of biscuits daily. There was a pot of gruel per man for breakfast every morning, variously supplemented with sugar or butter. Dinner consisted of either beef, pork, or plum pudding and there was pea-soup four times a week.

Everyone on board soon discovered that Coghill had a fetish about cleanliness. Wardens were warned, on threat of being sent back to the ranks of convicts, that the area below decks was to be kept dry and clean. Each deck in turn on a two day rotation had to be well fumigated with hot vinegar, then sprinkled with cold vinegar and a solution of chloride of lime on other days. All convicts were required to wash every other day and wash and change clothes at least once a week. Finally every day each man was served an ounce of lime-juice and an ounce sugar and made to ingest it on the spot, to guard against scurvy.

"I don't know where he came up with such a regime" surgeon Anderson was heard to say after a month or so at sea, during which time the number of sick men had dwindled down to almost no one, "but it most certainly works."

All convicts not on sick call were required to work on the ship, except the wardens. Scrubbing, swabbing, scraping or holy-stoning the decks was an everyday activity, weather permitting. The work not only kept the men occupied and healthy, it focussed any resentment the convicts might feel at being made to work upon their fellow convict wardens rather than on the ship's company. On most days there were classes in simple arithmetic, English and even geography, usually carried out by convicts able to do so, under the supervision of surgeon Anderson.

On Sunday there was religious instruction, also by the surgeon.

Weather permitting convicts were allowed on deck during the day to take the air and sunshine and were allowed to sing, dance, play games of dice or draughts and generally entertain themselves as they wished in order to while away the long and boring days under sail - once their work duties were completed, that is, and always under the eye of armed sentries. Soon after the ship had sailed from Falmouth Cooke was summoned to the Captain's cabin. Coghill had already drawn a detailed plan of the work he wanted carried out pointed out walls to be moved and furniture to be replaced or made. His own quarters were to be enlarged and a number of guest cabins constructed. Rooms allotted for the surgeon and officer commanding the army guard would be reduced, while the space allowed to the soldiers and their families on the upper deck would also shrink. At no time did he ask if what he wanted was possible. Cooke was to have two helpers, men who had described themselves as carpenters "and if it turns out they lied and they aren't carpenters, they will be flogged and replaced."

Finally Coghill pointed out that the three men doing the work would be watched at all times.

"Be aware, Nelson's boy, if one thing goes missing, no matter how small, it is you who will be flogged, not the thief."

The very next day Cooke set to work, first task being to open his precious chest. Old Tom had handed him the key on the Sheerness dock and it turned smoothly and easily in the lock.

As he expected, the chest held more than just his tools. Firstly there was Lord Nelson's bucket that Cooke had picked up the day he had left the Victory. The tool chest had been built to fit the height of the bucket exactly and inside there were warm clothes - breeches, shirts, two jackets and a belt. The sharp tools - plane, saw and scrapper blades - were wrapped inside the clothes. There were chisels, planes and scrappers, a drill brace, level, saws, callipers, various hammer, axe and adze heads. None had handles, all of which would made later. From Maria there were his favourite sweet cakes, and a letter.

The letter he carefully put aside for another time. Then his heart stopped. His precious telescope was not there. Sitting back he noticed that the chest had been modified. The lone key now turned three tongs that slid smoothly into the reinforced front and sides of the chest, making it almost impossible to force open once locked. On one side a chest of drawers had been fitted. Opening the draws he found they held blades, drill bits and other items necessary to keep his tools sharp and in good condition. Only when he touched the fine craftsmanship that old Tom had lovingly installed did he notice what Tom had added what only another cabinet-maker would see. Cunningly installed on either side of the small set of drawers were a row of ornamental brass lugs that did not need to be there. Will had seen similar lugs before. Looking around to make sure he was alone, he slid the centre two lugs backwards and lifted. Smooth as silk the top half of the drawers came away and there, nestled tightly, lay the telescope in its pigskin carrying case. Carefully easing the instrument out he unclipped the lid to quickly make sure the scope was still there, then quickly replaced it and reattached the drawer top. Sitting back he closed his eyes.

"I must learn to trust my fate" he said softly, "and all will be well".

Cooke's helpers turned out to be William Oram, who was indeed a carpenter, and John Kelling, an Irishman who Cooke soon enough divined was not a carpenter. Forced to confess, he said he had indeed worked with wood - but as a fencer. Despite Kelling's exaggeration, there was never a possibility Cooke could have informed on the man. If there was one crime that was unforgiveable among convicts, it was 'mosing' - informing on fellow felons. Any convict accused of informing would soon find his life a misery, shunned by his fellows and treated to every indignity cunning minds could devise.

The 'moser' - flash talk for informer - would begin to trip downstairs; sudden rolls of the ship would find other convicts crashing shoulder first into him, accidently stamping on his foot or accidently knocking him into a stanchion. Night-time below decks would hold more terrors, such as being awoken with a blanket over his head while men battered him with fist and foot. In the worst cases, a man might even 'fall' overboard.

In the event both Kelling and Oram turned out to be willing workers and quick learners and the three men set to, fabricating partitions similar to those found on warships that could replace solid walls and be quickly removed before action. The partitions were designed to divide the captain's working and living quarters from the stateroom he desired in which to hold court.

For a trained craftsman like Cooke the actual work was easy, the hard part was working around Coghill who, despite wanting more space, was less than willing to sacrifice his immediate space and comfort. Late one afternoon, five days after leaving Falmouth, two soldiers arrived to escort Cooke to the captain's quarters. As they walked away those left behind exchanged quizzical glances. Everyone knew of the work Cooke was engaged in, but everyone also knew of the Captain's fiery temper.

"I hope all's well" said Oram, 'or perhaps we may not be seeing the man again."

Even the two soldiers exchanged raised eyebrows as they knocked on the Captain's door.

"Come" came the response. They marched Cooke in and then stood slightly behind and on either side of the felon, ready for any eventuality.

"That will be all," Coghill said with an imperious wave of the hand. After they had left, he called the convict over to where he was bent over a map spread on his small table.

"Any idea what you are looking at here" he said, nodding toward the map. Cooke, unsure of what was happening, cautiously stepped forward. Spread on the table was a marine map and Cooke instantly recognised what he was looking at. Bending forward to look closer, he reached out to touch a pencil mark on the paper with a hesitant finger.

"Is this where we are" he asked, "about 30 leagues north of Cape Trafalgar?"

Now it was Coghill's turn to be intrigued.

"Where did you learn to read a map?" he asked sharply.

"Sir, Lord Nelson himself taught me just a little. Yes sir, he did" he said in response to the look of disbelief on Coghill's face. Then, realising he had gone too far, he backed off.

"Not a lot though sir, just enough to explain what we were doing off Trafalgar at the time."

Bending again to look closer, he swung around in amazement.

"We are near where the battle took place!"

"Well done, you never cease to amaze. Yes, at present we are off Cape Vincente, scene of another very famous battle, but later tonight we will pass not far from the site where thousands of good French and English sailors rest on the ocean floor."

"Shortly after that we reach the Pillars from where we catch the Canary current which will boost our journey down the coast of Africa."

The battle of Trafalgar had been a momentous event in Coghill's life, as it had been for so many men, and the presence of Will aboard his ship had triggered a wave of nostalgia.

"Ironic isn't it" he pondered, more to himself than to Cooke.

"Trafalgar was such an important moment in the history of England. Indeed in the history of the world! And I was there! Now, as I sail my own vessel past those once bloody waters, the only person to reminisce with is a cabin boy turned convict."

Cooke didn't know what to say to that and so said nothing. It was the right choice because Coghill continued talking to himself.

"In all my many voyages between Africa and the Americas I have never come so close to this place, the place where the fate of the world was decided. Indeed, to where I helped decide the fate of the world. Aye, me, and then but a lad. Ah, but that world is changed has it not?

"Changed and gone forever. Now we go to a new world."

With that he lapsed into a reflective silence.

For a moment Cooke thought he might have fallen asleep, but Coghill would never allow himself such latitude.

"Alright Nelson's boy" he said, "be off with you. Guard!"

Back below deck the men from his mess crowded around.

"What n'all was that aboot" asked Kelling, "wouldja be perhaps 'avin' a noise cuppa tea with the Captain, or was it a noight cap n'all" he asked to general laughter.

Cooke merely smiled and turned into his bed, as confused as the rest of the mess. Carried along by the Canary current and pushed along by some friendly winds blowing off Africa *Mangles* made good time as it hurried southwards. As the distance from England increased so did the temperature, a change which at first was welcomed by the convicts huddled in their thin slops under a lone threadbare blanket. But as the ship surged nearer the Equator the temperature surged and that, combined with frequent tropical downpours, meant the crowded space below decks became at first humid, and then fetid. Aware of the danger of the conditions impacting on the health of the convicts, possibly leading to the deaths of some, which would strike Coghill where it hurt - in his pocket - he increased the tempo of washing the decks with the vinegar solution. He also tried a technique he had seen utilised on the ships he had served on moving between Africa and the Americas that was used to cleanse the accumulated grease and filth from the areas that were most densely populated. It involved heating sand in the ship's oven and then scattering it over the deck that needed cleaning. The grease and filth adhered to the sand and was easily swept up.

Finally he forced the convicts to wash daily, a regime that initially was resisted by the majority of convicts, which necessitated another flogging and two days without convicts being allowed on the quarterdeck.

Resistance quickly crumbled.

As quickly as the weather had become hot north of the equator, so the temperature dropped as *Mangles* hurried south, driven by favourable winds and the sweep of the Benguela Current which roils down the African coast. Some of the lags who had spent time before the mast in His Majesty's Navy whispered that in keeping close to shore in order to pick up the current and favourable off-shore winds, Coghill must be familiar with the coast, or have some very good charts of the area.

"Lad, let me tell you, this Captain is a deep one who has his secrets," said one old lag. "Dark secrets, if you get my drift?"

Questioned about his meaning the old lag hesitated.

"I'll be talking about slaves my friend. Black Gold. There still be plenty of ships ferrying black gold from hidden coves and ports along that coast. There's little risk of being caught running them over to the America's from these parts, and I'd not be surprised if our Captain learnt his way about this coast, or got his charts, by dipping his cup into that well."

Cooke listened closely to the old man.

It made sense and he had no doubt that when it came to making money, Coghill would have few scruples.

The kind weather that had blessed their passage south down the West Coast of Africa had allowed Cooke and his two man team to make good progress on the refurbishment of Coghill's quarters and the captain had already expressed his satisfaction at the way the work was progressing, although two of the ship's officers, the military commander Lt. Matthews and Surgeon Anderson, were less than thrilled at their newly shrunken rooms.

"Yes, you have a good eye and a sure hand at this work Cooke" Coghill said one afternoon while stalking the poop deck after an inspection of his newly completed sleeping quarters and his adjoining chart room. "Tell me, why are all of these partitions lying about up here on the poop? They are causing consternation among the officers of the watch."

Will nodded.

"Sir, I am just taking advantage of the kind weather to use the deck space to pre-fabricate what I can while I can. I have no doubt we will run into some foul weather at some time, and when that time comes if I have already done some of the work which requires room in which to work, I'll be able to continue work in the more cramped space below deck so that no time is wasted and, of course, without inconveniencing yourself."

Coghill pursed his lips and nodded his approval.

"Good thinking! Yes, we are doing well. In the next fortnight I should be passing the Cape of Good Hope and after that you can indeed expect some rougher weather." He walked off without another word, but after a few steps stopped and looked back at Cooke.

"In recognition of your good work so far I will authorise an increase in the wine and rum rations for you and your team, though if you ask me you would be better to avoid both, for they are both the devil's brew."

With that he was off to his cabin, leaving Cooke and those crew manning the helm to exchange bewildered looks. Praise was not something Coghill was known for. A week later, as the ship neared the Cape of Good Hope, the temperature above and below decks plummeted and heavy squalls hit the ship regularly. There was speculation that the weather might force the Captain to change his mind and call in at the famous port at the bottom of Africa which was something most of the crew, as well as the soldiers and convicts all wanted, if for different reasons. But it was not to be. Port calls cost time and time was money, as the canny captain well knew. And should either a member of the crew or a convict escape and disappear into the charming city sprawling in the shadow of the fabled flat topped mountain overlooking the harbour, the delay dealing with authorities could turn very costly indeed. But with his human cargo showing no signs of the dreaded scurvy, or any other sickness, in no small part because of his strict attention to cleanliness, Coghill was able to swing past Africa well below Cape Town and burst out of the cold Atlantic into the southern Indian Ocean.

A few days sailing past the Cape, Coghill swung *Mangles* east-south-east into the belt of wind known as the roaring Forties. Blowing just short of a gale from the west-south-west from behind, the wind propelled the sturdy ship even more south into the West Australian Current which, like the Roaring Forties, ran from West to East between the 40th and 50th latitude.

The two great forces of nature combined to fling Mangles across the Indian Ocean towards the Great South Land at breakneck speed. For the first week, despite steadily rising seas, the ship averaged almost 200 miles a day, but it could not last.

The Southern Ocean

On the eighth day a violent storm drove down from the north west, lifting huge seas which began to ram the ship mercilessly. Tossed about in the huge swells like a cork, *Mangles* seemed much smaller and vulnerable than it had in the warm calm waters off West Africa. As the ship drove headlong into giant waves, it began taking in more and more water which made its way below decks and to the lower deck convict messes in particular, while the wind-driven spray found its way through each tiny crack and crevice.

Clothing and bedding quickly became sodden and freezing cold. The slops the men had been issued at the start of the voyage and which had been perfect near the equator and, no doubt would be suitable for life in New South Wales, were useless against the slicing cold of a Southern Ocean gale.

With waves hitting *Mangles* athwart, the ship was constantly corkscrewing in all directions and soon there was a long line of men outside the Surgeon's room suffering from bumps and cuts after being thrown into stanchions, downstairs or across slippery decks.

After a few days of this endless dizzy whirling, sea sickness struck and the stench of vomit and diarrhoea added to the tense malevolence stalking below deck.

Tempers shortened in direct ratio to the loss of sleep and comfort. Hot food disappeared as it became dangerous to keep the large ship's stove alight, and soon after that the sounds of coughing and wheezing that had not been heard since the convicts had left *Retribution* returned as the cold seeped into bodies which had no defence to offer. It was a battle without any possibility of victory, but one that had to be maintained around the clock to prevent total defeat. Above deck the sailors also waged a constant war against the elements, straining desperately to keep at least some sail aloft in order to maintain steerage, but even with protective clothing the men could only spend a few hours exposed to the bone-chilling wind and constant freezing spray that numbed hands and faces.

After a week of water torture Coghill summoned Cooke to his quarters.

"Cooke, some time ago I said that I required you to be my eyes and ears below decks, now the time has come to deliver on that request, and you'll better have prepared yourself.

"You know the sea, though not as you have seen it the past week, and you'll no doubt have guessed the crew are reaching breaking point. I need you to identify those men who have served aboard ship in the past, be it navy or merchantmen, to fill in for crew members who can no longer continue to work all hours.

"I need ten to a dozen men, more if possible.

"They will not be required to go aloft as I accept they may not be up to that task, but they will be required to help pull the sheets, secure rigging and so on. I especially need reliable men to relieve crew manning the pumps. Can you point out such men?"

"I can do that Sir, but I will need just a little time to pick the best men. Below deck many men who could do the task are sick or injured. Can I say, Sir, by way of inducement, if they will receive any reward?"

Instantly Cooke knew that he had asked the wrong question at the wrong time. Coghill's face reddened.

"Tell the blackguards they may survive the voyage if they do the damned job well!"

"Yes Sir" was all Will could say and upon Coghill's wave of the hand he turned and almost ran from the cabin. In truth, after almost three months at sea Cooke did know most of the men who had been tars, and running the faces rapidly through his mind as he ricocheted down to the convict quarters, he was sure he could find the right men.

It took but an hour to find not only the dozen, but almost double that number who fit the bill. All were prepared to do the work, each recognising their own lives might be in the balance. Reporting back to Coghill, he was rewarded by a curt nod and told to divide the men into four shifts and present them to the duty officer. For the next four days crew and convict worked side-by-side to keep *Mangles* afloat and on course. The first group of able-bodied convicts were drafted to work the cumbersome chain pump, which was in constant action trying to rid the ship of the endless streams of water rushing down from above into the bilges and lower deck. Those with more knowledge of sailing, including not a few who had fought for their country in the King's navy, threw their backs setting the rigging, hauling sheet and tack lines, as well as yard hoist lines, all under the direction of those sailors able to function. For a short time there was no distinction between prisoner and guard, free man or felon, all battling a common foe. When weather permitted, other less able-bodied convicts were drafted into work the Elm Tree pump, suctioning up clean sea water used to rinse vomit and worse from the decks and wash soiled clothing.

Those not able to work took to spending day and night huddled in their bed, curled up beneath whatever could be scrounged in a desperate attempt to keep out the cold, or huddled together in a desperate attempt to thaw frozen hands and feet.

Then, just when it seemed that no one could endure the wet and the cold and the fear any longer, there came a break in the weather. The wind abated and occasionally the sun even shone, a simple gift that had all the men cheering. After the storm broke most of the crew slept for 24 hours, leaving just Captain Coghill and a few dead-eyed crew and convicts, watched by armed soldiers, to keep the ship on course. Throughout the ordeal Coghill had been the mainspring around which crew and convict alike had turned. The man seemed never to sleep and to have an almost demonic energy he miraculously uncovered wherever and whenever it was needed, giving orders with a sureness and authority that brooked no question. On the third day after the storm broke Coghill summoned Cooke. Somehow the man must have managed to catch a few hours of sleep because he looked almost normal except for the dark rings around his eyes.

He even managed a wry smile as Cooke stood before him.

"Aye. Well Nelson's boy, it seems we live to fight another day, though I admit to thinking at one time that that would not be the case. Those rogues from below deck made the difference.

"That makes the second time you have helped me at a difficult time, though I ha' no doubt I would have made it through by myself on both occasions, nevertheless, as I have said before, I recognise when I have a debt of honour to pay.

"Or at least, to reciprocate. I am not sure how that debt will be repaid, but be assured it will. As for those who assisted, I need you to give me a list of their names and I undertake to make a point of putting in a good word for them once we dock in Sydney Town."

Until then Coghill had been looking down at his desk, but as he finished speaking, he lifted his head to look at Cooke.

"You are an enigma. Clearly you do not belong with that rabble below."

Leaning back in his chair he placed his palms together at his chin for a minute, looking down and clearly lost in thought.

"I will share a thought with you Cooke. At some time in the future I believe I will settle in this new colony.

"From all reports there is a future to be had in a new land where nature is the enemy, not the English gentry.

"Certainly I have nothing waiting for me in Scotland, or England, apart from a wife and children in London. I cannot undo what the court has done, but I also undertake to mention you to such friends as I have that they may assist you as they can.

"I further undertake that should I settle in the colony - if fate allows - I will make a place for you with me should you need it. After all, it seems you may a good talisman for me!

"Despite what you may or may not have done, you are a good man Cooke, and believe me, they are few and far between.

"Now be off with ya."

Outside the cabin Will stood for a long moment, unsure that he had actually heard what he had just heard. He understood that in essence the man had promised nothing beyond goodwill, but he perceived that any goodwill could well be an important factor in what lay ahead for him.

Three weeks later Will stood spellbound on deck and watched as a pair of magnificent opposing headlands, gates to the new world, opened before him to reveal the most magnificent harbour he had ever seen.

For the previous week he, along with the other felons, had stood on the deck as the new world had passed by, to all evidence unoccupied because not a town or village or even a dwelling had anyone spied. After sunset the occasional fire had been spotted, whether the result of the hand of man or the hand of God, no one knew.

Until *Mangles* approached Sydney Town, all that anyone had seen was a long, seemingly endless coastline of heavily forested virgin land interspersed with golden beaches.

It seemed at once both amazing and impossible that such a land should be unoccupied.

"It seems this is an empty land" Cooke pondered to the man beside him.

"For some reason, God may have brought us to a land where our past can be erased and we can be who we will be."

Sinking to his knees he put his hand together in prayer and to the amazement of the watching guards, many other convicts did the same.

PART TWO

AUSTRALIA

Chapter Five

Cooke and Haynes sat looking at each other, neither quite sure what to say. Cooke was astounded that he had revealed so much of his secret life to this young man.

'I have said far too much' he thought, regretting that he had ever taken such an insane decision.

'What was I thinking? I have gained nothing by this.

'Vanity. That is what this has been about. Me, William Thomas Cooke, giving in to vanity. 'After all this time, disaster rides on me talking about me. Me thinking I was important; that my life mattered; that I had a story to tell that was somehow important.

'And now my whole new life - all the hard work and careful scrimping and saving - will all come to nought. For so long I have lived quietly. And made my children live quietly, and in the end it may be my vanity which brings about our downfall'.

Haynes was equally astounded, but for an entirely different reason.

'Is that it' he thought. 'Can that the terrible secret'?

'Can this be the heavy burden that this man has carried for so long, all the while thinking that it was a mark of Cain that would somehow destroy him? He really does not understand.

He does not comprehend the reality that this is not only a new land, a new country, a new nation, but a new dawn which will break the chains of the past that have held back good people for no reason. That is the real sadness here, not that a man made a mistake, but that he feels he has to pay for it for the rest of his natural life!'

It was Haynes who finally broke the silence.

"Can that be it Mr Cooke? The fact that you were once a convict? Is that the secret that you have harboured and borne for so long? Sir, I must say, that was long ago. You made a mistake, as did so many, but you have paid the price. A terrible price.

"Sir, from my heart I say to you that your story is not a story to be ashamed of and kept secret. It is a story to be shouted from the rooftops because your story is the story of Australia!

"This is the story not only of a new land, but of new ideas and new values. No longer will we be held hostage by the remnants of a corrupt and decrepit aristocracy!"

Taken aback by his own emotional outburst, the journalist sat back in his chair. Hayne's outburst seemed almost ... well, almost like treason to Old Cookie, who had been and remained, despite all that had happened to him, a loyal British subject.

Such had he been his entire life and as such he intended to die.

"As I said earlier Mr Haynes, we live in different worlds. Such is the case with all young people, their world revolves around themselves only, but many worlds exist Mr Haynes.

"Not too long ago there were different words for the different people in this new land of yours? Those of us who were shipped here were called felons and we were seen as incorrigible and beyond redemption, perhaps even rightly so. But even our children who were born here, they were not born free! They were called - are still called - 'currency children' and that, young man, is a mark of Cain they neither earned nor deserve. Children born of free settlers, or born in Britain, were called 'Sterling children' and seen as being made of better stuff. It was expected that currency children would grow up to be criminals and for that reason they oft weren't even allowed to go to the same school as Sterling children. It would indeed be wonderful if that were no longer the case, but mark my words, it will not be erased by simply saying it should be!

"That, Mr Haynes, is why I have kept my secret. I was born free but will never again be free. As far as anyone knows, my children were born free and will remain free only, but only, if no one knows I was a convict and that is how it must remain."

"I believe you gave your word on that, did you not?"

Haynes slowly nodded.

"I gave my word and my word I will keep. It's of no matter that I believe with all my heart and soul that you have suffered a grave injustice, because in the end it is your life, not mine."

19 Colony of New South Wales, Circa 1828. Stretching from just below Botany Bay - abandoned site of the original colony - north to Port Jackson (Sydney Town), Port Hunter (Newcastle) and Port Macquarie, the colony comprised just a miniscule part of the entire country.

The journalist sat back and slowly shook his head. Both kept their silence for a long time, both lost in the past. It was the journalist who dragged them back to the present.

"I can only wonder at the things you have seen and heard and experienced. I have so many questions, indeed even more questions.

"When did you arrive in Australia?

"What was Sydney like back then? I live there now and cannot imagine what it must have looked like back then.

"And the people you must have met in those early days? What about Captain Coghill? Was he really" - he looked down at his notebook, "James Dott? Did he ever keep his promise?

"And how did you come to end up here in Morpeth of all places? You have lived here a long time, in fact I had thought you had always lived here! And what of your wife? Where and how did you meet? Dare I ask, is...was she also a convict?

"But Sir, I know it's late. This interview has been nothing like I thought it would be, and I can't imagine how difficult it has been for you to dredge up so many of the unspeakable things you have seen and experienced.

"Can I suggest we end this interview now and continue tomorrow? I need to try and digest all you have said and I am sure you do as well, but one thing before I go - I want to assure you that I fully intend to stick to every word of our agreement. I would never write anything that could harm you or your family and I give you my word on that again here and now."

Old Cookie appeared at the hotel the next afternoon as agreed and Haynes breathed a sigh of relief at the sight of him, for he had half expected the old man to cancel the whole story. A tot of rum was placed in front of each man without the necessity of ordering.

"Good afternoon Sir" Haynes began after the pair had sat down.

"Thank you for coming, I was afraid that after your concerns last night you might have cancelled the whole thing" he said, involuntarily letting out a small embarrassed laugh.

Cookie took a sip of his rum, savouring the taste before putting the glass down slowly and deliberately. Haynes could see that he had something to say and steeled himself for the end of the interview, and the article. Cookie gave out a large sigh. "I considered doing so, I must admit. But I made an agreement and, as you have said you would adhere to your side of that agreement, my wife Mary decided that it behove me to stick to my side of the bargain. And besides, Mary has said she wants to speak to you."

"Of course' of course" agreed Haynes. "It would be an honour to meet her. I am interested in your wife's side of your family history as well. I even made a note of that last night" he said, smiling and holding up his notebook as proof.

"I would like to hear about your early years in Australia. What you thought of the country and how you survived? I don't know too much about what the country was like back then."

Old Cookie nodded. "Well, as usual, the best place to start is the beginning."

20 Cockle Bay (now Darling Harbour) the centre of Sydney, circa 1820. Original painting by Major James Taylor of the 48th regiment. Engraving by R Havell and Sons, 1821. SLNSW.

The Great South Land
August 7, 1820

Under full sail *Mangles* sliced through the mile and half wide crevice in the stone wall guarding the most magnificent harbour in the world, all hands on deck to manage the manoeuvre and all convicts confined below, clamped in leg irons.

"Just a precaution" the guards assured everyone, "they'll come off again', if we get through the gap that is. If we don't, well it won't matter then will it" they laughed.

Once through the gap the ship made a sharp turn to larboard and then, as the seas quickly subsided, the crew moved to reduce sail and soon the ship was gliding serenely through deep, calm waters. Back on deck convicts and crew alike crowded every possible viewing spot as the ship moved slowly down a wide natural harbour past sheltered little bays and coves that opened up one after the other like the leaves of a book. The water beneath the ship was crystal clear and the deepest dark blue, lightening to azure and green in the sheltered bays as the water shallowed to shorelines fringed by golden sands or rocky crags. Cooke noted that along the shore there was nary a building or man-made structure to be seen.

'This is paradise untouched' he thought, feeling a sense of freedom and peace that astounded him once he recognised it, 'surely a man could live and prosper here in this empty land.'

As the ship inched further into the harbour it passed several small canoes with natives standing, fishing spears in hand, completely naked. Almost an hour later a pilot and two row boats arrived to guide *Mangles* into Sydney Cove, the inlet around which the capital of the New South Wales colony had been built. From where he stood Will could see a small fort guarding the western side of the cove, sitting above what appeared to be a fine looking stone warehouse and wharf. It was surrounded by what looked to be private homes, each and every one with orchards and gardens stretching back up the side of the headland. The headland on the eastern side of the cove also featured a small fort, but the area was more sparsely occupied, with open land where horses and cattle grazed. A number of windmills dotted the highest ridge line, while closer to the water stood a double story stone house surrounded by gardens and orchards, with a path leading down to a small wharf.

'Perhaps the town home of a squire' Cooke thought, only to learn later it was the residence of the Governor of the colony. Closer to the heart of the colony the buildings became denser with a large number of smaller timber or mud daub dwellings and hovels taking up the space in between the fewer stone buildings. A small stream ran down through the buildings, ending at the apex of the Cove, and beside it a dirt road led up the hill to the most imposing building of the town, a large three story building surrounded by a strong-looking wall with towers at each corner and gatehouses between.

'A fort, or a prison?' Cooke wondered, 'or both.'

Well short of the shore where the stream entered the cove, several ships similar in size to *Mangles* were moored and *Mangles* soon joined them. No sooner had the ship secured its mooring than a small fleet of lighters and row boats began to make their way out to the ship and instantly Coghill appeared, pistol in hand, warning them to keep their distance as ordered the convicts to be hustled below deck. No sooner had that been accomplished than the first official visitor climbed aboard and proved to be no less than Governor Macquarie himself!

Coghill had barely time to don a jacket before meeting the great man, who insisted on a quick tour below decks to inspect the human cargo and assure himself all was well. Pleased with what he saw the two men had a private discussion in the captain's now impressive cabin which saw Coghill invited to dine at the Governor's residence the following night, the Governor pleased to have discovered the men shared not only a Scottish heritage, but a Highland Scottish heritage!

Once the Governor left the ship and before Coghill could move to prevent it, the ship was swarmed by visitors, their numbers bypassing the few guards on deck. The passengers on the small boats were mainly businessmen and shop-keepers looking to buy whatever the ship had in its cargo hold, or to sell what it lacked, but the boatmen themselves were businessmen of a different kind.

They spoke the 'cant' or 'flash talk' language of the convicts and one and all they knew their way around a convict ship and where to find what, or who, they were looking for. The men were the new colonial face of the age old schemers and con men who had perfected their craft over hundreds of years in the back alleyways of London and the other cities of Britain. During the 25 years of Sydney Town's existence the scams of the old country had been grafted onto the roots of the new by experts in the trade - convicts. While the administrators, backed by police and soldiers, controlled the formal economic and social life of the colony, by 1820 a hidden parallel underworld had been well established and by the time Cooke arrived both networks needed the same thing - skilled workers, of which there was a chronic shortage in the colony.

While the wealthy, well-connected aristocratic farmers and businessmen could rely on their friends in the administration to assign much needed workers to them, the underworld had to find the same kind of men in a different way - but the sole source of recruits for both parallel economies were to be found in the same place - on the convict ships. Most of the boatmen were themselves convicts and their task was to recruit the right men the underworld needed, literally from beneath the upturned noses of the authorities. The boatmen slipped smoothly into the convict messes and soon had the ear of men desperate to learn the real story about their new homeland from the only men they really trusted - fellow criminals.

One sly-looking fellow dressed in white slops emblazoned with the broad government arrow and sporting a fine-looking broad-rimed hat found his way to Cooke's mess and, theatrically signalling to all those men nearby to come forward, soon had a rapt audience.

"Oy, any of you fellas here wot are tailors or shoemakers, or maybe jewellers? Any of you wot can read and write and do accounts? Listen up, I can make sure that anyone wot fits that bill can have a real cushy number here very quickly.

"All I need is your name and your craft NOW, before his lordship finds out wots about and sends us packing. Believe me gents, you do not want to head up to the barracks wiffout knowing what's the go."

Cooke, immediately suspecting a trick, demanded to know who the man was what he wanted. "You're all flash talk. You're a lag. We don't know who you are or what you want."

The boatman looked him up and down coldly before replying.

"Well, ain't you the toff wot finks he knows it all, and you sittin' on this tub wif chains around your ankles is calling me a criminal."

"That's a bit rich ain't it?"

The gibe hit home and drew a laugh from most of the convicts. In reply Cooke could offer only a wry smile. Looking Cooke in the eye and now wearing a victorious grin on his face, the lag went on.

"I'll tell you wot I wants, guv, and that is to see that you all don't fall in a big hole on your first step, don't I. Now you might be Cock 'o the walk aboard this tub matie, small as you are. But let me tell you, it's a whole new world out here and believe me I know, 'cause I bin here for ten years, ain't I.

"There is a system to be played here for a sharp man 'cause let me tell youse, you don't want to end up 'aven to work out in the bush as a clod-hopper farmin' for nothin' and chained hand and foot, to boot, if you'll 'cuse the pun."

The felons laughed and the at that point flash-talker had them where he wanted them.

"Even worse, you could end up burnin' your skin off in the government quarrie; choppin' stone for years afore you manage to figure out that it didn't have to be that way."

He had their attention now and clinched it by anticipating their next question.

"Do I get a wad out of it? 'Cause I do, but so wot? That's the whole point aint it? Now listen up maties, here's a tip. Whatever you do, don't be sayin' you's a mechanic, especially a builder, carpenter, mason or the like, 'cause if you do you will be grabbed to work for the government and you will never get away from 'em. Even worse, some toff official will assign you to one of his farmer mates and you'll be stuck in the bush, livin' hand to mouth, wif a real chance that one day the black fellas will kill ya and eat ya."

The lag paused as he looked around the circle of faces, all of them showing the same apprehension and fear of the unknown he had seen so often before.

"I can help you not only end up livin' free and easy in this fine little town, with plenty a wimen and grog, but also ensure you make a nice little bit on the side. Pretty soon you might end up even havin' a house of yurn own, maybe even a wife and kids. I know that sounds like a dream but it can come true 'ere, believe me, 'cause I already did it. There's blokes in the know, you know what I mean, wot run the real show on the streets, and 'ere and now is the time get on their right side.

"Trust me, you can do it 'ard here, or you can do it easy - up to you".

It was a well scripted and well delivered pitch which precisely targeted the deepest hopes and fears of all the men and while Cooke was sceptical, he was literally knocked aside as the men rushed to give their names and skills to the flash talker who managed to quickly scribble down the names of a dozen skilled men - names that would earn him a pretty penny from his boss once the appropriated bribe to the right convict clerk had assured they would be assigned to him. At the evening meal that night the only conversation in the messes concerned the revelation the boatmen had delivered.

"I don't trust 'im, not a jot" said Cooke, but he was drowned out by the howls of derision from his fellow inmates.

"Those fellows are the same ones wot ran the show back 'ome" said one, "and makes sense to me they'll be doin' the same 'ere. I don't know 'bout the rest of you, but no way I'm letting on about my trade 'til I know the lay of the land for myself."

Most men nodded their agreement.

Early the next day Surgeon Superintendent Anderson reported as required to Major Frederick Goulburn, the newly appointed Colonial Secretary, and handed over his official account of the voyage, in the process setting a date a few days hence for the official reception of the convict cargo. Cooke happened to be outside Coghill's cabin securing his tool chest when the surgeon reported back that all was well.

He informed the captain his report had been cordially accepted by Goulburn, who professed his pleasure with both the report and the good health of the convict cargo, adding that the following day the Colonial Secretary would conduct a muster on board at which the convicts would be officially handed to the custody of the colonial administration.

"The process seems entirely tedious and officious" he heard Anderson report, "far more so than I had expected, but it does bode well that all will go smoothly and there will be nothing to prevent a speedy turnaround."

The Governor had included the surgeon in Coghill's dinner invitation and the following afternoon the two men, both dressed in their finest - Anderson in dress naval uniform and Coghill in formal civilian attire - were rowed to the Governor's private wharf by a mixed convict and sailor crew - of which Cooke was one. They were escorted up through the gardens to the governor's residence where Governor Macquarie met them on the covered patio that ran the length of a fine residence with wide views of the Sydney Cove settlement.

"Welcome gentlemen. Welcome to Australia, to New South Wales, to Sydney Town, and to my humble abode," he laughed, evidently in a fine mood. An Indian servant brought a tray of drinks to the patio and the Governor took a mischievous delight in introducing him as George Jarvis "my Hindu slave". Given that slavery had been abolished these past 13 years, as the newcomers were well aware, the two men were at a loss for words, more so Coghill.

Having received the shocked looks he had jokingly played for, Macquarie recited the well-honed story of how he and his first wife Jane had purchased the young man 25 years ago in India and that Jane - since deceased - had even given him her surname. Long since freed, George had not only stayed in service with Macquarie ever since, but had recently married one of the governor's convict chambermaids, Mary Jelly. Macquarie offered Coghill a whiskey, which the Captain politely refused.

"Sorry Sir, I mean no disrespect, but I dinna touch the stuff."

Macquarie laughed. "Well, you are the first seaman I have ever met to refuse a drink, especially a Scots seaman! But nevertheless I wish you well" he said, lifting his glass.

"I am told that you safely delivered young Charles Throsby to the colony. Well done! His uncle is highly regarded in Sydney Town, not only as a fine settler, but also a daring, indeed intrepid explorer. As we speak he is on an expedition to the south which I am desperately awaiting the results of."

"I believe it is time we burst from the shores of this great land into the hinterland. Who knows what we will find out there!"

Coghill instantly saw the chance and explained how he had become firm friends with Throsby, a man he had in fact barely spoken to. Macquarie introduced Coghill and Anderson to his second wife, Elizabeth, as well as to the Colonial Secretary Major Goulburn and one of the colony's most successful businessmen, John Campbell', yet another Scotsman. Anderson and Goulburn were soon enmeshed in a conversation with Campbell on the general state of health in the colony, while Macquarie was listening earnestly as the Captain gave a detailed account of the dramatic week of storms *Mangles* had endured in the Southern Ocean.

"So are you telling me that the convicts actually came to the rescue of the ship during the storm? That truly is a remarkable story."

Coghill looked a little embarrassed. Being rescued by convicts was not how he wished his first voyage to the colony to be remembered.

"Aye, well I'd no be saying that they came to ma rescue exactly" his thick Scots accent having been momentarily resurrected by Macquarie's similar brogue, "I have no doubt that myself and the crew would have prevailed, after all *Mangles* is a fine sturdy vessel.

"The seas of the Southern Ocean are well known to be a wee bit rough, so we were fully expecting a bit of a bouncy welcome, but the problem, your excellency, was not the ferocity of the seas, as powerful and monstrous as they were, but their duration. The storm did not cease pounding us for all of ten days and at the end of that the crew were literally asleep on their feet. A convict on board who had served in His Majesty's navy helped me round up some former sailors and that allowed me to rotate the crew and place the freshest men where they were most needed. That said, I'll no be denying it was not a near run thing. Once we were past the worse the better convicts worked on under the direction of my officers and the guard, so as to keep the ship on a steady course and enable the crew to get some sleep.

"I did not close my eyes that I can recall for the whole time. The felon who helped is a fine carpenter and cabinet-maker by the name of Cooke who I would heartily recommend to your excellency should you need a good man."

It was a fine story and Macquarie tucked away in his memory to retell at another time.

"Well Captain" he said, raising his glass, "here is to your outstanding seamanship and to the pluck and courage of British seamen. With men like you, long may we rule the waves."

"As for the carpenter fellow, Cooke you say? Well I may indeed soon have need of him and quite a number of other good mechanics like him. There is a terrible shortage of skilled men among the rogues being delivered here, and the fact of the matter is none of the new arrivals want to work out on the farms - and I don't blame them. It's a hard and rough life and unfortunately land-owners are not above charging good men with petty crimes so as to extend their servitude and so ensure they keep their labour.

"Then there are the businessmen, and government officials who, I am sorry to say, assign themselves and their friends skilled convicts. Then, instead of utilising the men in productive roles, they sell-on their labour to others at a profit. I believe some even indulge the convicts to establish their own businesses, pocketing a percentage.

"There's not much I am able to do about the problem at the moment, being under the yoke of a pompous investigator from England by the name of Bigge, but let me tell you there is enormous potential here my friend. Enormous.

"I am planning a new settlement a few hundred miles north of here to allow fine farmland around the port of Newcastle and its interior to be opened to settlers, but that aim is stifled for lack of workers.

"The numbers of newly arriving freemen and freed convicts are increasing by the day and demand for land is far outstripping what is officially available, even in this vast territory. In fact, I'm having a major problem with free men simply heading out into the wilderness and staking their own claims beyond the reach of law and civilised behaviour.

"Can't blame them I suppose. They firmly believe there is an almost inexhaustible supply of fine agricultural land out there and it is impossible to arrest them from seeking it out and making it their own. Such is the way of the world, and especially the way of the British, and long may it stay so!

"You should yourself consider settling here Captain. This new country needs men of your character and determination and, might I add, of your fine Scots heritage. There are a lot more of us here than you might imagine."

Up until that point Coghill had been on the verge of losing interest in the Governor's monologue, but mention of him possibly settling in the colony rekindled his attention.

"It's interesting you should mention that your excellency" he said, giving Macquarie his full attention, "I have been advised to look into that very matter by, shall I say family connections. The former head of the Transport Board, Mr Macleay, a close relation of my mother, being one of them. Indeed, one of the reasons I bought an interest in *Mangles* was to facilitate my journey here. I have recently consolidated a number of investments and should such a venture be found to be viable I could make a solid investment in this new land."

Macquarie raised his glass.

"Well, as I said, I believe you are exactly the kind of man we need in the colony. I would go so far as to say I would commend you a grant of land, should you so desire."

Coghill could barely conceal his delight at the turn the conversation had taken. It did not take much subtle prompting on his part for the Governor to offer to undertake some investigation as to where his fellow Scot might well be granted an initial fair-sized grant. It was dark by the time the dinner ended and as he took his leave of the Governor, he noticed Cooke was one of several men waiting with torches to escort he and Anderson back to the wharf.

Signalling, he called him to come forward.

"Your excellency, this is the man I told you of - William Cooke."

Macquarie nodded. "I heard of your fine work on *Mangles* from Captain Coghill tonight Cooke, well done. Keep up that spirit and I am sure you will do well here."

Cooke was dumfounded, but had the presence of mind to mumble 'thank you Sir' before stepping back into the darkness. Long after the evening had ended, Coghill sat in his cabin, the Governor's words ringing in his ears. Finally he dared ask himself the question: why not?

"Why not indeed settle here in this new country?" he said, talking aloud to make the possibility more real. He had long since come to the conclusion that advancement in Britain was completely stifled by English aristocratic dolts blocking the rise of stronger, better men.

"Men like meself, let it be said."

Since leaving the navy not too long after Trafalgar, Coghill had done well. In fact he had prospered to the extent of purchasing a London residence in a salubrious section of the city and setting up his growing family there, far from the stares of his some of his Scottish relatives he was certain looked down on him because of the circumstances of his birth. He also had a second London property and not inconsiderable funds banked in the city.

Although a fine seaman and natural leader, he was constantly at odds with his employers, chaffing at having to explain and justify himself to men he considered his inferior, simply because they were wealthier or, more often, because of the aristocratic circumstances of their birth. His total belief in the rightness of his decisions, combined with a haughty intolerance of other's opinions, had led to him have more than his fair share of confrontations both physical and legal.

Since he had been made captain these past six years, his reputation of being both ready to fight at the drop of a hat, and of being ready to take a chance, had already led him to take commands others had shied from. He had spent a few years commanding ships ferrying the King's armies to and fro' across Europe to fight the that Corsican upstart Napoleon, a role that arose from an introduction by 'uncle' Alex Macleay, secretary of the Transport Board, the august body which decided such things. Macleay, who had spent many years in the wine trade, had even played a role in Coghill meeting his wife Jane in Portugal following an introduction to her wine merchant family.

Napoleon's defeat at Waterloo ended the plum Transport Board jobs, but his reputation and availability next led to him being approached by another distant relative, asking if he might be interested in undertaking voyages 'that it would be better if the authorities did not know about', but which, he assured Coghill, would most certainly turn a huge profit. Coghill easily divined what the mysterious voyages entailed. After all, the huge profits from the slave trade were no secret among the Scots, and indeed in his own family.

Ever ready for adventure, a challenge, and the possibility of making a lot of money, he grabbed the offer and was very soon making regular voyages around what came to be known as the golden triangle.

Trade goods such as clothes, tools and trinkets were loaded in England, supposedly bound for the Americas or the East, but which found their way to Africa. The goods were sold or bartered for slaves bound for America where slavery remained legal.

Profits from the sale of those slaves were invested in cotton, sugar, tobacco and other raw materials bound for the growing markets of England and Europe, reaping still more profit.

Then the circle recommenced, profits growing with each loop.

But while the profits were enormous, so were the risks. After Britain abolished the slave trade in 1807, British navy ships had begun to patrol in earnest the vast empty spaces of the Atlantic in search of rogue slave runners. Two years sneaking around the golden triangle not only earned Coghill a fair fortune, but the trade in black gold also taught him a great deal about the darker parts of the nature of man, possibly even about the darker recesses of his own mind, and he knew he did not want to travel any further down that road. He had made a lot of money, but well understood it would need to be husbanded carefully and judiciously if it was to grow. He had been lucky in the evil trade, but he knew his luck could not continue forever and had already decided to opt out of the trade when family connections again interceded on his behalf, offering the option of another trade, also in humans, albeit a legal trade this time - carrying felons to far off New South Wales.

During the first night in Sydney Cove Coghill had kept the convicts locked below lest anyone try make the short swim to shore, leg irons and all. But as Governor Macquarie had explained, there was no point in convicts risking life or limb attempting to escape - because there was nowhere to go.

The problem, as Major Goulburn pontificated to the guests, was 'how to get that message through their thick skulls'.

Getting messages through thick skulls was something Coghill specialised in. The day after the Governor's dinner he assembled the convicts and laid out their situation in plain Scottish.

"As you may be aware I had the pleasure of dining with Governor Macquarie last evening and I raised the topic of keeping you men fettered. You will be pleased to know he gave the opinion that it was of no need, so off they shall come. Now, once the chains have been struck off, should any of ye be thinking ye might slip overboard to get to shore, fettered or no, I'll just say this to ye - go ahead.

"The Governor informed me that waters here in Sydney Cove abound in large sharks that have been attracted here from all over this vast harbour by the offal and waste from the town.

"I'm told most who attempt the swim ashore simply vanish. So if you fancy your chances, go ahead. Should you get past the sharks and should you then get through the town without being recognised, captured and sentenced to a chain gang for the rest of your life, I'm told that the chances are quite high that those that do reach the empty wilds beyond will be killed and eaten by the natives - and sadly, no one will care - certainly not I."

"I was contracted to deliver you safe and sound to Sydney and that is what I have done. Surgeon Superintendent Anderson has reported your safe arrival and that has been officially noted, so the fact is I have no further interest in your safety. That said, my suggestion is that you should instead take time to look closely at what his new world has to offer you, because it offers you - one and all - a new start. Good luck."

Sydney Town

Their chains struck off, the business of ingesting the convicts into New South Wales began in earnest. Firstly yet another set of prison garb was ferried out for the convicts who, one and all, were less than pleased with the slops they felt were clearly designed to humiliate them.

Each man was provided a striped cotton shirt, a pair of white 'duck' trousers, a coarse woollen jacket, a yellow and grey waistcoat, stockings and shoes, a neckerchief, and a woollen or leather cap.

The clothing itself was of good quality, but lest the convicts think they could escape custody and blend into the townspeople and settlers, each piece of clothing was 'branded' with the broad government arrow daubed wide, thick and often in both black and red paint, signifying to all that the wearer was 'government property'.

Used to degradation and even ridicule, this last humiliation proved a step too far for some men and Coghill was obliged to order the guard below decks armed with cudgels and knotted ropes to restore order.

The next day Colonial Secretary Goulburn and a squad of soldiers arrived on board to register - yet again - the personal details and statistics of each prisoner. Each of the men was required to give his name, age, and birthplace, as well as the time and place of his trial and the sentence handed down. Each convict's height was carefully measured and the colour of their eyes, hair and complexion noted Any scars, birth marks and marks such a moles were carefully described, the information becoming the basis of identifying a particular individual at any time in the future. Each man's conduct during the voyage was noted as a warning to future 'masters', and any trade or occupation was recorded. Mysteriously, many men who had previously said they weren't mechanics when they were arrested in England, seemed to have become tailors or shoemakers or hatters - trades much in demand by businesses in Sydney Town.

The new register of convicts was given to the members of the Board of Assignment, a voluntary body consisting of businessmen and government officials. The Board decided where and to who each convict would be assigned, Board members not shy to assign those convicts possessing prized skills either to themselves or their friends. After the re-registration process, the felons were lined up on the quarter deck of *Mangles* and asked to come forward one by one to receive any goods, including money, they had handed over to the designated Receiver of Convict Property at the beginning of the voyage, each convict confirming receipt of all their property in good order either by signing or making his mark. Cooke stepped forward when called and signed for his tool chest and some money he handed over, almost 15 pounds, money which old Tom Hobbes had managed to gather, to be added to the 20 pounds which lay hidden in the tool chest he had retrieved earlier that morning from Coghill's cabin.

The *Mangles* was then towed across to the public wharf and now came the moment each man had looked forward to with both dread and anticipation for over three months, actually setting foot in their new 'prison'. Although it was but a mere step down onto the wharf, each man recognised it for what it was; the final irrevocable step from mother England and onto a new world from which there would be no return. When it came time for Cooke to leave the ship he hesitated. Faced with carrying both the heavy toolbox and his bedclothes he was at a loss of what to do, but was gratified when his fellow 'carpenters', Oram and Kelling, both stepped forward to heft the heavy toolbox.

Standing on land for the first time in over three months he took the time to look around him while his legs adjusted to solid ground.

Up close the stone commissariat building in front of him looked a lot smaller and dirtier than it had from the ship's mooring in the past week. A knot of natives lounged outside the building, smoking pipes, seemingly disinterested in the new arrivals. Once all the men were ashore they were formed into a line four abreast, ready to be herded up the street running parallel to the shore, George Street it was called.

On the other side of the road a large sandstone quarry had been gouged out of the hillside and several dozen convicts were slowly hewing sandstone from the quarry walls, cutting it into building sized blocks and stacking them ready for transport.

Even though it was only mid-morning the men were sweating and Cooke could see it was brutal work.

After a half an hour of waiting, a few disinterested guards strung themselves out fore and aft and began herding the men up the dirt road up toward the large building over-looking Sydney Town Cooke had noted from ship. The felons couldn't help but notice the poor condition of the buildings along what passed for the town's main street.

Most were constructed of undressed timber roofed with thatching, giving the town a village look.

Towards the top of the hill they paused to rest next to a group of natives. Unlike the tall, well-built men he had seen fishing from canoes on the harbour, this group looked decidedly ill-kempt.

There were several men, one naked except for a loin cloth, another wearing just a shirt. Two were lying on the edge of the road while the others sat around. A number of women sat nearby, a few wore shift dresses but the rest were almost naked.

All appeared to be drunk.

Around them a number of naked children stood looking openly at the convicts. Cooke thought the group looked worse than the worse reprobates he had ever seen in Britain, and wondered where the natives fitted into this new society.

"That's the old gaol" a guard standing next to Cooke said, pointing to a large ramshackle timber building, "you don't want to end up in there me mate. Boiling hot in summer and bloody cold in winter and liable to burn down at the drop of a hat, just like the last one did."

"They could do with some good carpenters and builders here" Cooke said aloud, even thought he was actually talking to himself.

"How many do they squeeze into that shed then?" a convict asked.

"Too bloody many" came the soldier's simple reply.

On Eastern side of the street was a smaller, fine looking double story building which the talkative guard said was the government printing office "where the Gazette is done".

Further on was a smaller version of the prison, which the guard described as "the orphanage", while directly across a muddy intersection he pointed out a lumber yard.

Trudging on the convict caravan passed a row of three fine stone houses the guard said were the homes of the chief judge, deputy judge and colonial secretary 'in that order an' all'.

Swinging back up the hill he pointed out the Governor's Observatory which, he suggested, "commands a very fine view over bugger all".

Further up the street - Macquarie Street - the guard added "that fine building there is the new General Hospital, also known as the Sydney Slaughter House which, so rumour 'as it - 'an' I ain't partial to rumour normally - was built on the profit of the sale of rum."

"Well, a poor ignorant soldier such as meself wouldn't be knowing about that, but a very fine building so it is; finest in all the land if you ask my opinion, which of course, you ain't. That said, I'd also stay out of that one as well if'n you have the option."

"Furver up the street is the Governor's Guard House. Wiffout a doubt you fine gentlemen is gonna be livin' in the best part of town," he said, laughing at his own well-rehearsed joke."

Opposite the observatory were a number of streets bordered by small, nondescript private dwellings and what amazed Cooke was that even these humble houses were all built on their own plot of land, each with their own garden. Most of the land had been planted to vegetables, but a few even boasted flowers!

Children played in the yards or on the streets, stopping to watch the convicts pass by with only mild interest. Finally the men arrived at the large gates which had been their target.

The three-storey brick building was built in the simple, austere Georgian style, with the façade dominated by a large clock, the guard cryptically assuring one and all it would soon come to be the most important feature in the life of convicts working in the town.

The building boasted a strongly built enclosing wall with squat towners at each corner, as well as a gatehouse around the main gate.

21 The newly completed Sydney Barracks building, circa 1820, exactly as Cookie would have seen it when he arrived in the colony.
George Evans. SLNSW.

At this point a Sargent of the guard appeared - a big brute of a man, full of strutting self-importance and, like the talkative private, clearly relishing his moment on stage - so he took his good time before speaking, waiting until he had the full attention of the men.

"Well, well, well, 'ere we are then gentlemen, the Sydney Barracks.

"Brand new it is, finished less 'n a year and just waiting for the likes of your good selves to make yourselves at 'ome 'ere and enjoy it. But before you takes your ease inside, let me please inform you of the day's program. Once inside the gate you will form up in ranks in the square. Shortly the Governor will address you and thereafter you will be inspected before being handed over to the masters you have been assigned to work for, thereafter no doubt to be taken to even more luxurious accommodation. Should you at any time wish to make a disturbance or voice loud opinions while his lordship is speaking, be aware that I will take you aside and thrash to you within an inch of your life. Understood?"

After waiting a theatrical moment, he resumed his monologue.

"Very good. Well, shall we proceed then?"

Ushered inside, the convicts were herded into line to await the governor, their line made straighter with the help of knotted ropes the guards carried.

"Come on! Come on! Don't you clever people even know how to make a straight line! You!" he shouted at one laggard as he swung the rope across his back, "get in line or get a week in chains!"

The example worked and the men began to shuffle into a vague resemblance of a line.

"Who does he think we are, the bloody household cavalry" Oram whispered? Soon the quips were flying back and forth until the huge Sargent stepped forward to glare them into silence. As the convicts waited, groups of what looked to be businessmen drifted in and gathered in knots around the compound, some calling to convicts they knew and talking to them, others looking at lists they carried and trying to ascertain who they were there to secure. Finally the Governor arrived accompanied by Captain Coghill, Surgeon Superintendent Anderson, the superintendent of convicts, John Gandell - once a convict himself - and a troop of police constables.

The Governor then mounted a small dais to address them. Firstly he asked if there was anyone who had any complaint to make about his treatment on the voyage, especially as regards the rations provided, which raised a general snigger - as if any of the assembled convicts would ever think of voicing such a complaint. He then asked if anyone had not received all the property they had deposited with the ship's officers. Receiving no reply, he cleared his throat and, in a broad Scots accent, got down to the business at hand.

"Today each of you will be assigned to various tasks and masters and I must stress to you that you are required to carry out the tasks and jobs given to you under the law. If you shirk those tasks, or abscond, or wrongly refuse to serve, let me be clear there will be real punishment.

"The point I want to make to you men today is that if you obey the law, once you have served your punishment you will be free men in a free land. This is a vast new land of untold wealth, and untold opportunity for those who choose to work hard. This 'punishment' of transportation could also be seen as an opportunity you have been given, and I invite you to look at it that way. Consider that carefully for a moment. I urge each and every one of you take full advantage of that opportunity and for those to do, I say 'good luck'."

The governor then began in his inspection, accompanied by a troop of soldiers and followed by Superintendent Gandell who asked each prisoner his name, and after looking it up on a list he carried, loudly read out the name of the prisoner followed by the name of the person or station to whom he had been assigned.

Men assigned to individuals or businesses were immediately escorted to their new master or his agent, who was required to pay a fee of one pound for each convict assigned to him. Those whose occupation had determined they could be of use to the government - mainly mechanics - were noted as being assigned to the chief engineer and were ordered to stand aside. The men assigned to outlying districts for government work were told to collect their belongings at the end of the muster, after which they would be marched down to the harbour for transfer by boat to Parramatta, the odd-sounding name being a settlement at the mouth of the river which fed into the harbour, from where they would be marched further inland.

Cooke noted that the flash-talker who had spoken to his mess mates on *Mangles* had arrived with a few colleagues and they were assigned about ten men. The process had obviously been carried out many, many times and was well practised so that very soon there was just a small group of about 50 'government men' remaining after the last assigned convict had walked out through the gates; Cooke and his carpenter 'mates' William Oram and John Kelling being among those chosen to remain. At the end of the procedure the Sargent once again stepped forward to address the remaining convicts.

"Well then gentlemen, it seems you lucky individuals have been chosen to work for his majesty's government in New South Wales. You will stay here in these wonderful premises tonight and no doubt for a while after that. There is a secure place for your possessions to be stored should you wish to deposit them, over there" he said, pointing to a desk manned by a corporal, "and I strongly suggest you do so. You will be required to give a list of all the goods you wish to deposit. "

After that you will go directly to the Prisoners' Barracks, over there" he again pointed.

"There you will report to officers of the Superintendent of Convicts, Mr John Gandell, who from this day forth will own your miserable lives. You will no doubt have observed there are a number of buildings attached to the walls of the Barracks. Let me explain what these buildings are.

"Firstly, on the southern wall - over there on my right for those wot don't yet 'ave their bearings - are two long halls. These are the mess rooms where you will eat food prepared in the kitchen, which - logically - is in the middle of the two messes.

"Behind you on the Eastern wall are the privies, very important places in which you will no doubt be spending a lot of time. On the Northern side of the compound is a private area which is the 'ome of the Deputy Superintendent and his family. This area is strictly out of bounds and anyone found inside that area will become intimately acquainted with another feature of the compound, namely the fine-looking triangular pillory standing over there in the south-east corner, an object many of you will no doubt already be familiar with.

"That instrument is not an ornament. It is a fully functioning and well-used piece of equipment. Should you break any of the rules of this establishment, you will become very intimately associated with the lovely lady wot comes wif it - Madam Lash I calls her.

"Now, by way of general explanation. I don't know what you may or may not 'ave 'eard about this 'ere wonderful establishment, but the first thing you need to know is that this beautiful Barracks building is not a prison, it is a place to sleep and eat when you are not at work or until you find a residence worthy of your own no doubt refined tastes.

"However, again I warn you there are rules and regulations which will be explained to you and you will obey them or face the consequences. After you deposit your possessions you will be shown to the sleeping quarters. You will no doubt be surprised to find that the doors are unlocked and will remain so.

"You are free to explore you immediate surroundings, but you must return here by eight bells tonight or you will be regarded as having absconded and I assure you, you do not want that to happen.

"The large clock you see at atop this lovely building will enable you to see what time it is from almost all parts of the town.

"Just one more word of caution. While Sydney Town may seem to be a lovely, calm and peaceful place, I assure you it is not. If you end up in a dark alley with a lady of the night, or drunk in a tavern, you will in all probability also end up being beaten and robbed. After which, if you are late returning, you also will be charged with absconding from government work and probably flogged. So, because I am such a good, caring person, I urge you to be careful. Good day."

With that he turned on his heel and marched into the guards quarters.

Cooke and the other men looked at each other in astonishment. None of them had been prepared for this sudden dose of freedom and for a few minutes they stood, dumbfounded. Oram was the first to react.

"Right, let's get his stuff recorded and stored away and get indoors to find a bed, in that order."

It took almost an hour for the men to have their possessions recorded and stored in a locker to which the owner had the only key. Then the trio carried their bedding into the barracks to search out a bed in the cavernous building. Completed just the year before, the main Barracks building had 12 large sleeping wards, designed to hold a total of 600 men, but at times had held as many as 1000. Luckily at this time the barracks were below capacity. The trio of 'new men' wandered through the cavernous building, overawed at its size.

The three-storey building was 130 ft in length and 50 ft in breadth with a high-ceilinged passage separating each side's sleeping rooms from the other. Each floor was accessed by a staircase in the centre of the building, and there were four rooms on each floor, two long rooms and two smaller rooms. In each room two rows of hammocks were slung from wooden beams supported by stanchions fixed to the floor and roof. A space of two foot by seven foot was allowed for each hammock; the two rows separated from each other by a three foot passage. Each long room slept 70 men, with 35 in the small ones. There was a convict 'wardsman' appointed to each room, who was responsible for the conduct of the 'residents'.

Another dormitory in one of the long buildings on the north side of the yard, 80 ft in length by 17 ft wide, was where newly arrived convicts were usually lodged, sleeping on mattresses they had brought with them from their ship. Convicts employed in the kitchens and bakehouse were allowed to hang their hammocks in the same rooms they worked in.

As with most aspects of the British penal system, convict wardens were employed to bring order to their fellow convict's lives. Each hall had a number of these convict wardens who were responsible for keeping the barracks clean and maintaining order.

They issued the newcomers with flax hammocks and directed them to vacant places in which to string them.

Cooke, Oram and Kelling were pointed to a vacant area by the wardsman and there found three adjacent places to hang their hammocks on the ropes provided, careful not to take any spot already taken - a mistake that might prove fatal. After stringing their hammocks the three companions sat and looked at each other, then looked around at the cavernous hall that was their new home. Inside the building everything looked surprisingly fresh and clean compared to the bridewells and prisons they had come from.

The crisp scent of the recently cut eucalyptus timber still lingered in the halls; the white lime-washed walls were clean and the windows allowed in plenty of bright sunshine. Again it was Oram who spoke first.

"So, wots the go here then? Are we just free to go wherever we want to now? That can't be right can it? Is it some kind of trap? Or a test? I dunno wot to make of this, do you?" he asked of the other two, only to be met by slowly shaking heads. Finally Cooke spoke up.

"I reckon what Captain Coghill said is true; there's no need for cells or chains or the like because there just ain't no place to go. It's like it really is wild and empty out there and so the whole country is one big bloody prison. I was lookin' about as we walked up here and I didn't see one person who was fettered, and not many constables or soldiers."

"What I did see is that everyone seems to have their own home, with actual land around it to grow things. I ain't never seen the like at 'ome, so's I reckon the other thing the Captain said is true, that this 'ere country is like nothin' I've ever seen or heard of."

Again the trio lapsed into silence, but then Kelling suddenly stood up.

"Seems like everything I know has been turned on its head."

"The world is gone upside down. Well, the only way to find out if it's true is to give it a go. I'm going for a walk."

With that he stood and strode purposefully toward the door. Cooke and Oram looked at each other, confusion writ large on their faces. They watched as he walked out through the open doorway, then sat and watched for at least ten minutes, each second expecting their friend to be frog-marched back into the hall - but nothing happened. The few men present in the hall went about their business, whatever it was, unconcerned at the arrival of the newcomers. Finally, with a quizzical look at each other, the two newcomers rose and treaded softly in Kelling's wake, down the hallway, out through the doorway, across the parade ground, out of the main gate, past the two bored sentries standing there, and then on to the dirt street which led into their new and vast unfettered prison.

The street, not much more than a track really, meandered downhill and they followed the path, each second expecting a hue and cry to be raised behind them. Shortly afterwards found Kelling sitting on a small hillock looking out over the harbour and the land stretching endlessly beyond. The two sat down beside him, no one saying a word. Below them the town was silent, emptied by the heat of the afternoon sun. The only sound disturbing the warm silence was the occasional bark of a dog or a child's squeal.

The three had been sitting in silence for some time when knots of convicts began to appear on the track, making their way up to the barracks. Some sat on the grass near the trio of newcomers and smoked a pipe, while others simply looked out on the vista as the sun slid quickly down the into the empty land. At the main gates the guard had grown to almost a dozen soldiers and they were ticking the names of returning men off a muster and searching them for alcohol, which was banned from the barracks.

After the gates were closed just before 8pm there was another muster, carried out it seemed to Cooke in a rather half-hearted manner. Some names called out went unanswered and when he mentioned this to the man beside him, the man merely shook this shoulders.

"If someone ain't here today they'll likely be here tomorrow. If they ain't here the day after that they might go look for 'im at his assignment. No one much cares 'cause everyone turns up eventually. There's nowhere else to go."

After the gates were locked at 8.30pm the men sat around in groups on the parade ground, smoking pipes and talking in low tones while huddled around fires to keep out the cold wind blowing in off the ocean. Cooke spoke to a couple of groups and from what he could gather the groups consisted in the main of men who not only had been transported together, but more often than not were men from the same area who had also been arrested, tried and sentenced together.

When the warning bell for 'lights out' sounded the convicts began to trudge up the staircases to their allocated wards to swing into their hammocks. Each area was lit by a hanging oil lamp and after the final bell rang the lights were doused, although no one seemed to bother, with men talking long into the night.

"Yep" said Oram before sleep took him, "this world is upside down."

The order for Cooke to go to Gandell's office arrived just days after he had been initiated into the Sydney barracks and to an entirely new life he was still struggling to comprehend. Shovelled into the office, he stood while the Superintendent ignored him as he laboured to read a document, brows beetling over small spectacles and a mouth silently forming sounds underlining the difficulty he was having.

Despite being a former convict, Gandell had worked himself into a position of importance in the colony, in large part because of his intelligence and ability, but also largely because his arrival had coincided with the liberal reign of Governor Macquarie, who not only believed that convicts could be rehabilitated, but that they might well be the future of the colony. As he stood and waited, Cooke pondered over what he could have done wrong given that he had only been in Sydney Cove a few days, days of confusion and apprehension equally mixed with astoundment at the level of freedom convicts enjoyed in this open air prison compared to the dungeons of Mother England.

Along with Oram and Kelling, he had watched with wonderment as each morning the convict residents of the barracks would rise early, eat breakfast at their own pace, and then saunter down the hill to Sydney Town to be at their various assignments by 7am.

Most would return for the main meal of the day around midday, returning to work until sometime after 3pm, when 'government work' ceased, the men would begin to trickle back to the barracks, the last arriving just before the gates closed at about 8 o'clock.

Like everyone else who had arrived on *Mangles,* the trio had been astounded to learn that convicts worked just eight hours a day for the government and after that, their time was their own to do as they wished! Even stranger was the fact that many convicts who had skills had been allowed - in fact encouraged - to find a 'second' job outside the prison system and they were allowed to earn their own money working at that second job.

Within a short time these 'half free' convicts, as Cooke came to call them, also often managed to find a 'second' home, usually with their new employer, but sometimes with a convict family who had previously taken the same path.

He was astounded to learn that a few relatively wealthy convicts had even been reunited with their own families, the man's wife and children having managed to secure passage to the colony, either by paying their own way or by convincing the crown to pay.

The *Mangles* trio struggled to make sense of it all.

"Upside bloody down, that's what I first said of this world and that is what it bloody well is" said Kelling, "seems to me like it's the gaolers are imprisoned here, not us."

Much later Cooke realised that in a roundabout way, Kelling had described the situation perfectly. While the 'gaolers' - the administrators, soldiers, police - all longed to be back in predictable and ordered England, away from the hot and pestilent backwater they felt they had been exiled to, most convicts quickly realised they had luckily landed in a world blessed with more freedom than they could have ever thought possible back in the England they had known. He also understood that, while at first impression the upside-down system seemed to be not only contrary, but dysfunctional, first impressions were misleading.

Casting his mind back to the explanation of the colonial economy by the boatman who had first climbed aboard *Mangles* to recruit skilled workers, he realised the inverted system not only worked, but that it was difficult to see how any other system could work given the unique conditions that prevailed in the colony.

In a hot, dry country packed with what seemed to be endless stretches of trees and, from what he had seen and heard, very little farmland, there were never going to be any slave plantations in New South Wales to make slavery profitable for the new owners.

Nor were there any riches to plunder from the local inhabitants, or strategic territory to be occupied. The only reason for the whole exercise seemed to be to house those people the rulers of England had decided they did not want in 'their' country.

Given that primary reason for the colony's existence, the 'upside down' system was the only one that allowed the private economy of the town to function in favour of the rulers, while at the same time saving the crown money it would otherwise have had to spend imprisoning those people it no longer wanted. The upside-down system allowed everyone to be a winner, even the convicts.

Finally, Gandell finished reading, made a short note on the bottom of the sheet of paper, and lifted his eyes to look at Cooke.

"Ah. Cooke isn't it? Well Cooke, seems like you have managed to settle into Sydney remarkably quickly. Well done! It took me years to come to the notice of the powers that be, but you have achieved that in just a few days. Well, what have you got to say for yourself?"

Cooke's astonishment was written clearly on his face, causing Gandell to burst out laughing.

"Nothing to worry about young man, all is well."

Picking up another sheet of paper he again squinted his way down a list.

"You're a carpenter I see. A cabinet-maker in fact. Is that true?"

Cooke could only nod.

"The Governor himself has conveyed to me that you have been given a glowing recommendation from the captain of the *Mangles* - I forget his name - who said you completely rebuilt his captain's cabin into truly spacious and well-appointed rooms even while the ship was at sea. In addition you helped save the ship during a storm.

"On the Captain's recommendation His Lordship has asked me to find a suitable position for you."

"I have decided you'll be orking at the lumber yard just down the street for the time being. However I should tell you the Governor has his eye on you and you may well be destined to take part in the establishment of a new penal settlement up north.

"Let me share with you a small secret you are not to share with anyone else. If, when the time comes, you should volunteer to go to that settlement, the chances are you will be offered a ticket of leave after a short time.

"In other words" he said in response to the silent question written large on Cooke's face, "you will get out of gaol well before your sentence is up. Just keep your nose clean. Don't get into any kind of trouble or wrong-doing and you may well make a success of yourself here just as I have. Now, do you have anything to say?"

Cooke's mind was racing. Did he say an early release was in the offing?

"Sir, did I hear you correctly that there was the possibility of an early release in return for taking on this task?"

Gandell looked down his nose and over his glasses at the man in front of him, noting the confidence behind the deference in his speech and, for the first time, his sharp blue eyes.

"That is what I have been told," he replied cautiously.

"Well Sir, can I ask one small thing?".

Seeing the frown cross the Gandell's eyes, he forged on quickly.

"Would it be possible for my two carpenter friends who worked with me on *Mangles* to join in that endeavour you speak of? William Oram and John Kelling are their names Sir. Both are good men and also carpenters. We work well together and I believe they would be a boon to such a task, Sir."

Gandell stared at the man in front of him, then nodded his head slowly.

"Well said and good for you to have a thought regarding your workmates welfare. Your captain seems to have read you correctly. I shall see to it. That's all"

Early the next day the three friends, unguarded and unaccompanied, walked from the barracks, down Bridge Street and then a short distance down George Street to the lumber yards. Standing at gates set in the high stone wall which surrounded an area of several acres, they looked into a hive of activity, with dozens of men hard at work.

It was clear to Will's knowledgeable eye that the area was divided into a number of different work sections. Each section boasted a rough wattle and daub 'office' housing an overseer and a clerk, while in the open air convicts were busy cutting, sawing and stacking timber into racks to dry and season. There were two large roofed workshops; a section for wheelwrights; a coopers workshop; small foundry and even a harness and saddle workshop.

"This is the heart of the colony" Cooke blurted out, "this is where we need to be."

The three men reported to the chief engineer who consulted a list and then immediately assigned both Oran and Kelling to stacking sawn timber into drying racks. Cooke was told to report to carpenter's shop number two, which turned out to be the building where items of joinery and furniture were made. The convict overseer gave Cooke a quick tour, pointing out about a dozen work benches, each tended by its own cabinet maker, all hard at work producing bespoke pieces of furniture.

"Each man is responsible for making a piece, from beginning to finished product," he said, "are you able to do that?"

In reply Cooke merely nodded and smiled. The sweet smell of newly cut timber; the aroma of oil and shellac and resin, the solid 'thunk' of mallet on chisel and the rasp of sawing, all told Cooke he was home. Within months he had been promoted to convict overseer, a development neither he nor his fellow long-time workers were particularly pleased about. The promotion entailed him doing much of the military overseer's work, but in recompense it allowed him extra time off and, more importantly, the right to find extra work of his own outside normal working hours.

Early in 1821 Cooke found himself working in the home of Stephen Partridge, a former sergeant of the 46th Regiment who for services to the colony in a few journeys of exploration had been appointed supervisor of convicts at the lumber yard, responsible in particular for the making of bespoke furniture, and also for running of a school of apprentices set up to train convict and orphan boys. Using his position to his own benefit, Partridge had forged an illicit and lucrative sideline, providing skilled labour to friends and colleagues, either for cash or a favour to be returned. With so little skilled labour, just as the boatman had first told Cooke aboard *Mangles*, common sense dictated that those in charge of skilled convicts would always find a way to turn their position into a money-making racket.

So it was that many of the best convict carpenters and cabinet-makers were to be found working away from the lumber yard, surreptitiously constructing cabinetry and producing furniture for the administrative and military hierarchy of the colony. The materials for these 'off-site' jobs came from the government stores at the lumber yard, with no questions asked. As usual, there was no honour among thieves and the convict cabinet-makers working off-site soon learnt to request extra material for the 'special' jobs, knowing the request would not be denied, and this material was then either sold on the black market or used for their own business.

Love at First Sight

It was at the Partridge home that Cooke met Rebecca Evans, a free woman working as a servant for the Partridge family. Older than himself by a few years, she had been forced into servitude a year earlier when her soldier husband, a corporal of Partridge's old regiment had disappeared, presumed drowned, during a drunken attempt to swim across Sydney Cove.

His body had never been recovered and because of that the military bureaucracy had decided he couldn't be listed as dead, and instead he had to be officially listed as a deserter, meaning his pay was stopped, leaving Rebecca and her two children penniless.

The army 'kindly' let her stay in the small house provided to her soldier husband, but with true military inconsistency had discontinued vital rations to the family until the corporal reported for duty or his body had been found.

That meant Rebecca needed to work, but with so many convicts available, work was scarce, especially for a free woman with a family. That was when Partridge stepped into the breech and, in an offer he described to colleagues as a 'generous gesture to the wife of a fallen comrade from his old regiment', he offered the stricken woman employment in his home.

With two young children under the age of four, Sarah Partridge was at first thrilled when her husband told her he had managed to find her some domestic help, but was less enthusiastic when the saw the flame-haired Rebecca - much the same age as herself, deporting herself well and with her natural beauty still apparent.

She suddenly decided she did not need any help, but Partridge was not to be thwarted.

'Help is help' he pointed out, adding that it would be wrong to begrudge a poor woman assistance.

Privately Partridge told Rebecca he could only offer her a modest wage, but hinted that would be enhanced by not revealing her income to the army, hence safeguarding her home.

He also hinted he would do all he could to restore her rations and might even be able to secure Rebecca's eldest son, eight year old Nathaniel, an apprenticeship at the lumber yard. It was an offer Rebecca could not refuse and initially she was overwhelmed with gratitude, but the hook was soon revealed. Partridge made no bones about emphasising he had done Rebecca a huge favour by helping her and that at some time payment in kind would have to be made. Cooke soon saw that Partridge, when he thought no one could see, would let a hand stray to Rebecca's waist in a way that implied ownership.

Rebecca was be the first to admit she was no beauty. Her alabaster skin burnt red at the merest touch of the sun; her rarely brushed forest fire of hair was already showing flickers of grey; her hands were chaffed from washing clothes, dishes and children and, after having two children, she admitted her figure was more 'mature' than she would have liked - but Cooke was spellbound from the instant he saw her.

From the first it was the simple things that captivated him: the way she unconsciously blew her hair out of her eyes when concentrating; the way she could at times sit absolutely still, her eyes closed, as if the world did not exist; the way she always swayed her hips with simple grace before starting a chore, as if she was dancing into her work. To Cooke she was the epitome of female elegance, or was until the moment her blue eyes flashed and she leaned forward and her hands flew to her hips, ready for war!

Then she was an irresistible force.

In the time he spent reconstructing the Partridge home, adding two extra rooms, building cupboards, beds, a fine entertaining table and chairs, Cooke spent every free moment he could as close to Rebecca as he could, though for the first few weeks he barely said a word to her. Mrs Partridge, on the other hand, did not have any such difficulty, ordering Rebecca about in a brusque and authoritarian manner which a silently outraged Cooke who thought it was a most improper way to treat a free woman of such obvious good character. Long after he had finally gathered the courage to speak and the pair began to spend what little free time they had together, 'Bec' told him Partridge was threatening to dismiss her and at the same time tarnish her name by labelling her a loose woman if she did not let him into her bed.

"I may not be much of a catch William" she said late one afternoon as the pair sat at the rear of Rebecca's tiny house, "but I have never done such a thing in my life. I am a good woman" she said, instantly bursting into tears.

Cooke sat shock still, terrified, not knowing what to do or say, desperate to reach out to her, but mortified she would run away screaming if he did. In a moment of sureness he simply placed his hand atop hers, saying nothing.

That was the moment she said she fell in love with him.

The usual working day for convicts at the lumber yard ended at three in the afternoon, after which convicts were free to do private work before heading back to the barracks by six for the evening meal.

Cooke asked Rebecca if he could start a small garden in the back yard of her shack that he would then tend, sharing the produce with her and her boys. As the days passed he began spending most his spare time fussing over the garden rather than doing extra work. It was but a small step to making repairs left undone since Corporal Evans had gone for his last swim.

First came a solid new door to replace the flimsy plank door the corporal had fashioned; then came a resting chair; then a lean-to with a bed each for three-year-old Guy and eight-year-old Nathaniel.

A smooth-topped table and matching chairs drew a hug and kiss on the cheek from Bec because it meant the boys no longer had to sit on boxes around a rough-hewn slab of wood balanced on mud bricks. Inevitably one afternoon when Bec was not working, Cooke was asked if he would stay to share in the meal of a large fish he had bartered some work for.

"Please William. It won't take long and you can still be back in time before the gates close," she smiled. When he protested he had to head back at the barracks, her smile instantly faded in a way that cut him like a knife. He stood for a few long seconds, not knowing what to say.

"I … well, it's just that, well, I'm a convict Bec. You shouldn't even be seen talking to the likes of me! You are such a fine person and …"

"William Cooke how dare you say that! You are a fine man. A good man. I will not listen to you say such a thing. You've told me what happened to you so don't you dare talk about yourself in that way," she said, hands on hips in what he called her 'take charge' voice.

"Now go wash your hands, and take that silly cabbage tree hat off your head and sit at the head of the table. Nate! Guy! William is staying for supper so get in here now!"

As he sat down to eat, a sudden thought literally shuddered through his body. He realised that this was the first time he had sat at a table with a woman and children since he had left home twenty years ago.

Taking a moment, he looked at the scene before him; two young boys digging ravenously into their food as if they had not eaten in days; Rebecca looking at him quizzically, a slight smile playing around her mouth; the remains of the day's light shining weakly through the thin gauze curtains covering the two small windows cut into each wall. In front of him were the table and chairs he had made. Beside him stood the cupboard he had fashioned and in the corner was the easy chair he had worked at lovingly every afternoon for several weeks.

The simple scene brought a lump to his throat that made eating impossible. It felt as if he were part of something; that he had come home. After the meal the boys were quickly ushered to bed and

Rebecca and he sat silently at the table sipping some locally grown tea Rebecca had 'borrowed' from the Partridge house.

"I know it's wrong, but I do miss a cup of tea and they have so much," said softly, her voice trailing off, tears welling in her eyes.

This time Cooke stood and went to her, resting one hand on her shoulder, the other slowly stroking her hair. He had meant only to console her, but without warning she stood up, her arms went around his waist and she leant her head on to his chest. Cooke thought his heart would smash to pieces inside his chest it was beating so madly as his arms went around her in turn. They stood frozen for a full minute before she lifted her face and kissed him.

Cooke wasn't totally inexperienced when it came to women.

His had experienced occasional moments of passion with a number of flirty tavern wenches, and like all sailors had paid for pleasure with 'port princess' who plied their trade in most docks, but this moment was something he was totally unprepared for and had no idea of what to do next. Bec had no such confusion.

Blowing out the candle she led him to the curtained off cot that was the bedroom before taking off his jacket and lifting his shirt to rub her hands across his chest. Her breathing became urgent and she stepped away to unbutton her dress and in a moment they were wonderfully naked and then almost instantly joined together.

Within a minute both were spent and lay in each other's arms, the only sound in the world their laboured breathing.

"You'll be thinking I am but a harlot," Bec said, a lilt in her voice.

"I will not be doing any such thing!" he retorted indignantly, which triggered her laughter and letting him know he had been fooled.

"Ha, ya little daemon" he laughed, mocking her accent as he reached out for her. This time their love-making was slow and tender and carefully drawn out, but ended the same way with both clinging together so tightly that they were almost forced to breathe alternately.

Cooke lay still, Bec's head upon his shoulder, her hair cascading across his chest. He had nothing to say but his mind was racing.

Nothing even vaguely similar to the love-making he had just experienced had ever happened to him before and he had a flash of insight that such powerful and compelling intimacy could only be the result of a of a woman giving herself to a man she loved, rather than just hiring herself out, which was all he had ever experienced.

'This is what love is' he thought. 'This is what the poets write about; this is what keeps men and women together forever.'

Looking down at Bec he lifted her slightly.

"It has never been like that for me before," he finally managed to utter, which just made Bec hold him even tighter.

"Shussssh. Me either. I don't want to talk lest it end."

But a few minutes later, just as Cooke's breath began to deepen into sleep, it did end when 'take charge' Bec emerged.

"You must get back to the barracks" she said, pushing him off the cot with a laugh, "you can't be seen leaving here in the morning. I'm a married woman after all!"

At the door she stopped him just as he reached out to open it and kissed him long and deeply, then he was quickly shoved out into the semi-darkness. He didn't remember the walk back or the ribald comments from the barracks guard or even swinging into his hammock, all he could remember was the milky soft touch of her skin and her hair scattered over his chest.

Time passed by quickly once Cooke and Bec had become lovers, the near intolerable heat of a Sydney summer eased into autumn almost unnoticed except that the cicadas stopped their perpetual chirping and the temperature dropped down to barely bearable. Cooke always managed to make it back to the barracks in time and was sure their secret was safe, although Bec felt the neighbouring wives knew.

"It's what they don't say rather than what they do say" she said one late afternoon as Cooke tugged his shoes on for the walk back up the hill to the barracks, "but they are good women and they know my plight so my secret will be safe with them."

"But I'm not so sure about Mr damn Partridge. He keeps making snide remarks, saying he has my life in his hands, that I don't appreciate what he has done for me and that no one else could do as well for me.

"He says he could make my life impossible and see me out on the street if he wanted to.

"William, he is such an evil man. People don't see it because he hides it so well when others are around, but I am scared to be alone with him. Mrs Partridge knows something I'm sure, but she is afraid of him as well so she keeps quiet when he is about and then takes it out on me when he is gone."

Then, as the new year loomed, disaster struck. Bec learned that Partridge was to be transferred, to where she knew not, and as the time for his departure drew closer, so his demands became more forceful. A final refusal of Partridge's advances infuriated the man so that she was summarily dismissed, with no amount of pleading able to move the soldier's heart once the ultimatum had been given. Not only did he dismiss Bec, but immediately took steps to have her evicted from the military-owned house she occupied. Then young Nathaniel arrived home ashen faced, saying he had been accused by Partridge of stealing from the apprentice school and had been dismissed.

"Oh William, what can I do? What is to become of me? Of my boys? Of us? I will not end up on the street William, that I vow. I will kill myself and the boys first!

"Oh I hate this forsaken country! I hate it, hate it, hate it! I want to go home", she sobbed through her tears. "I need to go home!

"My family are not rich, but they will help me, and my boys will be brought up properly."

Cooke tried to comfort her but she was beyond comfort, beyond reason, and he feared that soon she might be beyond caring. The thing was, from the first instant Bec had voiced her wish to return home, he knew he had the solution to her problem.

He had money. Money that would allow her to escape, but he was loath to use it because he knew for certain to do so meant he would never see her again. Shortly after he had arrived in Sydney Cooke had taken the money Old Tom had given him, combined it with that hidden in his tool chest, and deposited the entire amount into the newly opened New South Wales Bank.

The money was the nest-egg he had hoped would enable him to set himself up in business once he was free.

He had told Bec of the money and of his plans, saying the money was for the life he hoped they would share. Now those plans lay in ashes. Even though he had heard that Partridge had left Sydney Town, Cooke had no doubt he would do whatever he could to destroy both of then if he should find out about their romance.

In his heart he knew there was but one option, but he refused to say it, even to himself, for fear of making it come true. Daily he saw the fear and desperation growing in her eyes and every tear she shed was like acid burning a hole in his heart.

Finally he could delay no longer. He finished work early one day and walked to the docks in search of something he knew he would find and which he also knew would break his heart. The day after that he did not bother to even turning up for work, instead walking to the bank where he withdrew half of his money before heading down to the docks once again. Then he slowly walked to Rebecca's house. She and the boys were there, her eyes red from crying, but as soon as she saw Cooke's face she jumped to her feet and rushed to him, holding him close, her own pain submerges in what she saw in his face.

"What's the matter?" she asked, "what more can this hell do to us?"

Barely able to breathe and unable to trust himself to speak, he slumped into one of the chairs he had made and beckoned Rebecca to sit beside him. It took a long time to gather himself, finally taking Bec's tear-streaked face into his hands he held her to his chest before speaking.

"I have something to say that you will not like' he said, raising a hand to stop her as she tried to speak.

"I have been thinking about all that has happened and what can be done, and I want you to know that I can fix this".

Again he raised his hand to stop her from speaking because he knew that if she did he might not have the courage to continue.

"In the harbour right now is a convict ship is preparing to return to England via India. There is a cabin on the ship reserved for you and the boys and the fare has been paid.

"Here is the proof" he said, handing her a receipt for the cost of the passage. Then he handed her a number of bank notes.

"This is to get you and the boys to your parents, to your family. You cannot argue with me Bec, it is done.

"The die has been cast and there is no going back."

Bec squeezed him to her breast, sobbing hysterically, which triggered his crying. They clung together for what seemed like hours until the cries of the boys dragged them back to reality.

That night Cooke didn't go back to the barracks, instead sleeping the whole night in the arms of a woman for the first time in his life. Nor did he return to the barracks until five days later, after watching the ship make its way slowly down the harbour, and still standing and watching for long after the red shawl Bec had been waving was lost to sight. He watched the ship's sails blossom, then shrink smaller and smaller until finally they disappeared through the headlands and out to sea. Only then did he turn and trudge up the hill to the barracks to face whatever fate would once again bring down upon him.

The next morning he was dragged before Gandell. He told the weary-looking old man the simple truth, only leaving out the part about Partridge because no one would believe it, or care if they did. Gandell was sympathetic, but he had heard it, or variations of it, all before.

After a week back in irons he was dragged before the Sydney Bench of Magistrates, once again standing before men dispassionately, indeed disinterestedly, deciding his destiny.

By now Cooke understood enough about the legal system to know that the word 'accused' read to the empty court was merely a nod to a process long ago left far behind in England.

He had not been asked to plead because there was no need. There was no jury, no witnesses, no testimony given and no questions asked, the verdict having been decided before he had been shoved unceremoniously into the dock. All that was left to be determined was the place and duration of the sentence. After a brief discussion with his colleague the magistrate turned to address Cooke for the first time in the proceedings.

"William Thomas Cooke, you have been found guilty of being absent from government work without leave or permission.

"The usual sentence for a such a crime is transportation for life, however there is a note in your file - from Governor Macquarie no less - that you are of good character and that during a time of crisis on board the convict ship *Mangles* which transported you here, you acted in a manner so as to assist the Captain to survive a storm in the southern ocean. Under those circumstances this court is disposed to be lenient.

"You are sentenced to serve the remainder of your original sentence of seven years, with no extra time added, at the penal settlement of Port Macquarie. You are dismissed."

He was then shackled at the ankles before being escorted back to the barracks, where he was told to report to Superintendent Gandell.

"Well, how did it go?" Gandell asked.

"I'm to serve out the remainder of my time at Port Macquarie" he replied, with nothing more added.

"I was told that was a lenient sentence."

Gandell nodded slowly.

"Yes. Well you may not think so, but I assure you it could have been worse, much worse. You could have been sentenced to life on a work gang. It was my recommendation that you merely serve out your time, there instead of here, as you would have done in any event.

"It is still possible that your sentence may still be remitted, though less of a chance I admit, but as I have said, your future remains up to you. Let me say that I think you have the character to be successful here in the colony Cooke. It will grow and perhaps you will grow as well. I wish you well."

Cooke hesitated and so Gandell also waited.

"Sir, I have my tool chest stored here. Will that be safe here until I can either send for it or retrieve it myself? It contains the tools of my profession and, when I am eventually released, they are what I will need to start my life over, should the day ever arrive."

Gandell nodded slowly.

"I know this has been a huge blow to you Cooke, especially given that in your eyes you have done nothing wrong. I give you my word the chest will be safe and that I will have it sent to you at the earliest opportunity should you request it. Alternatively it will still be here until you serve your time and can come and retrieve it."

After retrieving his few belongings Cooke was placed in a small holding cell. He managed to leave word for his carpenter mates of what had happened, but sadly never had the chance to say farewell to them personally. Less than a week later, shackled and escorted by a lone soldier, he arrived on the public wharf to board the Elizabeth Henrietta, a small coastal vessel which had been built in the colony, for the voyage north into the unknown.

"Just where do you think you are headed all alone then me lad." Cooke swung around at the familiar voice. Standing behind him, sacks over their shoulders, stood Kelling and Oram.

"You think after all the time we put in training you we would just let you sail away? Not likely is it?".

The three men clung together for an instant before springing apart, embarrassed as men are at such times.

It transpired that the pair had heard of Cooke's sentence, there are no secrets in prison, even in an open air in a prison, and decided to volunteer to join him on the trip north.

Gandell had been only too happy to make it happen.

"Fact is, ain't no one can survive in this land by themselves can they," said Kelling, "you know that and so does we. We're mates now and mates face the future together or die alone.

"Come on, let's get on that tub and get a good berth before this rabble get them all."

22 Government House - seat of colonial government - circa 1809 by John Lewin. National Library of Australia. INSET. Governor Lachlan Macquarie. By Arthur Levett, copied from original. 1874. Victoria State Library.

Chapter Six

Haynes, having to an extent learnt his lesson, had been listening carefully as Old Cookie's life story unfolded before him, taking occasional notes for his own interest rather than for the article for The Bulletin. That story had already been mentally written. He had sipped his way through two rums while Cookie's first sat almost untouched, the old man totally lost in reliving the most wrenching times of his life.

"Ah, can I jump in there?" the journalist asked as the old man finally paused and took a sip of rum. Cookie sat back and waited. He had not realised how taxing dredging up the past could be; re-examining memories and feelings that had lay dormant, if not entirely forgotten, for decades as his life had moved inexorably on.

"I understand how hard this must be for you Mr Cooke, and I want you to know that I really appreciate your time. I thought maybe you could take a break and I could ask you just a few questions, not specific questions mind you, just perhaps general questions.

"The truth is I have become more and more enthralled in your story. It is exactly the kind of story that myself and my colleague John Archibald want to bring to Australians. Real stories of this great country, stories that reflect the people's lives, not the lives of people who live thousands of miles away in a foreign land who have nothing to do with us.

"I was wondering if you had ever heard or seen the young lady who seemed to be responsible for your, ah. For you being sent here in the first place. Liz was it? Elizabeth? Have you ever thought of her?"

"And what of Rebecca? Did you ever see her again?"

Cookie took his time answering, and as was his wont, savouring a small sip of rum.

"I thought about young Elizabeth often, especially during the times I was chained and treated like an animal for something I did not do, and I grew to hate her. But now I have my own children, my own daughters, and I know I would do anything to ensure their happiness. I have wondered whether she ever even knew what happened to me.

"As for Rebecca, well, she also had children to care for. They were her priority and that is also right and proper."

Haynes looked at the old man as he considered his next question.

"Given all you have endured, through no fault of your own, what do you think of Britain's treatment of convicts?"

As he said the word 'convict' he instinctively ducked his head into his shoulders and looked around to see if anyone had heard him use the word, suddenly recalling that in Morpeth, Cookie had always been seen as a free man. Luckily no one had heard his slip of the tongue.

"Well, you have my story Mr Haynes, I will leave it to you to tell. The one thing I would say is that while many of the convicts I knew were honest working men at heart, men who transgressed the law simply trying to feed their families, there were a great many convicts who were the worst of the worst and deserved what happened to them. But the reality is we all benefitted in the end by coming to this great land."

Haynes shook his head in disgust.

"Aren't you bitter about your treatment?"

Cookie didn't hesitate.

"From my great age I understand there is no point in being bitter; what has happened has happened and cannot be changed. As the good Reverend Nelson said, all a man can do is do his best and put his faith in the Lord."

Haynes was not getting what he wanted. He wanted Old Cookie to be angry and indignant, which, as far as Haynes was concerned, he had every right to be and which Haynes believed most of his readers would be when they read Cooke's story. He tried a different tack.

"I find it fascinating you ended up being sent to Port Macquarie. Of course I know the town very well, but it must have been very different back then. You must have been one of the first to be sent there when it was just a wilderness. What was that like?

"Oh, and what of the Captain" - searched his notes for a minute or so - *"Captain Coghill. Did you ever get in contact with him?"*

Cookie nodded, the memories flooding back.

"Port Macquarie. That was a difficult time, but in an odd way also uplifting time for me.

"In Port Macquarie I found myself in a place that sorely tested me.

"They were strange days, Mr Haynes, strange days indeed."

To the Unknown North
June 30, 1821

Once again Cooke was on a ship. At sea. At peace. He was heading to a town called Newcastle, so-called after the English original because of the vast coal deposits found there he was told, the town but a stopover on the way to another town called Port Macquarie, named for the Governor he had met. According to one felon in the Sydney barracks, Port Macquarie was nothing but a clearing in the forest.

"There be nought there I heard from one bloke who got sent back for trial," said the lag. "According to him there be not a brick laid upon another; not a turned sod; no wimmin, no grog and not much food" he laughed, "rather you than me, matie, that's for bloody sure."

As far as Cooke was concerned all that was of no concern. In the wake of Bec's leaving life had lost all meaning and where his life came to an end mattered little to him any longer. The ship he sailed upon was the *Elizabeth Henrietta*, a brigantine rigged schooner built in Sydney Town of local ironbark and stringybark and named for the wife of Governor Macquarie, an honour that, had she had the choice, Mrs Macquarie probably could have foregone because the vessel was short, squat and ugly. At just 150 tons she was just a quarter the size of *Mangles*.

The little ship had corkscrewed its way through the Sydney heads and swung north on a following sea for what the crew had told them would be an overnight voyage.

Cooke and his fellow convicts - 19 men and two women in total - slept but a little on the short voyage, huddled together on deck, each with just a single thin blanket to ward off the wintery wind because the few inside berths were reserved for paying customers.

Morning found the ship bouncing in the wild seas off the mouth of the Hunter River, the dangerous entrance to the port of Newcastle guarded by an island and rocky shoals which had given the port a bad reputation. The strong blustery wind scuttling in from the southeast had turned the blue sea to shades of grey, forcing the small ship to cast a sea anchor and constantly tack to and fro' into the swells to maintain its position.

Cooke's experienced eye could see only trouble ahead.

"There'll be hell to pay trying to get into the river in this wind, mark my words" remarked an old deckhand standing nearby, "this be my seventh time to cross this bar and each time it be worse'n the last."

"But this, this looks to be madness."

Looking out over a sea of grey topped by white fumes, Cooke couldn't make out a path to safety anywhere near where the entrance to the river.

"Will the captain take a chance on it do you think?" he asked.

The deckhand hesitated.

"Probably" the old tar said at last, "Cap'n Cunningham be his name and this his first trip as master. He were the pilot here for a while and knows this place as well as anyone. In any event he's better than the last one who tried - Cap'n Ross - who managed to ground a ship not once but twice on the bar. The second time cost him the life of his wife."

"What happened?"

The old sailor looked around before answering, not wanting to be accused of spreading tales.

"It were about four year ago on a sea much like this. Cap'n Ross made a run for it, but just as he passed the island some freak waves came through the gap betwixt the island and the shore and hit the ship just as it went over the bar. She turned over quick as you please. Everyone escaped 'cept the Captain's wife and one other wot was trapped below.

"This 'ere captain is new and to give him his dues he has not flinched once yet. Problem is, he seems determined to prove himself and those sorts take more risks than needs be, p'haps to show they're not scared. Speed is the thing runnin' into the Hunter, and while gettin' in is hard enough, that ain't the worse bit, it's the gettin' out. I've spent more'n a week here in the past, waitin' for the seas to drop, and believe me, this town is no place for a felon, or even an ex-felon, to be sittin' around with nothin' to do.

"The commandant 'ere is Morrisett and I'll be tellin' ya there's not a more evil, blood-thirsty tyrant on the face of the earth. If we be stranded here for a while, if I be you I'd stay aboard and out of sight. Felons can be flogged for looking sideways at the wrong man in this place."

After the old man finished talking he gave Cooke a hard stare.

"I bin watchin' you. You know your way around a ship."

Cooke nodded. "Was in the merchant marine and the navy for a sometime a while back."

It was the old man's turn to nod. "Same as me" he said. "Hard times. See any action?" Cooke hesitated. He didn't particularly want to share his story with this stranger, but the old man had spoken kindly to him and that was a rare thing and not to be abused by silence.

"I was at Trafalgar. A bit on *Defiance* with Durham and on *Victory* with Nelson." The old man scoffed loudly.

"Ha! Wish I had a penny for every man wot's told me they was on *Victory* at Trafalgar. Easy question, where was the *Victory* in the battle? And whereabouts on the poop deck was Nelson when he was shot?"

Again Cooke hesitated.

He didn't want to get into an argument with the old man, nor did he want to say too much, however he did not like the turn the conversation had taken and the implied insult. He could feel his blood rising.

"I suppose there are many chancers out there, but let me say I don't like your tone. *Victory* led from the front, as Lord Nelson was wont to do, and when he was shot he was on the quarterdeck where he was supposed to be, not on the poop. I was there and saw the sainted Admiral die and I'll not be questioned by anyone who was not!"

The old man raised his eyebrows.

"Oh, I were there all right, on *Bellerophon* with Capt'n Cook I was, him who died in that very battle, shot through 'e was, fightin' the French hand-to-hand."

"I apologise, I had no right to have doubted your word."

To cover his anger Cooke looked back toward the wild water smashing into the shore. In his seafaring days he had faced many a danger; storms, huge waves, cannon fire, musket fire and even belligerent bullies, but getting in and out of harbour had always been relatively easy. What would happen if the ship was wrecked he wondered? He could swim a bit, but he doubted that anyone could swim to safety in this kind of sea. An hour later he was still standing in the same place when the deckhand came back to order him and the other convicts to take position amid the animal cages, well out of the way of the crew because the captain had decided to run for the shelter of harbour rather than spend days being tossed about like a cork. Whatever the history of the captain, Cooke quickly saw he knew his job.

The tiny ship headed north before taking a sharp tack to larboard that pointed the ship directly to the small island, corkscrewing wildly as the seas came onto her larboard bow. As ugly as the little ship was, she was up to the task before her. Running almost parallel to the huge waves crashing into the sandy shore, the ship held a steady course to the island under almost full sail.

From his position atop a large crate, holding on to the rigging, Will could see the island getting nearer and nearer and huge waves breaking onto a reef that stretched at least a league into out sea.

Both passengers and convicts were now on the deck watching as the maelstrom came closer and closer. The tension on the ship was palpable to everyone except the captain, who continued to issue orders to the small crew in a clear and concise manner. The man's calm manner caught Cooke's attention and he turned to look at the captain rather than at the approaching cataclysm. 'If we are doomed, the captain will be the first to know' he thought. In the background he heard a woman crying.

Forced to turn to the sound he saw she had a small child clasped to her and both were clearly terrified. Turning back he was astounded to see how close the island was, but just as it seemed that there was no way the ship could avoid disaster, the ferocity of the waves lessened and at the same time the captain ordered the ship to tack starboard and then for the fore top gallant and fore top sail to be reefed.

A minute later he called for a quick tack to larboard and then ordered the main top sail to also be reefed.

Cooke watched with keen interest as the crew jumped to with practiced skill, then as the old tar who had been talking to him ran past to grab the main mast sheet, he stumbled and pitched headfirst, landing hard on the deck and lying still.

Without hesitating Cooke ran to take the man's place, seamlessly blending into the crew for the next crucial minutes. When he returned the old man was sitting up, bleeding profusely from a deep cut to the forehead and clutching his left knee, but he managed to put his hand out in gratitude.

"I seen wot you did, but couldn't move. Thanks matie, you'll do to run the river with."

The ship was now in the lee of the island and looking over the bow Cooke could see deeper, quieter waters ahead. He realised he had witnessed as fine an example of seamanship as he had ever seen and as that fact became clear to those on deck they broke out in huzzas for the captain - who stoically declined to acknowledge their cheers.

As the ship stalled the pilot boat appeared and within a short time the schooner had been towed to shore and made fast to a stubby wharf that projected off a street that headed straight into the heart of the tiny settlement. On the wharf a uniformed officer stood at the head of a detachment of soldiers drawn up in precise formation.

Behind the soldiers a knot of oxen drawn carts stood ready to receive the ship's cargo, while a gaggle of convicts and citizens stood by watching the show. Beside the wharf was a walled area that was clearly a lumber yard, being similar in design to the one Cooke had worked in at Sydney Town. Lashed to the rocks below the lumber yard were rafts of good sized logs, clearly having been floated down the river. Further ashore on a slight rise stood a surprisingly large church with a massive bell-tower stretching into the heavens amidst dozens of well-made houses, picket fences demarcating their boundaries. There was even a sturdy-looking windmill spinning furiously in the stiff wind.

23 *The brig 'Lady Nelson' and Schooner 'Francis' depicted entering Coal River (later Hunter River) Circa 1803. This engraving of the original painting by Lt. James Grant, which first appeared in his account of an exploratory expedition to the area, perfectly shows the dangerous entry to the river past Coal Island, later connected to the mainland by a causeway.*

'This looks to be far better run town than Sydney Cove' Will mused. The *Elizabeth Henrietta* sat in a broad sheet of still water nestled between the sandy coast to the east and belts of mangroves to the west before the river disappeared around a bend heading east.

"It's a fine body of water is it not matie?" said the old deck-hand who had sidled up beside Will, his head swathed in a blood-stained bandage.

"It's called the Hunter River now, but used to be called the Coal River. I spend a few years here way back in the early days before I got my ticket of leave."

"I was part of a group that did some exploration inland and I tell you, there is a paradise there just waitin' for those wot have the courage - and the money - to take it. Green grass and good timber as far as you can see, and land fertile as England. Used to be lots of Cedar, but I hear it's mostly gone now."

To Will the serried rows of grey trees looked uninviting and he said so.

"Isn't the land full of black fellas waiting for a feast of convict flesh?" he queried. The old lag guffawed.

"When I were here there were not a black fella to be seen, but then again that might have been as they didn't want to be seen. And don't believe that nonsense about the blacks being cannibals. They can be mean and vicious if riled, but for the most part I found they just want to be left alone. The bad things wot 'appen in Newcastle are all done by white men.

"See that smoke up the river? That be the lime pits. Not as busy as they once were 'cause the easy stuff has been worked out mostly, but they're still hell. Felons are forced to dig old shells out of the sand and mud, workin' up to their waist in water sometimes. They burn the shells in pits on shore to make lime and then carry the bags of lime out to ships on their backs because the river is too shallow up there for boats to get close to shore.

"The lime mixes with saltwater and that wot seeps from the sacks is so caustic it burns holes in men's skin, but if'n they dare to complain they are on the triangle for 50. I've seen men go mad there and kill themselves, or each other. Reckoned death from either the axe or the gallows were an escape they did. Some of 'em run away but they don't get far 'cause local blacks get a reward for trackin' 'em down. Most don't last more'n a day out, and then it's onto the triangle and back to the lime pits', with 50 for their trouble.

"Over there," he said, pointing south to an idyllic looking hill dotted with sheep, "under that hill, wot's called Shepard's Hill, at this very moment men are burrowing their way into the earth like animals, diggin' out the coal from seams wot can collapse and bury them in an instant. They crawl along the seams like rats. I know 'cause I've seen it with me own eyes.

"I know you'd prob'ly like to get off the ship and explore a bit, and no one will stop you if you do, but you saved my bacon so mark my words, if you do you may regret it.

"I reckon this blow wind will blow itself out in a day or two and the captain will take her out quick as a wink.

"If you aren't on board it'll be to the mines or the lime pits for you, so take my advice and stay aboard - it's safer."

Two days later the ship's holds had been emptied and on the high tide of the third day the tiny ship sailed serenely down the narrow channel into a calm sea. This time the voyage north was more like a pleasure trip, the sea an azure mill pond while a steady southerly breeze both cooled the skin and shoved the ship along at a fair pace such that as dawn broke two days later the ship began dropping sail as it approached the fledgling settlement of Port Macquarie nestled on the banks of the Hastings River.

Again Will and the deck hand stood watching the scene float by.

"See those three peaks to the south? They're called the Three Brothers. And far to the north you can just make out Smoky Cape" said the tar, now Cooke's firm friend, "named by Cap'n Cook they were, long before any white man stepped foot anywhere here abouts, 'cause of fires he saw burnin' there as he sailed past. Port Macquarie be sittin' right in the middle of them landmarks.

"That there peak just to the north is called Tacking Point. Named by Matthew Flinders I bin told, 'cause if'n he hadn't tacked out to sea at just that point, he would've run up on the rocks sittin' just below the surface, well placed to catch the unwary. The Cap'n says he's not goin' ter chance the run over the bar just to drop off some convicts and cargo. Not worth the cost of a ship he says, even an ugly one like this," he cackled. Both men laughed.

An hour later they were still standing there when they spied the Pilot's boat making its way out of the river mouth toward them.

"I reckon you'll be on that little boat soon, so I'd be getting' your gear together 'cause we won't be here for long."

He put his hand out and Cooke took it firmly.

"Been a pleasure meeting you and you never know" said the tar, "maybe we'll have the pleasure again one day. I owe you one and don't be afraid to ask for it to be returned."

When the pilot vessel arrived it turned out to be a whale boat. A double ended, ribbed vessel about 35 foot long with six foot of beam designed as a steady platform to harpoon whales, there was room for passengers or cargo amidships. Sturdy and lightweight, they usually boasted five men on the oars with a sixth handling the tiller oar, a job taken by the pilot, flanked by two armed soldiers, while felons did the rowing. As the boat came alongside the captain came to greet the pilot as he clambered aboard.

"Ah, Mr Neave. Good to see you again. How goes the building of the settlement? I hear that things have not been going too well. And what of the bar? I am loathe to even get close, let alone try to make it into the river in this vessel. What's your opinion?"

The pilot took his time lighting a pipe before answering.

"Well captain, the truth of it is you are wise not to try. As you know I have only been here a short time, but the fact is the only chart I have of the bar and its approaches seriously over-estimates the depth of the channel. I'm busy laying down some channel markers as I take a measure of the mouth, so p'haps you will be better able to enter in the near future.

"As for the future here, well it will need to be better than the present, that's certain. We are short of food and proper shelter and we need some proper mechanics wot understand how to build a house and coax some food from the soil. I see you have some more felons for us and p'haps they will suit.

"But fact is it does no good to complain. There're worse places to be. The huntin' and fishin' is good and so we will survive, of that there is no doubt. That said, I have some letters and reports from lieutenant Allman for the Governor and p'haps that will spur some help."

Taking the canvas sack the captain in turn handed over a satchel of letters and documents for delivery to Lt. Allman, and with that the men shook hands. Will and the other convicts climbed down among the pile of canvas supply bags and a crate of chickens which had already been squeezed on to the whale boat, and even as it pushed off for the shore Captain Cunningham was giving orders for the Brig to turn south to Sydney Cove.

The whale boat easily skipped over the small surf sounding on the bar at the river mouth and glided into a slow moving deep blue river which almost immediately swung to the north and shallowed, bounded by thick stands of mangrove as it ran parallel to the sandy peninsula protecting it from the sea.

Immediately to the south, where the river had for ages run up against the sentinel hill at southern side of the river mouth, a deep basin had been gouged out, revealing a rocky shelf which formed a natural wharf.

There, under the lee of the hill, huddled the new settlement.

Port Macquarie

At first glance Port Macquarie could not have been less imposing. Consisting in the main of a smattering of grass huts much like the blacks built as temporary dwellings which was but a number of saplings stuck into the ground, lashed together at the top with smaller stripped branches tied crossways from which grasses and leafy branches had been hung in a very optimistic attempt to keep out the weather. None looked like they would hinder even the slightest rain. Fires smouldered next to some of the huts.

To Cooke it looked more like a native camp than a British-run settlement.

'The blacks would do a better job of it' he thought.

Just to the west of the hut town rafts of logs were lashed to the shore next to a cleared site clearly destined to be the lumber yard. On a level section a field of tents had been laid out in a military manner, standing snow white against the green hillside. Further up the hillside a few rudimentary slab huts were scattered about, each with the beginnings of vegetable gardens beside them. To one side a gang of convicts were picking at the ground with hoes and shovels, possibly levelling the ground for some more buildings.

Finishing off the picture of isolation, further down river a small ship lay forlornly on its side on the riverbank, it's clean lines revealing what must have once been a fine vessel.

Now it was a resting site for seagulls, the river swirling around its barnacled flank.

As the whale boat moved into the lee of the hill the wind dropped and the heat of the sun bouncing off the water drove the temperature up dramatically, convict rowers and passengers alike breaking out into a sweat. Immediately the whale boat had been beached the crew off-loaded the sacks and chickens and lay in the shade while the pilot sorted through the sacks.

A slow, heavy feeling of lassitude settled comfortably over the two groups, the cries of the seagulls and the occasional desultory sound of a hoe or shovel striking rock the only sounds penetrating the stillness. A short time later a small troop of soldiers headed by a civilian appeared from the bush and struggled toward them along the loose sand. Peering out from beneath his cabbage tree hat at the approaching little procession, Will thought the civilian had a familiar gait to him. Then, as the man's face became clear, Cooke's eyes widened and he involuntarily sat back in shock.

Striding toward him was none other than Stephen Partridge.

"You men! Get up and form a line. Now!" Partridge shouted.

'That's definitely Partridge' thought Cooke, slowly drifting into line, 'nothing much has changed'. While he knew Partridge had left Sydney Cove some time ago, not for an instant had he given a thought to where the man had gone, or indeed why he had left, being merely relieved the threat he posed had gone. Now here he was, returned like an evil genie.

Thoughts of Bec, and the way Partridge had treated her, triggered another thought that sent a shiver of fear through Cooke. Was it possible Partridge knew about him and Bec?

Even though the man had left the colony before he and Bec became lovers, that did not mean someone may have told him of their romance. If he did know, then Cooke had no doubt Partridge would make sure his life became a living hell.

'How will I know if he knows? What will I do?' he thought.

The answer came as a revelation, a clear and certain course of action that had the effect of calming him.

'I shall kill the fiend here and now and that will be an end to it all' he resolved. 'There is no other way. It must be him that dies quickly, lest it be me will die a slow and painful death'.

GOVERNMENT AND GENERAL ORDERS.
Colonial Secretary's Office,
March 15th, 1821.
CIVIL DEPARTMENT.

His Excellency the Governor has been pleased to appoint Captain Francis Allman, of the 48th Regiment, to be Magistrate and Justice of the Peace of the New Settlement of Port Macquarie, and of the Territory of New South Wales:—He is therefore to be obeyed as such accordingly.

His Excellency has also been pleased to appoint Mr. Stephen Partridge to be Superintendent of Convicts and Public Labour, at the Settlement of Port Macquarie with a Salary of Fifty Pounds Sterling per Annum, commencing from this Date, and to be paid from the Colonial Police Fund.

By Command of His Excellency,
F. Goulburn, Colonial Secretary.

24 *The official government notice of the appointment of Captain Francis Allman as Commandant of the Port Macquaire settlement - as well as Magistrate and Justice of the Peace - and also appointing Stephen Partridge as Superintendent of Convicts and Public Labour at a salary of fifty pounds per annum. Colonial Secretary's Papers. 1821*

Just how he could carry out such a plan given he was unarmed, shackled at the ankles and facing a man a foot taller, well-fed and much stronger than himself, with armed soldiers to back him up, never crossed Cooke's mind.

All too soon a convict scribe was checking off the names and details of the new arrivals, and all too soon it was his turn.

"Cooke" he said in answer to the question the convict scribe asked him, "William Thomas; cabinet maker; seven years," his eyes focussed on Partridge who had been staring down river at the pilot busy opening the bags which had been delivered by the *Elizabeth Henrietta*, but the man swung around to face him at the mention of his name.

"I know you," he said. "Cooke? Was it Cooke?" he pondered.

Cooke braced himself.

"Cooke! The cabinet maker! You worked at my house in Sydney Cove, did a damn good job I recall. Well, well, well. You are just the man I've been waiting for."

Cooke immediately tensed, fearing the worse, but then a genuine smile lit up Partridge's face.

"At last they're sending me some decent workers."

At those words the pent up tension in Cooke's body dissolved, threatening to drop him into the sand.

"Are you alright Cooke?" Partridge asked.

"Corporal! Get these men settled in the convict quarters, get their shackles struck off, then bring this man Cooke to my tent".

"That'll be all."

With that he strode - Cooke recalled that Partridge never walked, he always strode - toward where the pilot was busy sorting the contents of the sacks. The 'convict quarters' were exactly what he had suspected they might be - the sorry collection of grass-roofed huts he had seen strung out along the river. Up close there were a great many more than he had seen, up to fifty or sixty he estimated, enough to sleep around 200 convicts or more. As usual the day-to-day running of the convict camp was left to convict overseers, so the soldiers merely handed the newcomers over to the old lags, the corporal telling them to report to him at the 'barracks' - meaning the cluster of tents he had spied earlier - later in the afternoon.

The felon in charge disinterestedly pointed out the unoccupied huts after Cooke, Oram and Kelling quickly let it be known they would share a hut - to which the felon shrugged, pointing out the communal cooking and eating area under the trees before leading them off to the blacksmith to remove their shackles. That done, he called the newcomers together.

"Right. Let's get a few things sorted. Aint't such a bad place 'ere; in fact, nice and quiet it is. Nuffink to do but work, eat, shit and sleep. The fishin' can be good if you know how and the blacks are mostly friendly and we all want to keep it like that, ok?"

"So, a few local rules. Firstly, no botherin' the black wimmin. The black men here about are big buggers and not afraid of a fight. They get real testy when somefink 'appens to their wimmin'. Usually they spear the next white fella they come across.

When that 'appens, work stops and the Lieutenant also gets testy and sends some soldiers out, who usually shoot someone, and for a month or two everyone is on edge and there's no huntin' so everyone goes hungry.

"So 'ard as it is, don't touch the black ladies.

"Two. Hard as the work is, as long as it gets done eventually, no one bovvers anyone. The commandant, Lieutenant Allman, an Irishman, he don't like to use the lash, so provided we look like we're workin' and some work gets done, he leaves us alone. So, life here has been nice and slow and we wants to keep it that way.

"The officers like to go hunting more than they do workin', and they like to take some black fellas with 'em to break the path so as they don't step on a snake or get bit by spiders, and a few felons to carry everything. In return we get some meat, which is always shared out. Always. Got it!

"Long as we all share, we're all good. Try to steal anyfing or keep anyfing out of the pot and you may end up being speared by persons unknown, if you get my drift. Mr Partridge, who you just met, is the supervisor of convicts. He can be a real bastard if he wants, but he's on the take, always lookin' for a bit extra for his own account and we like to help him whenever and 'owever we can and when we do ... well, then we all get along better.

"Now, get yourselves up to the stores hut - that's that big wooden hut up on the ridge there - give your names to the storeman and get your allotted rations.

"There's not much food about at the moment so be sparing how much you eat or you might end up going hungry, it's up to you."

His shackles removed, his hut mates sorted and some flour and hominy porridge stored in his sack and a water bag filled, Cooke walked off alone and sat on the riverbank in the thin shade of a small spotted gum. The presence of Partridge had shaken him, but at the same time made him realise once again that no matter how bad life might seem, it was worth fighting for. After a while he closed his eyes in silent prayer. 'Lord, you are determined that all I hold dear is constantly torn from me. I don't know why. I don't know your plans for me, but I will stay true to my vow to Reverend Nelson and I will trust my fate to you and strive to do the best I can, and ...'

He was torn out of his contemplation by a rude kick in the ribs, his eyes flying open to see the corporal standing over him, club in hand.

"Wake up you miserable bastard, you're not here to sleep! Come on, get up! Mr Partridge doesn't like to be kept waiting, especially by the likes of you. Get up or you'll be getting a pretty fifty across your back on your first day."

Ducking a swing of the club Cooke scrambled to his feet and away from the soldier in one move, only to take a whack across the shoulders from another soldier wielding a knotted rope that propelled him down the river toward the tents, followed by a steady flow of abuse.

Collared to a halt outside one of the tents he was confronted by the very last thing he expected to see, a group of a half dozen black fellas lazing about on the grass beside a camp table and chairs. As the corporal respectfully called out to Partridge, one of the black men stood up, looking Cooke squarely in the eyes with a dark gaze that left the convict feeling very unsettled. The man was a magnificent specimen, standing over six foot tall, he was naked but for a loincloth, his chest and face decorated in an intricate series of scars and white dots, with white strips down his arms and legs. Around his forehead a strip of red cloth held his long hair from his face. Pride of place high on his chest was given to a brass military-style Gorget, a crescent-shaped plate which Cooke took to be some form of official recognition.

In one hand the warrior casually cradled three wooden spears and a throwing stick, in the other he carried a short club, while tucked into a sling across his shoulder were a number of the curved throwing sticks he had heard were called boomer-things, or some other silly word he couldn't pronounce. Cooke had heard of the sticks, but had never seen them used and doubted the stories of them returning to the thrower.

"Ah Cooke, come here my man".

Partridge had appeared and sat himself at the camp desk. Cooke took off his cabbage tree hat and stood before him, once again tense and not knowing what was to come.

"I see you have met our chief tracker. I have named him Cook, after the discoverer of this great land. Hang on! He has the same name as you!"

The linkage of the name drew a cackle of laughter from Partridge, echoed by the soldiers.

"Well, that won't do will it" he said, carrying on the joke, "can't have people mixing you two up."

The image of the two men; one short, white and servile; the other tall, black and clearly a warrior to be reckoned with, again reduced Partridge to laughter.

"Wait. I have it! Because you have an 'e' in your name, and my friend here lacks one, we shall call you Cookie from now on."

In that moment Cooke's name was forever changed.

The joke again reduced everyone to laughter - except the black men. Partridge dismissed the soldiers and then told 'Cookie' to accompany him on a tour of the site, which proved to be much more extensive than Cookie had first perceived. Walking back to towards the ocean he spied a fine looking house with a verandah and enclosed garden.

"That is the commander's official residence" Partridge volunteered, "and behind it over there" he pointed, "the foundations of the military barracks are being laid.

"The huts you saw next to the lumber yard will hopefully soon be turned into proper convicts barracks, and just over there, next to that dirt track we call Clarence street, is where you are going to build a fine house for Mrs Partridge and I and our two lovely children."

Cookie must have raised an eyebrow or looked askance, because Partridge immediately stopped before laying a hand on the smaller man's shoulder.

"Now Cookie, you're not a fool. You were very quick to take advantage of the system that was run in Sydney Cove, where your services were made available to certain people in the settlement, to the benefit of everyone, including yourself. I know how you and your friends exploited my … ah, the system, and that is as it should be, and will be here as well.

"Everyone must benefit for any system to work. That upstart Irish so-called military hero Allman may be the commander of this settlement," he said, "but he is weak and will not last the distance.

He …" then he stopped speaking, clearly considering his words before deciding against saying whatever had been on his lips.

"Irish he may be, but hero he is not. The man was wounded and saved by a Frenchman for goodness sake, and spent the war as a prisoner," he said, shaking his head. "Well, whether he understands it or not, the fact is I am in charge here, and I have both the knowledge and labour needed to make this settlement succeed - but that success must also work for me. You may not be aware Cookie, for we did not converse much in Sydney Town, but I have been at times a soldier and a carpenter and many other things besides.

"I was one of the first men to explore this site years ago and I have the full support of the Governor, and many others who make these decisions, to decide what has to happen here and to make it happen.

"Finally, there is no stratagem, ploy or larceny unknown to me and should I find you have at any time tried to steal from me or in any way undermine me, your life here will be both brutal and short. Understood?

"On the othr hand, work with me and we will both prosper. Now, you will select a small team to help you on your first task. You will report only to mee. Let me know what men and material you need and it will be provided. Do not fail me Cookie - do you understand?"

Cookie said he understood perfectly.

"Sir, I have two mates, carpenters both, who can help me. All I need are the right tools, some labour and material and you shall have a fine house, a house *almost* as fine as the commander's."

Partridge laughed and slapped his knee.

"Exactly! Not as fine, but almost! I knew you would understand. The area of the house and garden has been laid out and it but needs to be levelled before work is ready to begin, and begin it must. Immediately.

"I have learnt today Governor Macquarie himself plans to visit the settlement before the year is out.

"I know Macquarie. He is out of favour and has to leave, but before he leaves he must have something good to show for his time here and that will be the settlement that bears his name.

"I intend to give him that cachet, but there is much to be done before then and so the lackadaisical tempo Allman has allowed to fester in this settlement is about to change. There will be teams working on the barracks, on a proper store and granary and so on. Be that as it may, and no matter who may order you to the contrary, your priority will remain my house, is that clear? The rest can follow. Report to me as soon as possible and let me know what men and materials you need."

With that the man strode off back to his tent, an extra swagger to his step. Kelling and Oram were delighted with the god news 'Cookie' returned with.

"Hah! Cookie! Luv it! Cookie you are!" Oram laughed, doing a little jig around the outside their new home with Kelling.

"I knew the wee fellow had the knack. Lady luck rides on his shoulders and we will also benefit from her gifts. In Sydney Cove I said, 'follow our mate' and I was right! Remember I pointed out that if we volunteered we'd earn a slice off our sentence."

As soon as the words had left his lips he knew he had erred, looking sharply at to see if Cookie had heard and understood.

Cookie merely smiled.

"Not to worry lads. It's the way of our world. I was to be here anyway, 'til the end of my sentence or 'til I die. It's well we are together, no matter the details."

"As you said in Sydney Town, and as we found on the *Mangles*, we must stick together and work for each other if we are to survive.

All three nodded, hugged and joined together in the jig on the sand.

"More madmen" mumbled a nearby convict, "that's all we need."

Three months after their merry jig on the sand the three men were back at the same spot, this time standing at attention along with the entire convict population of the settlement.

In front of the felons stood Stephan Partridge, his wife Sarah and their two children, Thomas and Jane.

To their right a small detachment of the 48th regiment also stood at attention, under arms, colours flying, with Commandant Allman and his officers at their head, along with wife Sarah and children William, Sarah and Maria.

In fact the entire population of the settlement had been on the beach since early-morning following news of the arrival off-shore of the *Elizabeth Henrietta* bearing Governor Macquarie.

All were waiting for the great man to arrive. And they waited. And waited. Lookouts on the bluff over-looking the river mouth scurried up and down passing messages to the Commandant, describing what was happening beyond the heavy seas pounding onto the bar outside the mouth, but neither soldiers nor convicts on the beach were considered important enough to be let in on the progress of the great man. So they waited. Eventually Commandant Allman, his wife and children departed to their house to await developments in comfort. Seeing this, Partridge decided he return to his home, triggering a ripple of knowing looks between the convicts who well knew the rivalry, if not enmity, growing between the two men.

"Me thinks there'll be a showdown between those two soon enough" Oram whispered, "and my money will be on the military. Partridge is getting too big for his boots. He has a finger in every pie and eventually he'll be caught. Methinks it may be time to get ready to jump ship."

Cookie looked back at his friend.

"Better the devil you know than the one you don't" he replied simply.

The past three months had been a busy time for the trio and the team of workers they headed. Not only had they finished the Partridge house, complete with enclosed garden, but had moved on to begin rebuilding the store and granary. In return they enjoyed good rations, including fresh meat and fish when it was available. Cookie had been promoted to overseer, so the trio were largely spared the attention of the whip and club used liberally on the other convicts as they were driven to make up for time lost at the beginning of the settlement.

Two hours later Governor Macquarie arrived and Allman and Partridge led soldiers and convicts alike giving three cheers, the later less enthusiastic than the former.

During the week Macquarie spent at the settlement he barely glanced at the timber buildings Cookie and his team had worked so hard to complete, instead devoting his time defining the parameters of 'his' town and touring the surrounding countryside.

The triangular pasture containing the few buildings and military tents, bounded on one side by the current camp and on the other sides by the Hastings River and the fresh-water Shoal Arm Creek running into the river, he named Allman's Plains, directing that the area should become the heart of the town. He gave names to the tracks bisecting the pasture and decreed where individual homes and buildings were to be located. He visited the trial plantings of sugar cane and tobacco outside the settlement, instantly declaring them a success, and ordered the hulk of the stranded ship - the *Lady Nelson* - be dragged out of the river so it could be repaired.

At the end of his visit he sailed away, happy that the town bearing his name would grow and prosper. The instant the whale boat carried him over the bar, life resumed its unhurried pace.

By now firmly installed in Partridge's orbit, Cookie firstly became overseer of the lumber yard, then deputy overseer of the stores and commissariat, at all times working to the tune called by Partridge who grew steadily richer and more influential at the same time as he undermined the position of Commandant Allman in private letters to his backers in Sydney Cove.

A year after Cookie arrived, Partridge seized a major chance to enhance his position. In September of 1822 a group of nine prisoners stole a rowboat and, using oars they had made secretly, rowed out to sea. Partridge threatened to hand a few fellow plotters the escapees had left behind over to his black guards 'to be eaten' unless they revealed the escapees plans, and one look was all it took for them to blurt out that the plan was to sail south to the tiny settlement of Port Stephens, 100 miles south of Port Macquarie, to raid the few farms there and hopefully steal a larger vessel in which to flee to America. Convincing Allman to allow him and his black trackers to give chase, Partridge commandeered a boat and a small troop of soldiers and surprised the escapees before they even knew there was a pursuit.

Partridge wounded one of the convicts with a pistol shot when they resisted, while two others were speared to death by the trackers. He sailed back to Port Macquarie in triumph, then moved quickly to ensure his exploit was the talk of Sydney Cove, writing to friends about the exploit with a hint that it be passed on to the press.

Although Lt. Allman tried to take credit by commending Partridge for his actions, implying he had ordered the operation, the damage to his reputation had been done and he never recovered from the humiliation. Sent for a time to Sydney 'discussions', early in 1824 he was officially recalled. A succession of weak commandants, three alone in the year following Allman's fall from grace, meant that Partridge's pre-eminent position in the settlement became unchallenged. Using his control over the key lumber and commissariat operations, both staffed by convicts overseen by a few picked men, he siphoned off quantities of scarce material for sale to both convicts and the small but increasing numbers of free settlers trickling into the area, while at the same time managing to supply them convict labour - at a price.

After harbour master and pilot Richard Neave was drawn into Partridge's circle, he was able to surreptitiously use government vessels to transport scarce commodities from Sydney Cove, such as furniture, sugar, tea, flour, gunpowder, flint and shot, on-selling them at a huge profit to both government and settlers. Cookie knew he was walking a fine line. If Partridges' crimes were uncovered Cookie had no doubt he would be one of those blamed and would probably spend the rest of his life in a hell such a Norfolk Island - if he wasn't hung.

If he did not do as ordered, Partridge made it clear he would end up in much the same predicament.

Trapped literally between the devil and the deep blue sea, Cookie did what he had learnt was the key to survival for a man in his position; he kept his head down, his mouth closed, and profited as much as possible from the crumbs that fell from Partridge's table. Disaster befell Cookie when Kelling and Oram, along with the other original Port Macquarie 'volunteers', had their sentences remitted by Governor Macquarie as promised. The three *Mangles* men had formed a cohesive, mutually supportive unit, but as free men it was untenable for the two to stay in the penal colony. After a tearful farewell they sailed on the regular packet to Sydney Cove and out of Cookie's life.

Yet again Cookie found himself alone, friendless, and at the mercy of forces far beyond his control. A desperate plea for a ticket of leave to enable him to join his friends was simply laughed off by Partridge, whose assent was the minimum requirement, the fiend candidly pointing out that Cookie was simply too valuable to him to be set free.

The Church of St. Thomas
August 1824

Shortly after his friends departed, Cookie was summoned to Partridge's home where he found the villain in a contemplative mood.

"Ah Cookie, come with me," he said, meeting him at the door.

Following Partridge into his office he closed the door as directed, standing nervously just inside. He did not trust the man, and the air of secrecy he was exuding heightened his concern even more. Seated behind an impressive desk, one that Cookie had made, he picked up a letter from the desk and studied it for what seemed an eternity. Cookie stood, slowly shifting his weight from foot to foot and waited. He was used to being left standing in the company of his betters, a ploy used by everyone in a position of power to reinforce their power. Eventually Partridge leaned back, balancing on the rear two legs of the sturdy chair Cookie had made for him, and looked squarely at the felon in front of him, fingers touching, lips pursed.

"A situation has arisen that may - nay, which will - have important repercussions on our cosy little operation here at the end of the world. This," he said, rocking forward to grab the letter and hold it up, "are orders from Governor Brisbane. He wants a church built. Have you ever built a church Cookie? A church to sit hundreds of people?"

Cookie knew an answer wasn't required, because Partridge knew the answer. Neither he nor anyone else in Port Macquarie had ever constructed such a massive building. Partridge eventually answered his own question.

"I didn't think so. But, nevertheless, as it says here" he said, waving the letter about his head, "it must be built, and built quickly. You won't understand Cookie, but this letter may have the unintended effect of undermining all that we have managed to build here."

Cookie noted the use of 'we', instantly divining that in the event of failure he would be the one who was held accountable.

"As you know, this settlement is supposedly run by the military. Supposedly. However the officers here are the most inept bunch of military nincompoops I have ever met. It is possible that our latest glorious commandant, Lt Rolland, might be the person in the settlement who knows the least about how to build a church, except perhaps for his incompetent so-called engineer and inspector of works, Wilson. So what does the military do? Why, obviously the army puts him in charge of building one! Soldiers! I doubt any of them could so much as hammer a nail into sand, so what has our military genius done? Yes, you're right" he went on, not waiting for an answer, "he has passed the problem on to me. And I am passing it on to you."

The look that passed over Cookie's face hit Partridge's funny bone and he roared with laughter, slapping his knee as he was won't to do.

"Yes, yes. I share your fear." More laughter.

"I am informed we are soon to have in our midst, from Sydney Town, one Thomas Owen, a real engineer and a real Inspector of Public Works, who the Governor assures me actually does know how to design and build such a church. Your job, Cookie, is - at my direction, of course - to assemble what capable men that are available - carpenters, brick-makers and so on - men who can actually build things. As well whatever materials Owen will need. More importantly, you need to do this very quickly.

"I anticipate that you may well end up as Mr Owen's convict overseer, in fact, that will be a certainty if I have anything to do with it. Who knows, if I'm lucky there perhaps may yet be a silver lining to be had. Whatever the case, the work must be done in order that the Governor be pleased and we can stay in business."

The man sat again for a long time, lost in thought, before looking up.

"That's all" he said, waving Cookie away.

Back behind his cramped corner in the government Commissariat building Cookie sat quietly and let the news wash over him. He thought he ought to be feeling fear and panic, but instead he felt strangely calm. Even a little elated.

At last it seemed he might be able to do something good. Even something important. It was true he had never undertaken such a monumental task before, but despite what Partridge had implied, he realised that it was not his head on the block should the task fail, but that of Partridge.

'What, after all, can they do to me that has not already been done?' he thought. But what a great thing it would be to actually build such a massive house of God' his thoughts continued. 'Perhaps I might still achieve something in this life after all. And in fact a church is just another building, a bigger building for certain, but just a building still.'

Cautiously his mind moved on to the practicalities. Having been overseer at both the lumber yard and the commissariat, he was uniquely placed to know what materials were to hand. He also knew the qualities of most of the felons in the settlement. What should a large church be built of he pondered and instantly the answer came.

'It should be built of stone' he thought, only to instantly reject the idea. 'But we don't have any stone. Nor any men or tools to quarry it or transport it.'

The answer came in one of those very rare moments when knowledge and clarity of thought combine to create a touch of genius.

"Bricks!" he said out loud. "It has to be built of brick. And Timber, because we have both". In fact the settlement had very few bricks, but it did possess an abundance of the clay needed to make bricks, while Limeburners Creek could supply all the lime needed for mortar.

Of timber there was plenty, but production would have to be increased.

'Where to build such a huge monument?' was the next question, but it was one he knew the answer to before he had even finished formulating the question. The site for such a church had long been laid out on a rise not 300 feet away from where he sat. A few minutes later elation collapsed into reality as the problems materialised.

'What we don't have is a design' he thought, 'a proper design by a good architect. And we need a good engineer to turn the architects vision into workable plans'. And mechanics! As Partridge says, we will need men who can build things.'

Cooke knew there were under 100 convicts in the settlement who were mechanics, or at least who said they were mechanics. On the positive side, brick making required just a few knowledgeable overseers. On the negative side, carpentry was a different matter. Counting out loud Cookie came up with about ten men who could do decent carpentry work, with another two dozen able to help. There were plenty of soldiers available of course, but Cookie almost laughed out loud at the thought of the idle military actually doing real work. After a long time he came to a conclusion.

"It can be done!" he said out loud. "If the Lord can provide a good engineer and architect, then it can be done!"

The next morning Cookie told Partridge he needed a large team of labourers to have the land cleared and begin the production of thousands of bricks, and good to his word Partridge issued the necessary orders, placing Cooke in charge - under the overall 'direction' of a military officer of course. Cookie was at once both consumed and energised by the idea of building such an edifice, but as days and weeks drifted by without any direction or help from the military administration, his enthusiasm waned in direct proportion to the number of bricks piling up. Faced with the insurmountable problem that had landed on his desk the aristocratic Commandant, Captain John Rolland, had done what most officers in the British Army did in such situations - he went hunting. The year 1824 was an exceptionally hot year in Port Macquarie, even by New South Wales standards. However in the finest military tradition Captain Rolland refused to allow the heat to justify any lowering of standards, insisting on hunting while wearing the full uniform of his beloved 3rd Regiment of Foot.

Known as The Buffs, the regimental uniform consisted of the traditional thick Red wool tunic featuring the beige coloured Buff facings that gave the regiment its name, in addition to heavy hemp linen trousers, black leggings and boots.

"It simply will not do" he had told the small officers mess, "even out here standards must be maintained at all costs. It behoves us to set the bar and keep it there."

He set off early one morning with his team of black trackers, who as usual foraged ahead to make sure the Captain did not step on a snake - he was petrified of snakes - or walk into any spider webs - he was equally petrified of spiders. Walking ahead and whacking the ground with their clubs to scare off snakes and grinning at the obvious futility of trying to find game while making such a racket, the trackers led the way south into land that even after almost five years of occupation few of the white occupiers had ever ventured into. Unsurprisingly nary a kangaroo or even a bird was sighted. It was late afternoon on the second day when, turning in fright at a slithering in the grass, Rolland swooned and collapsed. Suddenly scared, the black trackers stood around the drooling man.

"The white man as gone all red" one of them said, sending the rest to the trackers into peals of laughter.

"Not funny" said the leader of the hunt, "what do we do if he dies?"

"Well if he does die, I'm not going back to tell the soldiers" said another, "because then there will be two dead fellas instead of one"

That drew more laughter. Eventually it was decided to build a fire because as everyone knew, the white fellas loved a fire and could sit around them for hours. It was the next morning before Rolland revived and, true to form, as soon as he could move he sat up and put his hands to the fire. All the trackers nodded and smiled at each other. Rolland was covered in insect bites and on the march home occasionally staggered and stumbled, sweating profusely. By the time he reached the settlement he was speaking incoherently. The newly arrived military surgeon Francis Moran was at a loss as to what his illness was, let alone how to treat it and on November 16, after a fever that lasted 20 days, Rolland died, triggering a crisis of leadership that only ended with the timely arrival of Lieutenant Thomas Owen.

Taking control, he ordered that Rolland be buried beneath the site of the still to be laid foundation stone of the church, then rolled up his sleeves and set to work. Partridge ingratiated himself into the leadership vacuum, introducing Cookie to Owen as "a fine carpenter, cabinet-maker, builder and experienced overseer who would make a fine building supervisor".

Owen was pleasantly surprised to find that Cookie had anticipated the initial problems and set in motion work to address them, amassing thousands of bricks and a store of cured timber.

"Bricks? Yes indeed Cookie. I agree."

"Given the scarcity of stone and the cost, not to mention the time to secure stone elsewhere, we will indeed need to use bricks, a great many bricks, and a great deal of timber" he said as he was guided around the site the day after his arrival.

"I have spoken to architect Greenway in Sydney and we have drawn up some preliminary plans, including a simple ground plan and elevation of a stone church, but now these will need to be changed to suit the use of bricks. I need to go to Sydney Town, but will return as soon as possible and we can begin in earnest.

"In Sydney Town I will set in motion an order for all the glass work, windows and such, but in the meantime you must speed up the making of bricks and the stockpiling of lime.

"For a convict you have done very well Mr Cookie."

To say Partridge was pleased would be an understatement.

"I knew I could count on you Cookie. With a bit of luck I can get this job done! What a feather that would be in my cap! Well don't just stand there, get to work. And remember, all - and I mean all - lists of material and labour come to me first!"

God's and Nelson's Work
August 1826

Cookie sat at his makeshift desk in the cavernous building that one day soon would be the nave of the church of St Thomas.

Opposite him sat Stephen Partridge.

Around the two men sounds of construction reverberated through the fine dust that covered everything in the building, including the two men. Almost 18 months had passed since Thomas Owen had returned with an arm full of plans and a mind full of enthusiasm to build on the ground the church he had already built in his mind.

Cookie had officially become Owen's unofficial 'supervisor of convict labour' on the church site, meaning he was the actual building supervisor of the site, responsible not only for keeping the convict labour working, but also for ensuring the supply of raw materials met demand. Owen estimated that 380 000 bricks would be needed to build the church, as well as many hundreds of yards of many different types and qualities of timber. Meeting the demand had taken every ounce of energy and resourcefulness Cookie could muster, but it had been worth it. For the first time in many years he had been not only proud of what he was doing, but also proud of himself. Now all of that work and sacrifice tottered on a precipice.

On the desk between the two men lay a single sheet of paper. Both men stared fixedly at the same piece of paper, but it generated very different reactions from each of them.

"When did you get it?" Cookie asked, looking a squirming Partridge straight in the eye.

"On this last trip to Sydney. I wasn't expecting it. I had no warning it was due, in the madness of the past two years I never gave it a thought. I brought it to you as soon as I landed," he answered.

Cooke nodded. He had to admit not even he had given it a thought.

"What exactly does it mean? I mean, when does it take effect?" he finally asked.

Partridge looked at him with a mixture of both sympathy and disbelief.

"This is your certificate of freedom. It is dated almost a month ago and means, Cookie, that you are a free man."

"Right now, this minute, you are a free man."

Cookie turned his eyes back to the paper and after a minute a tear rolled from one eye, slowly forcing a track through the dust of his cheek to his chin where it vibrated for a moment before dropping onto the desk.

Soon it was followed by others.

Partridge stood and placed a hand on Cookie's shoulder for a few seconds - the first time he had ever touched him - before moving off to stare at a carpenter installing a window frame.

Five minutes later he returned and sat down. Cookie's tears had stopped, but the path they had forged through his dusty face remained.

He still sat rock still. Finally Partridge spoke.

"Cookie, if anyone deserves this, you do. You're a good man, probably a better one than I am, I might add.

"But, be that as it may, I have something more to say and, while nothing compels you to listen, what I have to say will interest you."

Cookie looked at him, saying nothing. He didn't like Partridge, in fact he might even hate him, but he still feared him.

Though he might indeed be a free man, he absolutely knew in Port Macquarie Partridge still controlled of his fate.

"I know you have some money saved which you have banked in Sydney Town and you have me to thank for that. You can walk away from here today, but I want to make you an offer.

"I need to have this church finished. It is sucking up the entire life blood of this settlement and I need for that to end so that I can return to business. You know that better than anyone. After I received this, while I was still in Sydney, I approached the new Colonial Secretary, Alexander Macleay, with a proposal.

"I told him I believed it was vital you remain here to help finish this crucial last stage of the construction."

Cookie's shock and anger must have blazed across his face instantly because Partridge instantly raised his hand and lowered his head in submission.

"Please wait. I know how you must feel and how urgently you must now need to be free. Completely free. But I have a plan that can help you make provision for your future."

"Mr MacLeay has agreed, albeit reluctantly, to allow me to hire your services, your services as a free man, at a good wage, until the church building is completed. I can offer you fifty pounds a year, with free food and lodgings, to stay until the church is finished."

"It's a good offer Cookie. Please consider it."

When Cookie said nothing, he pressed on.

"There is more. When MacLeay looked at your record he saw you arrived here on the *Mangles* under a Captain Coghill. John Coghill. Well, it turns out MacLeay's wife is Coghill's aunt, or some relation like that. Anyway, they are related and Macleay knows Coghill well. Very well it seems. Do you know this Coghill? According to MacLeay you do because he said that Coghill had enquired about you."

Cookie was struggling to give Partridge his full attention, his head spinning from the knowledge that he was a free man. A free man! And now Coghill was asking about me?

'Why? Why would he do that? What more could he want with me?' he thought. Even as he asked himself those questions, his mind was running through what freedom meant to him. What would he do? Where would he go? Could he go home to England? Did he want to go to England? Was England still his home? And what could Coghill and someone as important as the Colonial Secretary possibly want of him? Unable to say anything, he said nothing, which put added pressure on Partridge to talk on.

"Apparently Coghill has been given some grants of land. Large grants in fact. Given his uncle is the Colonial Secretary, that's not surprising. But in addition Coghill has powerful friends in high places, all bloody Scotsmen I might add, but so be it. It seems to me this Coghill could be an important and powerful patron to you, and we all need patrons."

"The thing is, it seems Coghill is back in England at present and only due back in the colony next year."

In fact Partridge was lying. He had in fact been told that Coghill was due back in Sydney sometime that very year, but after giving the matter a lot of thought, and after arriving at a plan to suit himself, the actual timing did not suit Partridge's purpose. So he lied.

"I have spoken briefly to Owen and he says the construction phase of the church can be finished in about six to twelve months."

"My suggestion is you continue to work here; earn some money; finish what you started; and then travel to Sydney to meet this Coghill, if that is what you desire.

"Macleay said Coghill had spoken of you and indicated that, should you come to MacLeay's attention, he should tell you Coghill would be willing to fulfil a promise he made to you to provide a place and work for you.

"You continue to surprise me Cookie. I had no idea you even knew such people! Be that as it may, I believe the timing of all of this is perfect. Should you decide to take this offer - which I truly hope you do - you will earn enough money to travel to Sydney to meet this Coghill not only as a free man, but as a man with enough money to be able to do what you want, not as this Coghill may want you to do."

Cookie remained maddeningly silent, so Partridge was reluctantly forced to play his ace.

"Look Cookie, let me be blunt. I hold all the cards here. The fact is at this very instant I can have you arrested and charged with …

well, almost anything really. Getting witnesses would not be a problem."

Seeing the shock on Cookie's face he rushed on.

"I don't want to do that, but the fact is I need you to do this. I'm sorry, but it's not an equal system is it? You know that."

Having said his piece Partridge stood up, looking down at Cookie.

"You have some time Cookie. Spend the time here. Finish what you started. Earn some money and then, when Coghill arrives, travel to Sydney to see what he wants."

With that he strode out of the building, leaving Cookie swirling in a sea of doubt and confusion. After a while he stood up and slowly walked down to the small shack at the rear of the lumber yard which had been built for him when the construction of the church had begun. Laying down in his hammock he pressed his fists into his closed eyes.

'Am I really free? What does that mean out here in the middle of nowhere?' he asked himself. 'What would happen to me if right now I walked into a free person's house? What would I do if some soldier ordered me about and threatened to have me lashed?

'What does freedom really mean. To me. Here. Now'?

The questions kept flooding in, questions about things he had not thought about, or dared think about, for what seemed a lifetime.

'Where is Bec? I wonder if she ever thinks of me.

"What would Rev. Nelson would tell me to do"? he said aloud.

Sometime during the afternoon he fell asleep, waking up only when the sun rose the next morning. On a whim he decided not to go to the church site. After all, he was a free man and able to do as he wished. Instead he chose to walk up the sandy path to a spot beneath the lighthouse overlooking the settlement where he sometimes spent time looking at the sea.

'Will I be stopped?' he wondered as he set off. 'If I am stopped, what will I say? Will I say, 'I am a free man and can go where I choose when I choose?'

Standing up he looked down at his clothes. He was wearing the hated canvas slops, a striped shirt and a jacket plastered with the broad arrow which signalled to the world he was the property of the King; a chattel to be mistreated at will by those in authority.

NUMBER,	96/5484
NAME,	William Cooke, alias Thomas Cooke
VESSEL,	Maugdeth
YEAR ARRIVED,	1820
WHERE CONVICTED,	Gloucester Qs
WHEN CONVICTED,	13 July 1819
TERM,	Seven Years
NATIVE PLACE,	Bristol
CALLING,	Cabinet Maker
AGE,	Twenty Eight
HEIGHT,	5 feet 1¾ inc
COMPLEXION,	Sallow
HAIR,	Brown
EYES,	Hazel Grey
DATE of CERTIFICATE,	20 July 1826
GENERAL REMARKS,	Was sent to Port Macquarie 13 June 1821 for the term of his original sentence for being absent from govt work

25 The official registration of Cookie's Certificate of Freedom, recognition he had served out his full sentence and was a free man. It was issued on July 20, 1826 - within a week of his seven year sentence having been served. His age is recorded as 28 – giving a birth date of approx. 1798. His physical description remains constant except that his once brown eyes are now recorded as 'hazel-grey'. It notes his conviction for being absent from government work and subsequent transfer to Port Macquarie. The certificate meant that theoretically he could return to Britain or engage in any legal activity in the colony, but in practice there were a myriad of barriers placed in his way. Ex-convicts were required to carry their actual certificate on their person at all times, which is why so few survive.
Register of NSW Certificates of Freedom. 1827-1867.

In the event no one bothered him on his walk to the top of the hill. The soldiers he passed did not notice his existence. The convicts he passed knew him and simply nodded. Sitting on the coarse salty grass below the lighthouse, Cookie looked out at the broad sweep of the land running south to Newcastle and Sydney Cove and to who knew what unknown wonders to the north. Inland, endless rows of tree-covered hills hid who knew what treasures. In his time at Port Macquarie he knew of no one who had ever explored that hinterland. In fact, no one he knew - soldier or convict - had ventured further from the river beyond that required to cut timber. Mentally exhausted he sat in silence and prayed for guidance.

Early in the afternoon hunger drove him back down the hill. Hunger and the firm decision to be someone and something new. Bypassing his shack at the lumber yard he walked to the commissariat and straight to the clothing store. No one bothered to stop him. There he shucked his convict garb, choose an outfit of 'civilian' clothes and, dressed as a free man, walked out, telling the astonished convict store-keeper he was now free and would pay for the clothes later. As he walked purposely up the hill toward the church several convicts stopped to look at him in astonishment, but said nothing. In a few minutes he arrived at his destination, the Partridge home. The home he had built. Cook, the savage sentinel who perpetually lounged outside the home, looked closely at Cookie as he arrived. Cookie had always felt the man's sharp eyes looked straight through him, but if the tall warrior noticed Cookie's new garb, he said nothing. Cookie the free man ignored him and was ignored in return. Partridge himself opened the door to Cookie's knock and for an instant was literally taken aback, but quickly recovered and roared with laughter.

"Cookie, you really are one for the books. Welcome back to the world of free men. From the look of you I assume you have a decision for me, so what is it to be?"

Cookie kept the man waiting a moment, fully aware that he had not been asked inside the home, then he nodded.

"I have decided to accept your offer," he said, purposely leaving off the word 'Sir' which would normally have followed.

"I will take 100 pounds, with suitable accommodation and food provided, and then we have a bargain."

Once again Partridge broke out laughing.

"Make it 75 pounds. Have a temporary home built for yourself, at government cost of course, and then a bargain we have indeed. I will even throw in the cost of your new clothes!"

"No" Cookie immediately countered, "one hundred or nothing."

Again Partridge laughed and after a moment's hesitation put out his hand. Cookie took it.

"You have made a commendably wise decision Cookie, well done."

Cookie was pleased he had out-bargained the notoriously sharp businessman and walked away content. Partridge was also pleased. He had been authorised to offer 150 pounds and now only had to figure out how to purloin the other 50 pounds for himself.

Apart from his clothes, not much changed in Cookie's life in the next year. He had a bigger shack built for himself in the grounds of the church, from where he exercised even more control over the construction. He ate better food, but not that much better, and while in theory he was free to come and go from the site as he pleased, in fact he found he spent far more time working on the church while free than he had as a felon. Away from work he quickly found that he had become neither fish nor fowl, instead falling neatly between the two groups in the settlement, those who had always been free, and those who might never be free.

To the few free citizens - soldiers, administrators and the odd local farmer and fisherman who drifted in and out of the settlement in increasing but still small numbers - Cookie had simply become a convict in civilian clothes, a man not to be trusted or welcomed into 'good' people's homes. Indeed as a former felon he was still officially and legally unable to hold a wide range of positions in 'free' society. To the convicts, he was no longer one of them and as such was not to be trusted or welcomed into their lives or their secrets. Work became his life and solace. In his mind he was not working for himself, he was working to create a lasting edifice to God, and possibly to his own self-worth. He threw himself into that work with such gusto that the main construction was indeed finished six months later, in February 1827, much earlier than expected,

Although he was by all rights able to leave the settlement at that time, he decided, with Partridge's enthusiastic agreement, to stay on to carry out a special task he had long reserved for himself - the building of a pulpit which, in his mind at least, would be dedicated to the memory of The Reverend Edmund Nelson. Partridge was happy to 'extend' his still unwritten contract because it also meant more money for him.

As he toiled on, deep in the back of his mind Cookie slowly came to understand there was another reason he wanted to stay - that he was afraid to leave. Alone at night he might he might ponder the delight of arriving back in Sydney Town with new clothes and money in his pocket. He had thought of going back to England, but doubted he could settle back into what he now saw was a dark and blighted country where, as a former felon, there was no hope of advancement, be he free or not. As a convict he had thought that as a free man he would have been able to look ahead and plan a new life, but when he did look ahead all he could see was more darkness and despair.

Free he might be, but he felt as trapped as he had been in chains.

What saved him was a memory that arrived unbidden but nevertheless strongly in his mind; the words Tom Hobbes had said to him aboard the prison hulk *Retribution*.

"Hold your head high" he had said, "there is no other way to survive, and you must survive."

He thought back to his friend old Nate Lusty, who he had often derided but who he had later come to respect not only for his irrepressible will to survive, but for his determination and ability to make the best of that survival. 'Reverend Nelson would be ashamed of me for my self-pitying' he concluded, 'I have been through so much, but not as much as others. I will do as the Reverend said; I will do my best and trust the rest to the Lord.'

Just before Christmas Cookie finished work on the pulpit. It's ornate woodwork had taken all of his skill to complete. Shortly afterwards Reverend John Cross arrived, becoming the first chaplain to the settlement, and when the initial service was held in the church in the last week of February 1828, Cookie was there to hear the words of God echo through his creation, albeit sitting on a chair stuck awkwardly between the private stalls of the powerful at the front of the church and the convicts standing behind a line of soldiers at the rear. Three weeks later he boarded the regular packet ship sailing to Sydney via Port Stephens and Newcastle to Sydney Town. In a final farewell to his convict days he paid for a private cabin, even though he spent most of the voyage on deck. That evening, standing in his favourite position near the bow of the ship, he watched as the sun slid behind the dark, dull olive green hills of the hinterland as he headed into unsettled waters and wondered what future this country held in store for him.

26 Cookie's last sight of Port Macquarie, circa March, 1827. The church of St Thomas dominates the skyline, looking down on the houses of government officials such as then Commandant Archibald Clunes Innes and the indefatigable Stephen Partridge. Artist Unknown.

Chapter Seven

Again it was Haynes whose words dragged him from his reverie.
  "Sorry to interrupt Mr Cooke, but I must say, you continue to amaze.
  "T'was you who built St Thomas?' I have been there many times and even thought I must admit I am not the believer that you are, I have often marvelled at the wonder of that construction and that it was built here in Australia.
  "That is amazing. Well done Sir! And to hear that not only was that magnificent church built by convict labour, but also at the direction of a convict, is wonderful."
  Cookie shook his head.
  "Convicts may have built it, and I played a part, but the concept and planning was the work of Owen and a fine job he did. He was a good man, which is more than I can say of Partridge who I believe made a fortune from the building of that church. A more conniving and evil man I have yet to meet, and I believe his perfidiousness tainted my life for years. It was a bad time in my life in many ways. I am ashamed to admit I lied and cheated and stole. All I can hope and pray is my sins were partly redeemed by my work on the church. I believe my hand was guided in that good work, perhaps guided by the hand of Reverend Nelson himself."
  Haynes nodded politely. He didn't believe in divine guidance, but so be it if others did.
  "And what of Coghill? His name arises so often."
  "Did you in fact meet the man?"
  "Yes, Captain Coghill" Cookie said more to himself than Haynes before lapsing into silence. "Well he also came back into my life, or rather should I say I re-entered into his?"
  "I have often pondered, young man, on the impact that others have on our lives. Have you? People enter our lives and so we do things we might otherwise never have contemplated and we may

never know the magnitude of their impact on our life or how it came about. I wonder what impact will you and your pencil have on my life John Haynes?"

"Looking back on my own life I can now see that certain people influenced what I did in my life not only there and then, but also for many, many years afterwards. One of those people who had an important impact on my life was Captain John Coghill."

"Let me explain."

Captain John Coghill
Kirkham, Outside Sydney 1828

Two hundred miles south of where Cookie watched the sun set on his time in Port Macquarie, John Coghill lounged comfortably on the verandah of the spacious homestead called Kirkham, watching the same sun slip below a similar set of olive green hills.

But while the strident reds lighting the sky for Cookie bounced into rainbows off a wind-tossed ocean, the gentle hues in front of Coghill were serenely reflected on the still waters of the pristine Nepean River.

In front of him green pastures swept down to the river and across to the other side of the newly built Great Southern Road, in reality little more than a dirt track, but still a valuable lifeline that had made Sydney Town just a day's ride away.

'I shouldn't denigrate the wee track, after all, it's made me a lot of money' Coghill thought to himself, 'but not as much as it has for that so-called gentleman on the other side of the river.'

That 'gentleman' was the colony's richest man, John MacArthur, the constant target of Coghill's envy, who lived about three miles away on the more gentile northern side of the Nepean on lush acreage known as Belgenny Farm. Moving down the road Coghill's eyes fell upon a fine looking windmill, the sight of which always cheered him. It was his pride and joy, the first in the area inland of Sydney Town known as the Cow Pastures, and it had been built by and belonged to himself, Captain John Coghill.

A windmill meant wheat and flour and bread and beer, and those things meant money.

27 An idyllic depiction of the area called 'Cowpastures' in the hinterland of Sydney, circa 1835. The name came about because a small herd of first fleet cattle that escaped Sydney in 1788 were rediscovered there in 1795. The fertile area was one of the first settled in NSW. Surveyor-General John Oxley was granted 1000 acres there which became Kirkham farm, named for his birthplace, and the Kirkham windmill was the first in the area. In the background is the village of Cawdor (Camden) on the banks of the Nepean River.
Artist unknown, possibly Thomas Woore. NSWSL."

Coghill was totally focused on making money, preferably more money than Macarthur. The fact that the great John Macarthur had to have his wheat ground in Coghill's mill was a constant source of amusement and satisfaction to him after the way Macarthur and his brood had treated him, disdaining his company socially. Coghill had attempted to cultivate Macarthur, using his well-tried ruse of appealing to his Scots heritage, but he quickly found what much better men than he had found when they tried to round Macarthur - that the man was arrogant and self-obsessed to the point of mania.

He treated Coghill with the same utter disdain he reserved for everyone, adding yet another name to Coghill's long list of enemies.

"Well, fate can be cruel," Coghill said aloud, "and delightfully wicked at times. I suppose I shouldn't begrudge the man some solace in his piles of gold, because there he sits, just over the horizon, a raving mad Midas chained to his golden throne."

As Coghill caught sight of some of the nearly 800 sheep he now owned, his eyes narrowed and he leaned forward, peering at the snowy bundles glowing orange in the sunset.

'Damn! How often must I tell that lazy idiot Evans to move the sheep away from the road in the evening. By God if so much as one lamb is missing I will have the skin off his back.'

"Mary!" he shouted. "Mary, come here." The assigned convict servant Mary appeared at his side almost instantly, wringing her wet hands on her apron, a look of abject fear on her face.

"Mary, get over to the windmill paddock and find that lazy idiot you call a husband and tell him to get those sheep into the back paddock. Mark my word, he will pay dearly if one beast goes missing in the night. Go!"

He watched as the woman ran as fast as her skirts would all allow down to the river, shouting for her husband as she ran.

'The sod is no doubt drunk again, as God is my witness those fools know not or care not that strong drink will be the end of them,' he thought, shaking his head. Mary came back apologising profusely but Coghill waved brusquely her away. He had no time for fools. He had long ago come to the conclusion that life was a continual battle which only the best, such as himself, survived.

The rest lived to serve the best.

Coghill understood that his own victory in life - for that is how he saw it - came from his narrow and perpetual focus on success. There had been some luck, he had to admit, but he saw luck as a succession of chances that floated by all men. The successful recognised luck and grabbed the chance. Those who did not were doomed to failure.

It had been luck he had the opportunity to ingratiate himself with then Governor Macquarie, but it was his ability to then seize the moment and convince Macquarie that as a fellow Highlander he would be a good ally should the Governor find him worthy of a land grant to entice him to settle in the colony that had led to success.

By the time Coghill had returned to Sydney on his second voyage in 1822, Macquarie could tell him he had been granted 2000 acres on the east bank of the Wingecarribe River in the fertile Shoalhaven district 60 miles south of Sydney Town. After settling in the colony in 1826, it had been luck to run into that fool of a Surveyor General

John Oxley, but it had been his ability to sense opportunity and the confidence to reach out and grab it after Governor Macquarie had let slip Oxley was in financial trouble.

Oxley needed money when Coghill had money and few others did. Oxley had status when few others did and Coghill wanted status. Coghill had lent Oxley the money he needed, at very favourable interest it should be said, in return for a one-third interest of Oxley's farm Kirkham, a fine 1000 acre property located on the southern side of the Nepean River not far from Sydney.

Oxley had no interest in farming, preferring to his spend time either in his large Sydney residence or on exploration trips into the interior. However having been granted the land for a song, it made financial sense to allow someone else to make a financial success of it while retaining part ownership and some income. It was a good idea but in the bargaining that followed the hard-nosed Scot ran rings around Oxley.

Coghill not only owned a part of the farm, but also - and more importantly - had the right to manage it on a daily basis. Under his sharp guidance Kirkham became a thriving concern, with much of the money it earnt coming from government contracts for the supply of all the necessities needed by road gangs and other government workers, contracts won with the support of Oxley and his aristocratic contacts.

It was thanks mainly to Oxley that the Great Southern Road from Sydney had not followed the easiest and cheapest route which lay to the east of Kirkham, but rather took a route that ran close to the farm. The road brought not only the hungry road gangs, and the contracts to feed them, but also an easy route to the city for the farm's produce, produce which came from the jointly-owned farm but which was sold for Coghill's profit alone.

He had no doubt one day the whole farm would belong to him and him alone. Coghill had also been lucky in having a powerful 'uncle' in Alexander Macleay, Secretary of the Transport Board, the powerful body responsible for contracting vessels to transport Britain's armies. But it was not luck but skill to use his uncle's position to leverage London ship owners Browns to appoint him captain of the *Martha*, a Browns' vessel which - under Macleay's guiding hand

- was contracted by the Transport Board in 1814. His well-paid position became the start of Coghill's fortune.

After the Napoleonic Wars ended in 1815, he continued to captain *Martha* on the regular trading route to India, but - afflicted with unbounded egotism - he quarrelled with the company and left.

Then came his stint running slave ships.

This was his dark secret, something not even his wife knew of. Then, when captaining slave ships became too dangerous, he used his family's connections to secure a job captaining for the respectable firm of Buckle, Buckle, Bagster and Buchanan - BBB&B - the largest ship owners and merchants on the New South Wales run. The arrival of 'Uncle Alex' as Colonial Secretary of the New South Wales colony just weeks before Coghill and his family had arrived was not a coincidence. Coghill had learnt of uncle Alex's appointment shortly after it had first been offered two years earlier, and immediately grasped the opportunity the appointment might represent.

'Such is the privilege of power' Coghill believed, 'and luck, like fortune, favours the brave' ... 'and the ruthless.'

Success begets ambition and now John Coghill was totally committed to take the role of Scots Laird in New South Wales which had been denied him in the country of his birth. He understood perfectly that being a Laird in the new world required the same assets it had required in the old world - land, lineage and patronage - and he had no doubt he had the ability to achieve all three.

Thus it was that he was driving an expensive imported two-wheel buggy behind a particularly fine horse one day in late May of 1828 when, arriving at the impressively large Kirkham stable block, he noticed a stranger sitting on a wooden chest, a naval rucksack beside him. The bearded stranger was dressed too well to be a ne'er-do-well, sporting loose-fitting tan-coloured long trousers, an open-necked white shirt under a short cut tan jacket, boots and a fine hat.

'Another of those damned English gentlemen down on his luck and fortune and looking to rekindle it in the colonies' was his instant conclusion. He had noted an increasing number of 'that sort' passing by Kirkham since the construction of the new road, 'vagabonds one and all looking for the fortune they won't work for but willing to steal if they can'. His horse cared for he strode over to take care of the interloper.

"Yes my man, can I help you in anyway?"

The stranger was a foot shorter than Coghill, but held himself with the poise of someone who was physically capable. Then Coghill noticed a pistol shoved into the man's trousers.

"You dare come to my home armed!" he bellowed, quickly closing with the stranger.

"Good evening to you Captain Coghill. I assure you I mean no disrespect, but I have been told that there are evil-doers afoot on the road from Sydney Town and felt it better to be prepared. I arrive merely to renew an old acquaintance with yourself, one that stretches back a long way."

Coghill hesitated. The voice sounded familiar, but he could not place it.

"And who might you be sir, to claim such an acquaintance?"

"Well Sir, I am William Thomas Cooke, formerly of *Defiance, Victory* and *Mangles*."

Cookie had never seen Coghill take a backward step, but he took one at that news. Then he stepped forward peering closely at the man for a moment before bursting out laughing.

Will laughed with him, but not as loud.

"Ha! Well I will be damned if it is not the bad penny who has rolled around again. Nelson's Boy! Back from the dead no less and looking all the better for it! I see you have forsaken the broad arrow."

"Does that mean what I think it does?"

Cookie had to smile and even gave a little embarrassed bow.

"Indeed it does. I am a free man these past twelve months or more. Free and independent, albeit looking for some honest paid work should there be any to be had hereabouts. If not, well I'll be on my way to wherever fortune should guide me."

Coghill threw his head back and again roared with laughter, causing the convicts and servants nearby to stop their work in alarm.

"Come! Come sit with me at the house. I have no doubt you have quite a story or two to tell."

The instant they reached the verandah Coghill was swamped by a stampede of children, all squealing in delight that 'daddy' was home. The captain swept them all up in his arms, clearly enraptured. A woman, certainly Mrs Coghill from her dress, appeared at the door. Coghill introduced him only as 'Cooke, an old acquaintance'. Mrs Coghill, a dark-haired, sallow-skinned and in her mid-thirties, nodded at Cookie and called the children inside.

Shortly afterwards a pot of tea was brought out by a female servant. It didn't take long for Cookie to relate his life story since last having seen Coghill, including the story of him meeting the Aborigine Cook and subsequently being renamed 'Cookie', a tale which reduced Coghill to tears of laughter and a promise to continue to use the name. At the same time Cookie was very interested to hear Coghill's brief recounting of what had happened to him in the same time.

Coghill had been very successful and was more than happy to boast of the reasons for his success.

"This is a land of opportunity for those able to grasp their chances" Coghill intoned seriously, pausing to look at Cookie before nodding to himself as if having made a decision.

"Well Cooke. Or Cookie. Or should I say Mr Cooke" again he roared with laughter, "let me say you are a sight to revive my flagging spirits on this week where I have laid to rest a friend who was my partner and part-owner of this fine estate, God rest his soul.

"The fact is I am just at the beginning of what I can do in this new country. Kirkham, this place" he said, sweeping in the entire valley with a swing of his arm, "is not yet mine, yet, but it is already a goldmine I can use to finance many other projects."

"I have 6000 acres of my own in a fertile area to the south which I intend to expand and turn into an estate to rival anything of which Scotland or even England can boast.

"The British empire is growing and this country has everything it needs to fuel that growth.

"There is land enough to supply all the food and raw materials Britain cannot produce itself. There are minerals in the land and grains and upon it, there are fish and whales in the sea - and it's all there for the taking for those with daring enough to reach out and take it," he said, clenching his hand into a fist as if doing just that. At that he paused and sat back, neither awaiting nor expecting a reply.

Cookie, who had barely spoken a word for the past half hour, remained content to listen. In fact he was already wondering how he might take advantage of his relationship with his former gaol-keeper.

"The problem at present is labour" Coghill started up again, speaking as much to himself as to Cookie.

"Convict labour is cheap, that I grant you, but they are nowhere near as efficient as good British workers. Felons are inherently untrustworthy, lazy, and dishonest," he said, oblivious to any possible insult to his listener, "they are unskilled and have no interest in becoming skilled. They prefer stealing."

"The sad fact is the very worst of Britain is being dumped here as if it were one giant gaol, which is perhaps what was intended in the first instance; but things have changed."

"The same goes for the English who are supposed to administer this land. Most of them could not organise a tea party, and that is also holding us back. It's infuriating. Bloody infuriating.

"So, to your question. Is there work here for you? Yes there is, though I doubt it is what you are seeking. What I need right now is a man I can trust. A man to oversee the idle idiots who work for me - both free and felon - and to help me run this large estate, and large it is I vow to you. At present I grow wheat and corn; I run sheep and cattle and horses - damned fine horses mind you - as well as producing flour and meal in my windmill yonder."

"I am contracted to supply all the government work gangs and officials in the district and in addition I have a store that supplies the farmers in this area and beyond with whatever they need, bringing in the goods in bulk by bullock drays from Sydney Town and selling it in smaller quantities. At a good mark up of course."

"Finally, I produce a fine beer and a few other spirits in a facility to the rear of the stable block. Unfortunately, all of these endeavours take too much of my time, time which would be better spent looking at other, more profitable, sources of revenue."

"I have friends and contacts amid the politicians and merchants of Sydney Town and as far afield as London."

He paused the monologue, sitting silent, before turning to face Cookie.

"There are a great many opportunities to be had, and I'm wondering that, possibly you could well be a part of them."

Cookie knew the man well enough to know an answer was not required, so instead he also turned his gaze to the land, waiting several minutes before Coghill spoke again.

"From what you have told me of what you did and how you took hold of your chances in Port Macquarie, and from what I saw of you on *Mangles*, you could be the man for me."

"I have seen you direct convicts and have no doubt you could do the same to free men, especially as you are now free yourself. Above all, the fact is that I trust you, and believe me, I do not hand out such compliments lightly."

"All that said, if cabinetry is the work you seek, there is very little of that here, or indeed in the entire district. One day I will build a fine big house on my land to the south and you would find work there, but that day is not yet at hand." Suddenly he stood up, signalling the conversation was at an end.

"It grows late. I will order the housemaids to prepare one of the spare upstairs rooms in the stable block for you. It is dry and comfortable and you can eat with the staff."

"On the morrow we can talk further. 'Tis good to see you again 'Cookie'," he laughed. "Good to see that you have done well and I ha'e no doubt ye can do better. Let's talk again in the morning."

That night, ensconced on a comfortable bedroll in the stable block, the comforting sound of horses munching hay provided the backdrop to Cookie's thoughts about the day's reunion. The Coghill he knew had always been a man dedicated entirely to his own success, if necessary at the expense of those around him.

While Cookie had managed to make himself a rare entry on the credit side of the Coghill ledger, more by luck than foresight, he had no doubt that at all times and in all circumstances Coghill would choose his own success over any others.

Any benefit to Cookie, or anyone else, would be purely incidental.

The question Cookie had to answer was whether there was a chance Coghill's success would spill over and form part of any future success of his own.

On the journey to Kirkham Cookie had come to the conclusion that, rather than be a paid servant to others, it was time for him to try a different direction if he were to make a success of his own life. The unanswered questions were what that new direction was and where it would lead. Given the lack of any immediate alternative, he decided he would accept the Captain's offer and see if he could fly on the great man's coat tails for a while.

If Cookie thought the decision to stay was difficult, the negotiations that followed put that idea into perspective.

The salary Cookie believed a skilled overseer/watchman was worth and what Coghill wanted to pay for one were a world apart.

Not too long ago Cookie would have been cowered into accepting whatever Coghill had offered, but not only had Cookie changed, so had the times. He understood from his own experience bargaining with Partridge in Port Macquarie and from talking to wayfarers he had met, that good workers, and more so skilled and trustworthy workers, were a scarce commodity in New South Wales at exactly the time farm profits were increasing and so, in the negotiations, though the captain railed and threatened, Cookie stood firm, ready to move on if needs be.

Eventually there was an agreement. Cookie would work for a salary of 50 pounds, with 'suitable' accommodation and food provided. Finally Cookie said they should draw up the agreement in a simple contract, an important provision of which, from Cookie's point of view, would be that none of the staff, or anyone in the neighbourhood, was to know that Cookie had been a convict. Coghill was taken aback, but had the good grace to shake hands to seal the bargain.

As he walked back to his house Coghill managed to fashion a victory for himself from the outcome.

'I believe I taught the lad well,' he thought to himself.

In the first colonial census - called a muster - conducted New South Wales in November of 1828, the name William Cooke appears, described as a 'watchman' working for John Coghill on the farm Kirkham, but as was the case with other convicts listed as being at Kirkham, the description, while not a lie, was less than the truth. Cookie quickly became the Captain's general factotum; a combination of foreman, works and maintenance supervisor, builder,

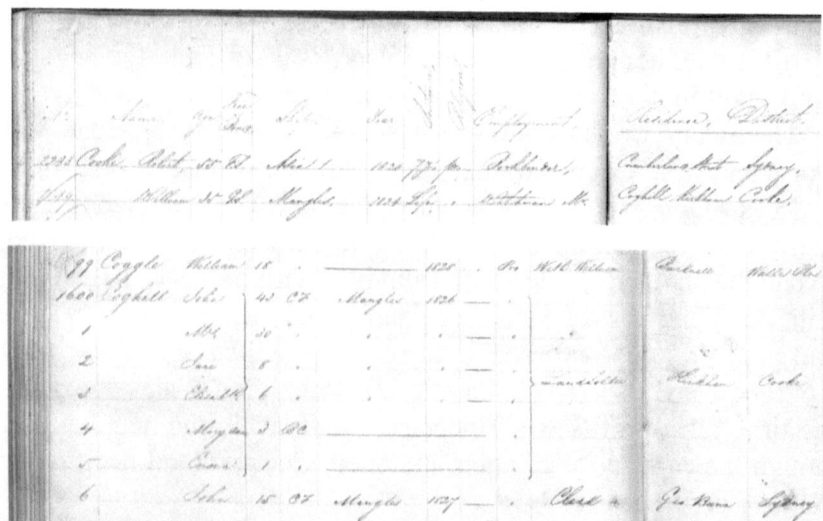

28 These two excerpts from the 1828 muster show the treasure and the trash to be found within such musty archives. The 'treasure' shows Cookie working as 'watchman' at the John Coghill-run farm, Kirkham - underlining the relationship between the two forged at Trafalgar.
Elsewhere in the same muster the 1826 arrival on Mangles of Coghill's family is noted, described as 'landholders' living at Kirkham. Coghill's eldest son, John, aged 15, arrived a year later, having stayed in England to finish his schooling. The 'trash' is that the final collated muster mixes up two different Cookes. It lists Robert Cooke, sentenced to 7 years, as arriving on 'Asia' in 1820 - but Robert was sentenced to life and there is no record of him being on Asia that year. It also shows William Cooke, aged 35, sentenced to life, arriving on Mangles in 1824, but Cooke arrived 1820 after being sentenced to seven years. The convict scribe transferring raw data into the official muster book mixed up his Cookes and almost spoiled the broth - an entirely understandable error at the end of a long day's work for an unpaid convict scribe.

shepherd, drover and personal driver, working at both Kirkham and the captain's southern property of Gillamatong.

He learned about sheep and cattle and horses, about fencing and shepherding, about how to grow wheat and corn and tobacco. He learned accounts from having to watch every penny he spent, for Coghill had no qualms about charging convicts and free workers for any shortages occurred, be it through careless or bad luck. Ensconced in his comfortable room in the stable block he became friends with the only other resident, John Dyer, storekeeper and bookkeeper who held a position the equal of Cooke even though as a convict he earnt nothing for this labour.

It was Dyer who explained to Cookie the agreement between Coghill and Oxley; that two thirds of Kirkham had belonged to John Oxley and one third to Captain Coghill, in addition to Coghill enjoying residence in return for managing the farm, and with any profits from the running of the farm to be split equally between them.

It did not come as a shock to Cookie when Dyer confided that since his arrival at Kirkham, Coghill had siphoned off much of the farm's 'joint' income for himself. This had only been possible because the captain had instructed Dyer to maintain two sets of accounts for Kirkham, one which reflected the true financial state of the farm, the other which reflected a much worse scenario, and it was this second set which was the basis for the disbursement to the Oxley family. Dyer said he had thought that when Oxley had died just a short time ago, in May 1828, leaving a widow and four young children without husband or father, the captain would do the right thing and honour the original agreement, especially as Oxley's will had stipulated that his share of the profits be paid to the trust account of his first born son, John, then aged just four.

He was disgusted when the stealing not only didn't stop, but accelerated.

"Mr Oxley's son be but a boy of four" decried Dyer one night over an illicit rum. "What can Mrs Oxley, a mere woman, know of running a large concern such as Kirkham? Granted she is well off living in her big house in Sydney Town, but I can't understand how the Captain can look her in the eye and steal from her purse at the same time.

"The sad thing is they trust Coghill, which only goes to make his crime the worse."

"He is a rogue worse by far than any felons wot work for him."

Hate the captain as he might, Dyer said he knew that to inform on him would be tantamount to suicide. The previous year Coghill had been appointed a magistrate and had already shown many times that he was not reluctant to use the power of the legal system and his position to enforce his will upon his staff. Dyer explained that most of Coghill's wealthy neighbours also sat as magistrates and from bitter experience convicts knew that the gentry were adept at using the courts to support each other; each willing to sentence his friend's staff to extended service for minor misdemeanours, knowing full well the favour would be returned should their staff appear before the bench.

"The captain and his friends are not even above bringing false charges against good men and women just before they are eligible for a ticket of leave, so that the application is refused. That means they can have the convict's services free for another year. And damn their eyes if a felon should complain because they will wear fifty for their trouble."

"If'n he were to find me with this 'ere rum in my hand there's no doubt I'd be up before the bench at Cawdor, and so my friend would you, free man or no."

"My friend Richard Mahoney; you know him, he be the ticket of leave man wot runs the mill. He has long asked the captain to sign his application for his wife and kids to be brought over, but the captain keeps puttin' it off an' puttin' it off 'cause he knows soon as that family arrives, Richard will contrive to leave this accursed place."

"He cut up rough about it to the Captain once and then, sometime afterward he gets hauled up on charges and ends up in the nick wearing twenty five on his back to keep him company. Now, like the rest of us, he just keeps quiet."

"He's a cruel, mean-hearted man is the Captain and he'll be having a long, long memory."

"You may think you've got away with a trifle or two, but he has informers and he knows everything wot goes on and when the time is right he will bring charges against you and you will pay. Oh yes. Fear not Cookie, cross 'im an' one way or 'tuther, you will pay."

While Cookie had little concern for either Dyer or the Oxley family, he now understood all too well that while he might think he had a good relationship with the captain, he was walking a perilous line. At times Cookie drove the Captain's chaise to neighbouring farms and especially to the magistrates court at nearby Cawdor, and Cookie suspected that task was demanded of him because the captain enjoyed arriving in a chaise driven by a free man.

Cawdor was a hamlet built on the Macarthur estate just across the Nepean river from Kirkham, and the Cawdor 'courthouse' was actually the sitting room of a government rest house built in the early 1820s as a stopover for government officials. Later a small police station was added on one side and a small inn soon appeared on the other side.

One day Coghill and James Macarthur, fourth and most capable son of John, were scheduled to sit as magistrates and by agreement met beforehand in the inn for a small meal - neither man touched alcohol - to discuss the cases due that day. Coghill invited Cookie in to have a meal at the only other table, introducing him to Macarthur as a former crewman on one of his ships. Macarthur looked him up and down and without a word sat down and began going through court documents. Coghill smiled at Cookie but said nothing. The Captain had spent some time attempting to cultivate a friendship with James, without success, despite the men holding similar views on the roles of the 'lower classes' in the colonial hierarchy.

Privately James looked down on Coghill as grasping social climber.

Privately Coghill thought the young man was a pampered brat, silently laughing at the pretensions of a man whose father was not only insane, but who - as Coghill was fond of recounting - had been a lowly-born draper before stumbling into wealth almost by accident.

Shortly afterwards a third magistrate, a Major Antill, arrived and joined the two magistrates in 'deliberations'. Cookie was joined by the court's lone police officer and as they ate their simple meal they became privy to the machinations of colonial justice as it was on carried on the border of civilisation of the British Empire. Over lunch the magistrates quickly agreed on the sentences to be handed down in a number of minor cases, mostly involving convicts absent from work, refusing work or drunk while at work. There was no need for the actual verdicts to be discussed, guilt was a given.

Then came the wheeling and dealing.

Coghill wanted a severe sentence to be handed down on two of his convicts to serve as a deterrent to other Kirkham workers. However he didn't wish to preside over a verdict in which he was also a complainant, not out of regard for fairness or justice, but because he knew that if the case were reviewed by a judge, as sometimes happened, such an anomaly would immediately be picked up and the sentences overturned.

Macarthur and Antill agreed Coghill could simply step away from the bench when his men's case was heard, provided that the same would happen when the case against one of Macarthur's men, charged with insolence, was heard. Major Antill chimed in about a case in which the woman servant of a friend of his was accused of drunkenness.

The woman claimed the charge was bogus and was brought about because she was due a ticket of leave, but her master did not want to lose her at this time because his wife was heavily pregnant and needed help. The major wanted her application dismissed. Coghill and Macarthur nodded.

On the drive back to Kirkham, Cookie was silent, not that Coghill usually deigned to speak to him anyway. The charade of justice he had witnessed had shocked Cookie to the core. He now understood that on those times when he had been the one in the dock, chained and ignorant, he might well have been the victim of a similar process.

It was not a process of justice, but of the helpless being punished for being helpless. He finally understood the justice system was not about right versus wrong, but about the powerful versus the powerless. He also clearly understood that while he might be free, he remained powerless and that if it was in Coghill's interest to detain him at Kirkham, he would not hesitate to do so.

Cookie realised had been living in a fool's paradise and he had to escape. He would see out his contract and until that day arrived he had to play by the same rules the captain and others just like him played by; using deception, deceit, duplicity, cheating, guile and hypocrisy to get what they wanted.

In the end Cookie's fate was decided by a racehorse. Coghill had long invested time and money into becoming known not only as a fine horseman, but as a breeder of fine horses. When he heard that James Macarthur was planning to expand the family horse breeding operation and intended importing the famous broodmare *Gulnare* to improve their stock, he immediately decided to go one better and import the even more famous stallion *Bachelor*, reasoning that while he might not be able to match their flocks and fine wool or their endless acreage, at least not yet, he could most certainly match them at horse breeding.

After all, as he said, horses were the natural pre-occupation of gentlemen - not sheep.

The captain's trips to Sydney became fewer and further apart as he concentrated on horses and spent more and more time at Kirkham, taking a keener interest in the operation of the farm. A week after his contract expired, Cookie saw his chance.

The captain was standing quietly at the entrance to the stable block having just finished issuing instructions to the shepherds and stable hands, hands in pockets, lost in thought.

"Captain, would you have a moment for me? Sir," he added as an afterthought. Coghill turned, resentful at having his peace disturbed.

"What is it" he asked brusquely. Cookie launched into his rehearsed plea. It did not go well.

"I have been thinking that perhaps the time has come for a change. For me, that is." He now had Coghill's undivided attention.

"I have been here for two years and I believe that in that time I have provided a useful service, but recently you have been spending much more time here at Kirkham, to the benefit not only of your family, but also of the farm and the staff, and it seems that perhaps it is a good time for me to move along and further my own fortune."

Coghill said nothing, but the frown on his forehead spoke volumes.

A thick silence enveloped the two men which lasted several minutes before Coghill broke it.

"I believe I did you a great service when I took you on here Cookie, at a time - I recall - when I did not need your services, doing it merely to help you as you once helped me."

Cookie knew that was a lie, but had no doubt that Coghill actually believed the lie to be the truth.

"I understand that Sir, and I will forever be grateful, but I truly believe that time is past. You are now here in your rightful position the majority of the time and my presence is not only no longer needed, but has at times become a hindrance. It may suit you that I should leave."

Coghill stared at him for a long time, saying nothing.

Finally he gave a slight nod.

"Perhaps you are right. Perhaps it is time you sought to improve yourself further. I canna argue with that idea, and indeed, I wish you well. When is your contact expired?"

"I believe a week ago Sir."

"And your money is paid?"

"It is in my bank account Sir, on time as usual."

Again Coghill nodded. "Well, that's convenient is it not."

For the first time Cookie felt that he had just scored a victory over the man he had come to despise, albeit a small one, and that freedom was at hand for him a second time.

Coghill nodded again before turning back to the view. It was Cookie's turn to nod, but as he turned away Coghill had the last word.

"Cookie, there is no need to tarry here. I believe when the time is come to take an action it needs be done boldly and quickly. I wish you well, but I suggest it best you leave sooner rather than later, so if you could be off Kirkham by the morrow evening that would be fine."

Cookie nodded to the Captain's turned back, but as he walked away he was silently screaming with delight. He immediately sent word to the regular cart which travelled from Cawdor to Sydney, and which he knew passed by on the morrow, to pick up him and his goods at the entrance to Kirkham. There would be no need for goodbyes.

Word moves quickly in a small village, which is what Kirkham had become, and he had no sooner begun packing after despatching the messenger to Cawdor than John Dyer was at his door.

"It's true then" he said simply.

"What have you done that he should treat you so?"

Cookie stood and took his hand.

"It is not that way. We had a contract and I have chosen not to renew it. It is time for me to go. I recall it was after speaking to you so intimately the thought first came to my head. My only regret is I cannot take you and others with me. I wish you well and safe John Dyer."

Dyer was but the first of many that made their way to his door that day, though none from the great house on the hill. The next day he was at the gate at dawn, his tool chest and navy bag at his feet, his mind racing ahead on the next leg of a journey to where he did not know.

Real Freedom

While escaping the clutches of Coghill had proved to easier than expected, the question of what to do next was a lot more difficult. Beyond a vague idea of working for himself as carpenter, builder or cabinet maker, Cookie no idea of how to go about achieving such a dream, for dream it was.

All his life he had been told what to do, as a child, as an apprentice, as a convict and even as a so-called free man.

'How does a man go about being really free?' he asked himself as he was bumped between barrels and bags on the back of the Sydney-bound cart. 'What tools do I need in order to make a fortune? Certainly not carpentry tools!'

The answer, when it came to him, was simple - money.

"Money is the tool people used to become rich. Money and a goal" he said out loud, pulling his hat over his eyes as the cartman turned to look askance at him. Money he had, at least some money, but he knew the few hundred pounds he had was not going to be anywhere near enough to run a successful business of any kind in the cut-throat world of Sydney Town.

It would not even last lounging about in Sydney Town.

'How did Coghill make his fortune so quickly' he pondered. Thinking back over the time he had spent with Coghill and all his wealthy friends he began to understand that the underlying foundation for the wealth of all those wealthy men was land.

They all owned lots of land, and that made all other things possible.

The idea came as a thunderbolt to Cookie. He had never even considered that he might one day be a landowner and so had never really considered the role of land in the life of wealthy people. But once the idea had been born, the answer to his dilemma was at once simple and obvious - he had to have his own land.

Once the idea of owning land became real, it gave birth to the next question: where will I be able to buy land?

From his time standing in the background as Coghill's driver when the Captain talked and dealt with this wealthy friends, Cookie knew that most of them had been granted their vast tracts of land because they were already wealthy, or aristocratic, or both. As were their friends.

All were members of a club of wealth, a club he understood he could never become a member of, at least not in or around Sydney Town. But even as that thought crystallised in his mind, he knew where he could get land - in the wild north.

The idea at once filled him with such delight that he actually shouted aloud, the driver turning around again and telling him to shut up or he would find himself walking to Sydney Town. The words of the old tar aboard the *Elizabeth Henrietta* on his voyage north to Newcastle and Port Macquarie came back to him.

"A fortune just sittin' there for the takin" he had said, talking about the vast hinterland lying west of the villages that were springing up along the coast. Lying back on some sacks he looked at puffy white clouds drifting through a hard blue sky edged by the dull green of the never-ending gum trees.

"I will do this" he said aloud, "or die in the trying."

Once the decision had been made to buy land somewhere to the north, he quickly realised he had no knowledge of where was best for him to buy, or how much land he could afford, or indeed even to how to go about actually buying land, so his first step had to be to find answers to those questions.

'Preparation and money, that is what I need' he concluded. 'And I must husband what money I have or it will soon drift from my hands and then there will never be enough to buy anything'.

After finding cheap accommodation in Sydney Town with a respectable family, he easily found enough carpentry work to ensure he not only maintained his capital, but added to it. After a year of working and speaking to people had a good idea of the cost of land and had identified where his goal lay - the hinterland of the coal port of Newcastle called the Hunter Valley - exactly where the old tar had said it would be.

By November 1831 he was ready to move, but first he had to put into practice one of the many things he had learned from Captain Coghill - the importance of presenting the right image to the world.

"Look like a vagabond and to the world you are a vagabond and the world will treat you as one," Coghill had said. "Mark my words, it's vital to look like the person you wish to be treated as."

Dipping into his precious funds he bought a suit of fine travelling clothes and suitable luggage, then splashed money on a ticket to Newcastle and beyond aboard the latest sensation to hit Sydney Town, the newly arrived paddle driven steam ship *Sophia Jane* - first of her kind to ply the waters of the colony.

Arriving on such a ship would not only send the right message to the people he would meet he reasoned, but *Sophia Jane* would take him to exactly where he needed to go - to the very end of the navigable section of the Hunter River to a village called Green Hills, the gateway to the Hunter Valley.

But there was another simpler reason for opting to take the expensive voyage. He desperately wanted to experience the sensation of being driven through the sea rather than sailing upon it.

Since *Sophia Jane* had arrived in Sydney Town in June that year he had watched astounded from the shore as the strange vessel poured forth smoke as it paraded the harbour waters with ease, so it was with more than a little apprehension that he bought a ticket on the mechanical monster, but in the end the worst thing about the voyage north was that it was over so quickly.

The ship had parted at exactly 6am as scheduled, in itself a miracle made possible because the vagaries of the wind and tide were not a factor in the timing.

Cookie had stood on the deck for the entire voyage, in part because he was afraid to go anywhere near the noisy, fire-breathing monster that turned the great wheels on both sides of the ship, but also because he quickly became enthralled at the way the vessel sliced through the water whenever and wherever the helmsman decided, no matter which way the wind happened to be blowing, sending the ship flying through the water at a thrilling 6 knots.

Apart from its engine the ship also boasted a standard Brig rigging, with two masts - fore and main - and could also fly a spanker behind the main mast and a jib and flying jib off the bowsprit if the wind was favourable, but in the event not a square foot of sail was hoisted aloft the entire voyage.

Cookie noted there were very few crew and he wondered what would happen should the engine fail and the sails needed to be hoisted quickly.

'No doubt myself and all those drunken oafs filling their bellies down below would have to be sent aloft', he laughed to himself, 'if'n so there'll be bodies falling left, right and centre'.

One of the ships officers walked up on deck to light his pipe.

"I must admit, after serving in the navy I can't get used to smoking on a ship" Cookie said shaking of his head, triggering a friendly laugh from the man.

"Aye, well I ken well your concern my friend, but it's a different world on this ship, nothing to explode and no sails to burn. I see you're no interested in the food and drink?"

"No, it's not often I get the chance to be at sea these days and this is my first trip on a ship without sails. It's quite an experience and I want to savour it."

"Aye, it's exhileratin', so it is," he said, proffering a hand, "I'm James Keppie, engineer of this vessel. It's a pleasure to meet another sailor."

"What brings you on board?"

"William Cooke. Call me Cookie, everyone does. I'm heading north looking for new land and a new start."

Keppie nodded, then fell silent, smoking his pipe as the big engine thumped rhythmically below and the paddles relentlessly tore at the water. After a while he spoke again.

"Tis a rare thing indeed to find a bonnie new country with so much promise and I ken your vision. T'is one I'm thinkin' I could share, even though it is only a short time I've been here."

"Tending the big engine is not a bad job, but like you I've a feeling that soon I might be wantin' a wee bit more."

"Can I ask where you be headed?"

Cookie took his time answering, reticent about saying too much to a stranger that might betray his background.

"I have no exact destination beyond the valley of the Hunter River in the hinterland of Newcastle. I'm told it's a vast area and very fertile, suitable for all types of farming and raising animals. I'm informed that land can be had cheap, indeed sometimes just for the taking, and that there are new towns springing up like mushrooms. I'm a … a builder, and a cabinet maker and carpenter, so I believe there will be opportunities to be grasped."

Keppie continued to smoke until the pipe was finished and then again offered his hand.

"Tis good to meet you Mr Cookie and I wish you well. I hope one day we will meet again and have the time to talk further."

Just before one in the afternoon the ship arrived off Newcastle, immediately swinging a tight arc around Coal Island in such an easy and elegant manner as to set Cookie's heart racing, before steaming gently to the town wharf. From the deck it appeared to Cookie's eye as if nothing had changed from his last visit. The lumber yard was still there, although it seemed unused. The dirt main street still went arrow-straight up to the Commandants residence and if there were more houses than there had been ten years ago, it seemed they could be counted on one hand. One welcome addition was a fine looking public house close to the wharf where none had been before, and ongoing passengers were encouraged to disembark and enjoy a beverage while cargo was unloaded. The appropriately named Ship Inn was a two-winged building but a minute's walk from the wharf. Small, but well-kept and clean, it consisted of three parlour rooms, five bedrooms and a kitchen in one wing; while four stall stables and a coach house occupied the other wing.

"Good day to you Sir, 'tis a fine day indeed to be arriving in the wonderful port of Newcastle" hailed the professionally friendly barkeep, "let me draw you a fine ale to start your visit," which he proceeded to do without the benefit of confirmation. Placing it in front of Cookie the jovial fellow then commenced to so what barkeeps do best - talk.

"Can I be askin' yourself, are you wishing to stay here in Newcastle, or be you bound for Green Hills or indeed elsewhere? I'll say now you have the look of man wot knows his mind and I'm guessing you are here in search of your fortune. Am I right?"

Savouring what was indeed a fine beer, Cookie took his time in answering the man.

"Well, you are a fine judge of men. Fortune is indeed my aim, as no doubt it is with many a man who passes through this fine establishment, though just where that fortune will be I am not sure. I am told that there be opportunities in the hinterland for a man such as myself. I'm a builder and I'm in no hurry to work so I'll take my time and explore the area before settling.

"And yourself good Sir, are you long in this area? I'm thinking you might be as well informed on the potential of the area as anyone."

Sensing a possible opportunity, the barkeep poured himself a beer and settled in for a chat, firstly putting out his hand in welcome.

"My name is John Hillier and I'm no Sir, that's for sure. I own this establishment and you are right, if there be anyone around these parts better informed than myself, I've yet to meet him."

Cookie took the hand. "William Cooke, but everyone calls me Cookie"

Jovial John laughed his professional laugh. "Aye, no long names in this country, and all the better for it if you ask me. When you say 'builder', what would you be meaning?"

"I'm a carpenter and a cabinet maker" Cookie answered, careful not to give anything to invite too close a discussion of his past, "and I have experience as a builder."

"Is that so. Well, if it's a fortune you be seeking you have made a fine start because a man such as yourself who can build a dwelling is worth a king's ransom in these parts. You'll not be wanting for work I warrant. I take it you are bound for Green Hills then?"

"It is my first stop" Cookie replied around a mouthful of ale, "but I have no idea of what's there. I'm not even aware if there's an Inn such as this in which to begin my search."

"Sophia Jane"—1831

29 Australia's first steam-driven ship the Sophia Jane shown steaming across Sydney Harbour. The ship arrived in Sydney on May 13, 1831, and was an immediate sensation. Built for speed rather than carrying cargo, it was 126 feet (38m) long and just 20 feet (6m) wide and could reach almost nine miles an hour - about 14kph! Creator Unverified.

John's laugh was genuine this time as he slapped the bar, slopping a little beer in doing so.

"Well, your good luck and good fortune has begun already Cookie. I have this very month bought the best Inn in Green Hills, called the Illulaung Hotel. Now don't you be worrying about trying to say that strange word, it be the native name for the settlement and it will soon be changed, that is for sure. Morpeth will be the new name I would bet, if I were a betting man that is" he laughed. "Cookie I would be honoured to have you as one of the first guests of my new establishment. It's right in the heart of the settlement and, as one of the first guests, I will give you a very affordable rate."

Cookie could only laugh at the costermonger attitude of the man, determining that John Hillier was exactly the kind of man he needed to befriend.

"That is a deal," he said, proffering his hand.

In the next half hour his new friend John Hillier gave Cookie more information about the Hunter Valley than he had learnt in a year in Sydney. He was honest, saying that while he felt Green Hills, situated as it was at the end of the navigable section of the Hunter River, was destined to be the largest and most vibrant centre in the area, "it's time has not yet come."

"As you will see, only now have parcels of land become available in the township, and those at a great cost, while further up the valley there is a surfeit of cheap land. But as the hinterland comes into production and goods begin to flow back and forth, Green Hills will boom. Trust me, if you have enough money to invest in some land, I would urge you to do so for it will only increase in value."

Soon it was time to go. The two men agreed to meet in Green Hills in the next few days when Hillier was due to arrive in the town himself, adding that he was sure that he would have need of a cabinet maker in the coming weeks to help with the refit of his hotel. At 2pm, exactly as scheduled, *Sophia Jane* set off on its three hour cruise up the Hunter River to Green Hills. Again Cookie choose the deck as his travel position, and as the country drifted by, he could not but feel elated as he thought over his position.

'Here I am, not even in the district yet and already I have a place to stay, perhaps an offer of work, and a friend to turn to for advice and direction. Surely the world is turning my way.'

Once past its wide open lower reaches, the Hunter River concertinaed, sometimes narrowing to little more than the width of a canal, at other times widening substantially, all the while remaining deep and placid. An occasional shepherd's hut could be spied through the trees, but there were no large houses to be seen. The whole area was heavily forested so as to deny the passengers any real sight into the nature of the land until the ship hove to at Green Hills.

The hamlet was exactly as Hillier had described it - a village in the making which straddled a bank high on the southern side of the river immediately before the river was shallowed by rocks, halting the passage of all but punts or small boats.

On the corner of the main street up from the makeshift wharf was the unprepossessing Illulaung Hotel. Little more than a dining room, bar and kitchen, with thatched rooms leading off a corridor at the back.

It nevertheless provided food, drink and a safe place to sleep and store his possessions while he explored the area.

Stowing his gear, he headed to the dining room for a meal and a beer and had not been at the bar long before he was joined by Keppie.

"I said I'd be meeting you again Mr Cooke - sorry, Cookie - but I dinna expect it to be so soon" he laughed.

"Please, let me buy you an ale."

"And please, call me Jimmy.

Cookie was keen to talk about steam vessels, which the engineer opined would soon replace all sail vessels. When Cookie expressed his doubts, Keppie pressed on.

"You saw yourself today how efficient and easy steam is, and it's free. All you need is water and coal, or even wood, and you have power to take you where you will. Not only that, but I'm thinkin' that soon steam will power every moving machine we can imagine. Think of windmills - expensive to build and no use at all if the wind dinna blow, but a steam engine will turn the mill stones day and night without let. Water pumps the same - not a problem with steam engines. "Tis the future."

When the talk turned to the pair's immediate future, Keppie made an interesting proposal.

"I've been thinkin' of our talk and of your plan to explore the hinterland for opportunities. It is something I desire to do meself, but canna do easily because of my work. At the same time, like yourself, I think it's time to go out on my own in some fashion if I am to make something of meself. I've been thinking that if a good man, like yourself, were to take a hard look at the possible opportunities in this new land, we might end up partners."

The two shook hands and parted, friends and possibly business partners.

A walk around the settlement the next morning revealed a few dozen plots marked out around the few streets, rough wharves beside the river and a number of warehouses holding goods brought up the river from Sydney for settlers further up the valley, but little else. Over the next few days Cookie scouted the area, finding fertile and well-watered farming land, but nothing to entice a fledging businessman in search of his fortune.

The 'owner' of the town was Edward Close, a former British soldier turned settler, who had founded the town and was its leading citizen and landowner, in effect controlling the town and all in it.

As Cookie spoke to more and more locals about a place to invest, the area most mentioned was Wallis Plains, sometimes called West Maitland. As he had been told early on, but did not initially fully grasp the importance of, deep draft ships plying the Hunter from the sea could only reach Green Hills, where a series of rocky shallow rapids restricted traffic and backed up the river into the Hexham Marshes.

West Maitland was the point at which the produce of the rich alluvial plains of the Hunter Valley, destined for Sydney and beyond, had to be unloaded from boats because below that point the same swampy land and shallow rapids stopped progress to Green hills, just six miles away.

Like Morpeth, West Maitland occupied a flood-proof site high above the river flood limit and consisted mostly of warehouses for storing goods destined for movement up or down stream.

The budding town's main street, appropriately named High Street, was noisy, unstructured and wild compared to quiet, tightly controlled Green Hills and its aura of adventure and potential appealed to Cookie's growing self-confidence. When the Illulaung's

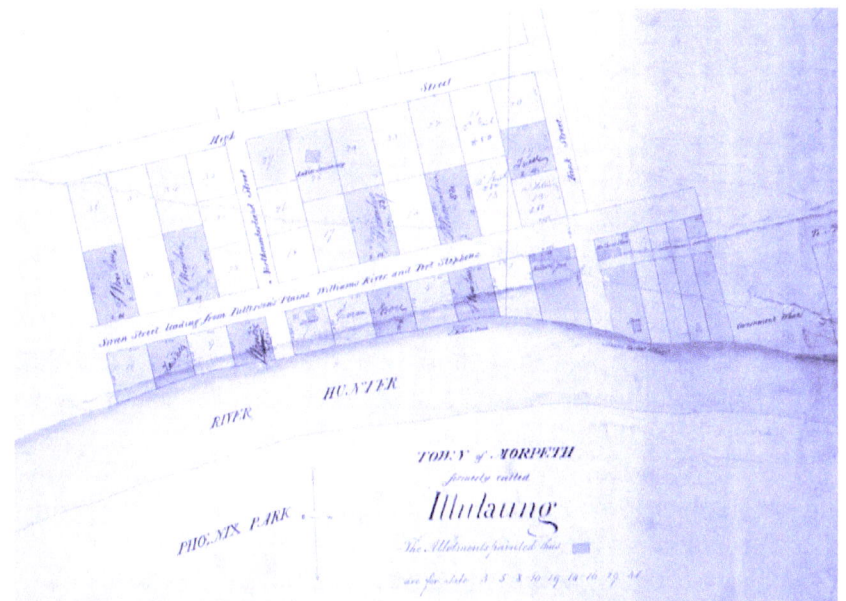

30 Map of the newly formed settlement of Green Hills, circa 1833. Known as Illulaung by the indigenous people, it was soon to be renamed Morpeth after an English town. Just twelve years after being proclaimed by founder Edward Close, 25 of the original 36 plots had been sold. The village boasted a school building (7 Swan St) and a 'Ladies Seminary' (25 High St.). A new wharf at the western end of the village was allocated to the regular 'Steam Packet' from Sydney Town. SLNSW.

owner James Hillier arrived at Green Hills he proved as good as his word, he and Cookie shaking on a deal whereby Cookie would supervise and help carry out renovations on the hotel, to be paid by the hour for work done and with free board and lodging, but importantly retaining the freedom to explore the region and accept other paid jobs if they arose.

"You'll have a base from which to explore the area without any outlay of cash, and I am not tied to paying a lot of money while the hotel is not making much," James enthused.

"We both get what we want without being tied down to unwieldy contracts."

In the months that followed Cookie travelled the length of breath of the Hunter, traipsing from hamlet to hamlet and farm to farm, meeting and talking to everyone and anyone, the experience confirming his choice of where his fortune might lie.

Luck was indeed turning his way and in early September 1833 a friendly voice whispered that James Nowland, scion of one of the area's earliest families, was leaving west Maitland and selling his prime allotment on the main street. Should Cookie want to buy land, he had to act quickly the whisperer added. Faced with the possibility of his dreams coming to fruition, Cookie was paralysed by indecision.

'Can this really be what I should do' he asked himself over and over. 'Am I really able to join respectable society? Can I own my own land? What if I am found out?'

Torn between fear and desire, he walked to the edge of the town and sat, looking down on the winding brown water moving sluggishly around the river bend below.

'What would the good Reverend Nelson advise?' he wondered.

'What would his Lordship Admiral Nelson do?'

The second question answered itself. Cookie knew exactly what Nelson would do when faced with a dilemma - he would attack.

His mind settled, on the fourteenth of September, 1833, Cookie's dream of becoming a reputable member of a society and overcoming his convict past took a huge leap forward when he bought an acre of land facing West Maitland's High Street for the price of fifty four pounds.

The purchase agreement - and subsequent sale - are recorded by the Deeds Branch of the NSW Registrar General, which defined Cookies allotment as "being in that part of the Town of Maitland known and described as west Maitland, in the Country of Northumberland and Colony of New South Wales ... bounded on the east by adjoining land belonging to Mr Cohen ... its southern border was two chains long forming its frontage to the Main or High Street while on the west and north it was bordered by a portion of Nowland's land now purchased and in the possession of Mr Joseph Waller."

In 1835 Waller bought the four acres of land from Nowland for two hundred pounds, while much later in 1837 Cookie sold his land to his then business partner, James Keppie, for seventy pounds.

The 1833 purchase was a calculated risk by Cookie because West Maitland was still an unproclaimed, unofficial, ungoverned and unruly town with an uncounted and unaccountable population of about 800 people growing wild and unfettered in what was the colony's wild, wild, west. The ambitiously named 'High Street' was a meandering dirt track that vaguely followed the sweep of the river, dodging stubborn stumps and fording small creeks as it wound its way west - impassable bog when it rained, a dust bowl in the dry, and at all times clogged by an unending line of bullock teams heading either East or West, their drays laden with produce for export to Sydney or beyond and with manufactured goods destined for the increasing number of wealthy settlers in the Valley.

The town's street corners and hotel bars were dominated by spruikers selling goods, or the promise of goods, and by businessmen looking to make a quick profit.

Buildings sprung up overnight and disappeared just as quickly, meaning the demand for skilled mechanics who could build them and dismantle them was insatiable.

Cookie loved the town's unpredictability and within a short time had built a small cottage/ workshop on his centrally located plot and was working as a cabinet-maker, carpenter, builder when his life was turned on its head by a chance encounter.

31 Extract from the Deeds Registration Branch of the NSW Registrar General's Office - 1822-37. This document records Cookie's land purchases and sales in the frontier town of Maitland West. The entry in the register details Cookies purchase of a one acre plot - described as being 'five chains long' (100m) by 'two chains (40m) forming its frontage to the Main or High Road' - from James Nowland for fifty four pounds. He later sold it in 1837 to his then business partner James Keppie for seventy pounds. See Page 322 for map.

Chapter Eight

Haynes finished scribbling the last of his notes and looked up at Cookie. The old man's second rum sat almost untouched in front of him and he looked tired, the first time that he had done so during the conversations of the day, and the journalist began to get an understanding of how gruelling the ordeal of retelling and reliving his life must have been.

"You look tired Sir" he said finally. "I'm sorry. I tend to get tied up in an interview, especially as one as interesting as this, and forget that how difficult it can be for the person being interviewed. It's a lot easier asking questions than answering them. Someone once said that interviews were so difficult because the biggest fool in the world can ask a question that the wisest man cannot answer," he said, ending with a weak laugh.

He had meant the banter as a light-hearted break, but instead of a smile or a laugh, the old man merely nodded, clearly not having divined the humour.

"It's late. We should call it a night. I am afraid this might be our last meeting. Tomorrow evening I take the coach to Newcastle and from there back to Sydney where my mistress awaits. That's the magazine" he explained hurriedly in response to Cookie's sharp look.

"And a far more demanding mistress she is than any woman could ever be," he added.

"Your story will find a page in our next edition and a fine story it will be, even though it must needs be but a fraction of what your real story has been."

"Australians such as yourself - good men and women - are the backbone of this new country, not the fake aristocracy who have managed to steal so much of the land and who want to reproduce here the rule they exercise in Britain."

"I know you see yourself as British Mr Cooke, and more power to you, for there is no doubt this land must be populated by the best the world has to offer and that is the British working man, most certainly not the riff-raff of other nations that have started to wash up on our shores in recent years. This new land is a wonderful opportunity for the real British people, the working people who day after day toil without the need for vain glory to fuel them."

"I'm sorry" he added, "I'm rambling."

The young man stood up and put out his hand to the older man he had come to admire.

"No" said Cooke simply.

"I'm sorry" said Haynes, visibly confused.

"I hope I have not insulted or offended you in any way, if so I really am most sorry."

"No" said Cookie shaking his head slowly.

"I mean that the story is not yet over and cannot end at this point because there remains another side of my story to be told, that of my wife Mary. I assure you it is more important that her story be told than it is mine. I'm sure you would not want to leave without getting the whole story - not only of who I am, but also of how my wife and family have survived and become a part of this land you call Australia. You leave on the afternoon coach.

"I will arrange for Mary to speak to you tomorrow morning and I will not take 'no' for answer" he said. Haynes was hoist neatly on his own petard and could only nod and smile.

"Can we make it 10am?" he asked and it was Cookie's turn to nod and smile.

The odd pair again shook hands outside the doors of the hotel and Haynes stood and watched as the old man, shoulders hunched and collar lifted against the chill wind, slowly weaved his way up the street and out of view. The next morning he tapped on the door of Cookie's modest two story home on Swan street at precisely 10am.

The door was opened by a fine looking young woman, dressed conservatively, who shook his hand firmly.

"Good morning Mr Haynes, it's a pleasure to meet you after all I have heard about you. My name is Caroline, I'm Cookie's daughter. At least one of them" she laughed a pleasant and confident laugh. "Please come this way."

The small 'formal' reception room was warmed by a fire. On one side of the room a small table was set for tea. On a two-seater divan sat the matriarch, Mary, her arm draped over the ornate arm of the divan. At first glance she seemed formidable, reminding Haynes of his own very formidable mother.

Caroline stood behind her mother in support, as did a younger man.

Cookie rose and formally introduced him to his wife, and the man as "my son, Alfred".

"I hope you don't mind my children being present" Cookie began.

"Caroline lives here in Morpeth and Alfred owns the 'Who'd a Thought It' Inn further up the valley in Qurindi, but happens to be visiting. I thought it might be good if they were present."

Cookie looked as if he was going to say something further, but held his tongue, as did everyone, until Mary broke the silence.

"Mr Haynes, it's a pleasure to meet you again. You probably won't remember but you often came into our store when you were just a lad, usually with your mother Margaret. I hope she is well?"

Haynes had done enough hard interviews to understand the old lady was establishing her position in charge of the situation.

"Yes indeed she is Mrs Cooke. She moved back to Singleton to be with family after my father died a few years ago, but she is still well. Thank you." There was a pause as the old lady visibly composed herself.

"I hope you don't mind, but I insisted William bring you here to meet you because ... well because the fact of the matter is our lives have been placed in your hands by what you have been told."

She raised a hand, stifling Haynes' objection.

"I am not worried. I know you come from a good family, your father was a school-teacher if I recall, and I know that you would never do anything to harm this family." Haynes squirmed uncomfortably, but said nothing.

"This family has spent a lifetime in the shadows, and not without reason. William has told you of his time as a convict and I too was once a convict. It is not an easy thing to admit because whether you like it or not, the stigma never leaves you. Nor your children. The lives of Caroline and Alfred and our other nine children would be changed forever if that side of our history were to become known, but I do feel that if you are to know our story, you need to know our whole story."

With that the 'grand old lady,' as Haynes mentally described her, sat back in her chair, leaving him to respond.

"I can only tell you what I have told Cookie ... er, sorry, Mr Cooke, that while I feel very strongly that neither of you have done anything to be ashamed of, I have given my word that nothing of that will be written, and I again give you my word this morning."

"Your husband has had an amazing life, and his - and your - achievement in overcoming your past and not only being successful but also raising fine and successful children is remarkable. You are a shining example of what can be achieved in our new country."

Satisfied, Mary looked at Cookie and her children before continuing.

"Well, what can I tell you John Haynes? Where do I begin?"

Haynes smiled. He was back on familiar territory.

"Well, at the beginning of course. What brought you to this country?"

"I was not brought here, Mr Haynes, of that I assure you. I was sent."

Mary McWilson
London. June 13, 1833

The crowd outside The Mansions, official residence of London's Lord Mayor, was growing larger and the few policemen on the street were worried. Walbrook Street was short and narrow and once the word was out that the beloved Queen Adelaide was to pay a visit to the Lord Mayor, it seemed everyone in the city wanted to take the chance to cheer her.

But the hard-eyed buskers were already out aggressively touting their wares and the pickpockets - flash boys and girls - were beginning to make an appearance. The guards outside the mansion also exchanged worried looks.

"If this keeps up then I shouldn't be surprised if'n her majesty doesn't just carry on by" Corporal Thomas confided to his two colleagues posted outside the imposing building.

"I reckon every ne'er-do-well and flash jobber in the city is 'ere."

The two sentries knew no answer was required and so gave none, but they also exchanged glances in which a mere lift of an eyebrow and slight twist of a mouth was enough to send the message they both thought the corporal was a worrywart. It seemed to them the crowd was happy enough and besides, everyone in London loved the newly crowned Queen, even if they did think King William was a tosser. Word was that Adelaide was a good and honest wife, but sadly she had not yet born an heir, a sad situation made doubly sad because King Willie's concubine had so far provided ten children and word was the King was trying his hardest for eleven. Across from the Mansions Ed McWilson nodded for Mary to stop trawling the street and join him in the quite corner where he had retreated.

"There's a lot goin' on t'day me lovely, no need to hurry, all good fings come to them wot waits. I see there's a few Peelers about, so you need to keep an eye," he said, finger to nose. Mary looked up at her husband and smiled. He was the most handsome man she had ever seen, and not only that, but he was always right, as he always laughingly said, even on those few times he was wrong. It was Ed who had rescued her literally from the door of the poor house when her mum had died, not long after her Dad had gone out one day, never to return. Not only had Ed rescued her and allowed her to stay in his rambling home, he had taught her how to make a livin' in the unforgiving city of London, pickin' pockets and enticing men to Ed's public house. He was quite the catch thought Mary and she reckoned she was lucky to have him, even if she knew she didn't really have him all to herself. But Ed looked after her and when she became pregnant with his baby he had even married her, after a fashion, in a ceremony performed by a former priest who was one of the regulars at Ed's pub.

She had lost the child sadly. Ed said it was 'cause was just 15 and so small. He knew so much did Ed. That was five years ago and even though she had not fallen pregnant again, she knew she would one day. Ed said so. Then they would be married proper.

"There" Ed said softly, interrupting her train of thought, "the toff with the green jacket. He's just left the bank, an' see 'ow he keeps touching his left pocket. That'll be where he has 'is purse tucked away, for sure. Alright, same as usual. I'll cause a bit of a palaver and then head up toward the bank. You shift the purse to me as soon as you can and keep walking and I'll see you back at the rooms."

Mary nodded, her eyes already focussed on the mark. Mary understood that Ed couldn't be seen close to any nefarious acts 'cause of his position as owner of a public house, so he always stayed 'out of the limelight' as he called it.

As for Mary, she was perfect for the role she played. Petite, with a mane of red hair, alabaster skin and a pretty face - not so pretty as to cause men to stare, mind you, just pretty enough to disarm them and make them smile. Her clothes were carefully chosen to complete her disguise. She was dressed in the style of a young lady of good family - not too flashy, not too rich. A pale blue bonnet demurely covered her hair and she sported a dark blue short spencer jacket worn over a white gauze shirt of moderate, but interesting, decolletage.

A full cream-coloured skirt, brown short lace-up boots and flowered shawl wrapped demurely across her shoulders completed the picture - projecting just the right degree of middle-class goodness. Drifting through the crowds, she approached Mr Green Jacket casually, to all intents just another young lady out for a stroll.

Moving in close she stood quietly until Ed started his diversion, suddenly tackling some bloke and yelling 'thief' before slipping away as the crowd surged forward. After a quick look around to make sure everyone was looking elsewhere, Mary's petite hand quickly and smoothly slipped into the man's pocket, fingering what felt like a silk purse before instantly lifting and secreting it into the folds of her shawl and blithely moving on, careful not to give the mark a backward glance, just like Ed had taught her.

Resting close to her breast the purse felt too light to be coins and her heart skipped a beat, thinking perhaps she had lifted some bank notes.

'Ed will be very 'appy if that's so' she thought, smiling as she threaded her way lightly through the crowd, taking her time, pausing here and there as would any young woman out for a stroll, failing to see Mr Green Jacket following her at a discreet distance. She was about to cross Cannon Street where Ed would be waiting when a heavy hand landed on her shoulder.

"This the girl Sir?" a deep voice asked.

She turned to see one of the dreaded Peelers beside Mr Green Jacket.

"That's her. I believe she has my purse hidden in her shawl."

With that he pulled at the shawl, pointing triumphantly as a silk purse dropped softly to the ground.

"Wot you got ta say fer yerself then young lady?" the Peeler asked.

Struck dumb with fear all Mary could blurt was 'that's not mine'.

"Well, we already know that then, don't we' the beefy" Peeler said.

Mr Green Jacket laughed.

"Let 'er go yer bloody rozzer" a big, rough-looking bloke standing beside the trio said, "she ain't done nuffink too wrong. He's got his money back, for goodness sake.

"You lot in your fancy blue outfits; just got 'ere and think you rule the streets don't yer. Bugger orf afore I thump ye."

His words brought forth cries of "let her go, let her go" from a small group that quickly gathered around. Police Officer number 197 Bill Edwards looked the big bloke in the eye and then looked about him, taking stock of the situation.

To his eye the crowd all seemed in good cheer. Ready, as Londoners always were, for a little free entertainment. Even though he had only been a member of the police force for a few months, he knew he and his fellow officers were resented by ordinary Londoners and the good mood could turn ugly very quickly.

It wasn't that Bill was afraid. As a soldier with twelve year's service behind him he could take care of himself, but the fact was he wasn't happy about having to arrest such a respectable looking young lady, and it showed in the pained expression on his face. Taking her cue from the crowd, Mary stopped sobbing for long enough to turn to growing mob.

"I just found it on the ground and picked it up. Honest."

Turning to Mr Green Jacket she sobbed "please let me go kind Sir" she said, reaching out beseechingly to take hold of a green sleeve.

The peeler sighed. This flash youngster knew her job.

"Does you want to lay a charge against this young girl then Sir? If you do want to proceed you'll have to come to the station to make a statement."

Bill waited, almost sure the mark would relent and tell him to let the girl go. He didn't see his role as arresting sobbing little girls, but the indignant victim was having none of it.

"Get your hands off me you trollop," he said to Mary, roughly knocking away her hand.

"Constable, I demand you arrest this woman immediately. We need to get this trash off the streets or the whole city will be soon unliveable."

That did not go well with the crowd who then turned their wrath on the unforgiving Mr Green Jacket.

"You bloody toff, let 'er go", said the big bloke said. Another grabbed Mary and tried to tug her from Bill's grip while another gave him a shove in the back. Tightening his grip on Mary he reached into his pocket for the whale bone whistle he had been issued with just that week and putting it to his lips gave three sharp shrill blasts, the signal he needed help. Then he then turned on the crowd.

"Orlright, you 'eard the man, now get off wiff yer or I'll take a truncheon to the lot of yer."

"Yeah, you and whose army?" the big bloke answered, triggering a wave of laughter which faded quickly as three other truncheon bearing rozzers appeared, forming a line between the crown and Mary, now on her knees and sobbing in terror. Seeing the mood change, Bill moved in and stuck the tip of his truncheon into the big blokes throat.

"Alright then big mouth, you want to take a trip to Newgate as well."

The bloke stepped back, a silent signal for the rest of the crowd to do the same.

"Sorry luv, you're nicked, come with me then," he said softly to Mary, before turning to the now less than confident victim.

"And you need to come as well, to make a statement."

As she was led away Mary looked around wildly, catching sight of Ed looking at her from across the street, but when she went to speak he shook his head, gave her the thumbs up sign that everything would be alright. Then he blew her a kiss and quickly disappeared into the crowd that was rapidly building.

That was the last time Mary saw her 'husband'.

At the police station next to the old Bailey it took less than an hour for Mary's details to be taken. She gave her birthdate as 1814, in Reading, Berkshire. Her height was measured at 4'11" and it was noted she had a "fair, ruddy complexion, grey eyes, red hair and a pug nose". It was also noted that she had a scar under her left jaw, the letters WW tattooed on her upper left arm as well as five dots tattooed on the back of her left thumb. Finally, it was noted she wore a blue ring on her wedding finger.

Shortly after Mary had been booked Sergeant Smith called Constable Edwards aside "for a quite word".

"It seems we have a bit of problem" the sergeant began, lips pursed, "the lass you brought in works for a, um, how can I say… the owner of a gentleman's establishment here in the city."

Edwards said nothing, forcing the sergeant to forge on.

"Yes, well. As I said, the man she works for owns a large public house in the city and dare I say he is well connected. Very well connected indeed, to say the least. He runs a big team of, ah, people, like that young lady, over there, but seems he calls this one his missus."

"Now, the fact is, a lot of very important people, including some politicians and even policemen, run a, well, let's call it a perpetual tab at that gentleman's establishment. Got my drift."

Edwards was not a particularly intelligent man, but nor was he born yesterday, but he was as honest as the day is long and he bristled.

"You aren't suggesting we let the young lady go free are you?"

Sergeant Smith shook his head.

"Too late for that I'm afraid. Far too late. But the fing is, no one wants to see her pretty little neck stretched for a few quid. Do you?"

Bill slowly shook his head.

"Well then, may I suggest that you have a chat with our poor victim of the crime, Jonathon Clark his name is, and he's a wealthy toff wot owns a very expensive perfume store. Put it to him politely that he might want to agree to lessen the charge? If he agrees, all good. If he doesn't, well I'm told his perfume business might not survive the night."

Seeing the shock on the policeman's face, the sergeant rushed on.

"But in all truth, I don't expect it to get to that. If necessary, send him over to me and I will take the necessary action. But if you can get him to agree, I think I can see a commendation in it for yerself, and perhaps even a moderate tab at said establishment," he winked.

Bill Edwards could only mentally shake his head. He had seen more than enough of the same kind of skullduggery by officers in the army not to know that such arrangements were a part of life. 'So be it' he thought to himself, 'I'm not here to change the bloody world'.

A short time later, before Mary had been formally charged with the theft of five pounds, Bill took Clark aside for a private talk.

"Now Sir", he started, "you look a reasonable man, not the kind to kill a young woman."

"What!" Clark exclaimed. "What the blazes are you talking about?"

"Well, you may or may not know that stealing a gentleman's purse containing five pounds, like your's did, will surely bring down the death penalty on that young girl over there" he said, pointing to the shivering wreck Mary had been reduced to. "Now, I agree wif you; can't have that lot on the streets. But you don't want to see her dancing on air? Do you?" he asked, a sympathetic smile spreading on his face.

"Well I don't see that that is any of my business" Clark said indignantly, "nor yours for that matter."

The policeman nodded. "Well, the fact is, I didn't see her nick anyfing from you and if it comes right down to it, I would have to testify to that fact. Didn't make anyfing drop from her shawl either for that matter - that was you. But if you were to say that she had stolen, say, a handkerchief. One werf less'n a shillin' for instance, then I would have to testify to the same and then in all probability the young lady would get to spend the rest of her miserable life in the colony of New South Wales, from where I suggest she could no longer prey on good citizens like yourself. On the quiet, I might add the young lady is the wife of one of the better known flash men in town, and 'e is furious and threatening all kinds of retribution.'

"I say, are you threatening me? I think I need to speak too your sergeant!"

"Of course Sir. Please do, but please hurry sir, 'cause I have to rush out. Seems a gang of ruffians is gathering outside a well-known perfumery shop in the city, threatening to burn it to the ground they are, for some unknown reason. If we can't get this issue dealt with quickly, we may be too late to save the building."

Clark went from red-faced anger to blanched-faced shock in one instant. Looking in the direction of the sergeant, he saw the man was looking directly at him with a stern face that silently, but most clearly, said 'do it'.

"Well, I suppose you are right, in a way. No need to hang the poor child. Alright, do what you must."

"A handkerchief it is then. Can I go now?"

"Good man!" said Bill, clapping him on the shoulder, "right decision".

A few minutes later Mary McWilson was charged with stealing a silk handkerchief, value one shilling, from the person of Jonathon Clark, the lawful owner of said handkerchief.

The formalities over with, Mary was taken on the short walk next door to a stinking, howling, over-crowded hellhole called Newgate.

Newgate Prison

As hard as Mary's life had been, nothing she had experienced could have prepared her for Newgate.

Immediately she arrived at the front gate a toothless male warder drew her aside and conducted a quick 'search' of her, pulling aside her shirt to feel her breasts before rubbing his hands all over her body and deep into her under-clothes as she stood rigid with shock.

He then whispered he had the means to make life better for her if she wanted when he came back tomorrow, before thrusting two blankets into her arms and walking her through a number of corridors, unlocking and locking iron doors them behind him as he went, before unceremoniously shoving her through a grated steel gate into the Chapel Yard - the open air section of the female wing of the infamous Newgate Prison.

Chapel yard was an open space of about fifty feet by twenty feet, bounded on all four sides by sleeping wards, each about forty feet by fifteen. The yard had been originally designed to hold about 20 people, but when Mary arrived at least 100 women of all shapes, sizes and ages were squeezed into the space.

Young girls sat in wide-eyed shock next to blowsy harridans.

Babies howled and children ran wildly.

Mary was shocked to see that many of the women were half naked, while others were dressed in the barest of rags. In one corner several men held down a screaming naked woman, while next to her another naked woman bathed at a spigot, with a group of well-dressed gentlemen standing nearby, ogling at the spectacle.

Some of the women were clearly drunk.

All looked dirty. All wore leg irons. All turned their eyes toward Mary.

Open mouthed and wide-eyed she stared back, arms clasping her two blankets to her chest in symbolic rather than actual protection, afraid to bring attention to herself and trying desperately to look unafraid.

No one moved until the sound of the steel gate clanging shut behind her triggered a howling and screeching such as she had never heard. Almost immediately she felt hands tugging at her clothes.

Her bonnet was quickly torn from her head and she lost one of her shoes and both blankets.

As she struggled to keep her clothes on she screamed at the top of her voice, the yard echoing the cacophony of madness. The group of men at the water spigot broke out in laughter at the spectacle.

Mary was saved by the appearance of a wards-woman, a massive female dressed in men's clothes, who waded into the melee swatting away the women prisoners with one beefy fist as she whipped others with a length of willow held in the other hand.

"Come with me" she said, grabbing Mary by the arm and dragging the terrified, dishevelled girl back through the grated door and into a small passageway. "Stay there" the Amazon said, "don't go anywhere and don't talk to anyone 'til I come back."

32 A forbidding depiction of the innards of Newgate Prison, circa 1833. Original drawing Arthur Griffiths. 'The Chronicles of Newgate.' 1884.

With that she strode away. Afraid to even look around Mary sat on the lone chair for almost an hour before the wards-woman returned.

"You got any money or valuables on you?" the Amazon said brusquely.

Mary could only shake her head.

"You're Mary McWilson?" she stated rather than asked. "Alright, seems you have friends outside. They have paid for you to stay in the master's ward. You're lucky I found you in time. Come with me."

Again the huge woman took her by the arm, unlocking a steel door and shoving her into a stairwell before shutting and locking the door behind her before unlocking yet another door that led into a dormitory which in turn led onto a closed off section of the main yard.

Inside were a number of wood pallets, neatly made up as beds, on which sat about twenty women, all well-dressed. They all looked up at the new arrival, but said nothing.

"You'll sleep here with Louisa," the Amazon said, nodding toward to a woman about Mary's age standing next to one of the pallets, "don't make any trouble and you'll live through this. Cause trouble and you will have me to deal with. Some flash fella has paid for your safety, but cause trouble and neither he nor anyone else will be able to save you - understand?"

Mary nodded numbly.

The Amazon looked her up and down in an open appraisal.

"You're pretty enough, and if you're clever enough you might be alright. Give me this shawl" she said, fingering the long length of fine fabric Mary still sported around her neck.

"No!" Mary said before she could stop herself, instantly regretting it as the Amazon simply backhanded her, sending her spinning to the floor. Standing over her the Amazon took hold of the shawl and ripped it off.

"Wrong answer luvvie" she laughed. "Living 'ere on the master side is expensive luvvie. Are you worth it? You better hope your fella thinks you are, otherwise, you will need to find someone to take his place 'cause you won't survive out there luvvie, that's for sure," she laughed, pointing a thumb over her shoulder.

Mary lay on the cold stone floor, bewildered, unable to even begin to comprehend the turn her life had taken. In what seemed to be just minutes she had been torn from a blissful peace, looking forward to meeting her husband and seeing a loving smile crease his face, to being thrust into a hell of filth and violence.

Time stopped and she had no idea of how long she sat there, totally unaware of what was going on around her.

"Give me your hand sweetie." Mary looked up to see the girl called Louisa with her hand extended in friendship and a smile on her face.

"Come, sit on the bed here."

That small hint of kindness jarred her back to reality and triggered the flood of tears that had been held back by the wall of terror. Deep sobs of utter despair racked her body, the spasms ending only when she fell into a tortured sleep. She awoke to silence and the dim glow of lamp lights. Jerking upright she looked wildly around, for a moment having no memory of where she was. Then the memories surged back, bringing a loud outburst of tears with them.

"Come on then, that's not helping!"

"Besides, you're upsetting people. Stop!"

The sharp command from Louisa had the necessary effect. Mary stopped and looked around. She was laying on one of the pallets, Louisa sitting beside her. In the glow she saw groups of women sat on pallets drinking and talking.

There were a number of men in the room, clearly on very friendly terms with the women they were talking to.

"It's a big shock, I know" said Louisa, squeezing her hand, "but believe me, it could be a lot worse. You're safe in here, so try to get some sleep. I'll be here and your stuff will be safe."

"No one will bother you here, I promise."

In the next few days Mary quickly came to fully understand that, as bad as her experience had been, it could have been much, much worse. Louisa explained that in the Chapel Yard, women had no money and so quickly had to sell everything just to buy food, and gin. The reason most women on the 'other' side were near naked was that clothes were the first thing taken in lieu of money to buy necessities. After they were gone everything else was quickly surrendered, including themselves. Gin - plentiful and cheap - was the only cure. Raucous gin-fuelled parties began in the women's quarters most nights shortly after sunset. The fun almost inevitably degenerated into anger, screaming and violence. Male prisoners with money bribed their way into the women's quarters because many women, and eventually all women, had to sell themselves for gin or clothes or food.

"It's alright in this side 'ere darlin', not great, but better'n out there" Louisa said, pointing vaguely. In 'ere we have food and our own space. There's no violence, no one gets raped, no one is beaten or killed. Out there" she pointed again, "it's pure evil. It's a living hell."

The key to such luxuries, Louisa needlessly pointed out, was the wards-woman. The Amazon who saved Mary was called Big Martha, though not to her face. Big Martha controlled every facet of existence for women behind Newgate's bars and she had to be paid for everything from food and gin to bedding and even water for washing.

Most of all she had to be paid for 'easement' - freedom from the leg irons that women on the other side wore at all times.

A few women inmates had their own money to pay for such 'luxuries', but that was rare and most women depended on family or 'protectors' to survive.

Mary knew Ed had to be paying for her, but as the days dragged by a nagging fear rose in the back of her mind. 'How long would he, or could he, continue to pay'? The thought that she might be abandoned and left to end her life in such a hell kept her on the edge of terror. Louisa was her saviour.

"Mary, you'll be fine. Your husband loves you and he will find a way to get you out of here, don't worry." Louisa had been behind bars for several months, ironically also charged with stealing a shawl, also worth just one shilling. She was a year older than Mary and had run away from home to be with an army officer.

He had married her, but deserted her after just a year and, too ashamed to go home, she had worked as a maid. She had stolen a shawl from her mistress 'cause I wanted to have something pretty'.

Luckily her parents had forgiven her and were working to get the charges dropped, even paying off the woman she had stolen from, but in Newgate the demands from everyone who worked in the prison were endless.

"I'll be fine, and so will you Mary."

"You are not a bad person. I know that."

That triggered another flood of tears.

"No, I am. That's what I am. My father deserted my mother and when the money ran out and … and, my mother killed herself. I was all alone. I was alone and Edward saved me and now I've let 'im down."

Louisa hugged her and some of the other young women joined in, holding her as she descended into an abyss of despair beyond any help.

Later, when she had cried herself out of tears, some of the other women shared their stories.

None were hardened prostitutes or thieves, most came from good homes but all told the same story; of how one stroke of bad luck, one unexpected misadventure, had tipped them from a precarious existence they had not realised they were living, into hell.

On her tenth day in Newgate Mary got a visitor, a wealthy-looking gentleman who, once he began speaking, sounded like anything but the gentleman.

"Blimey, bloody rough in 'ere innit? I knew it were bad, but … anyway. Ed sent me. Tol' me to tell ya not to worry, he's gonna sort it. Spoke to a lawyer he did, who says whatever you do, don't mention 'im, Ed that is. As the pro-pri-etor of a public house. Ain't no way 'e can be seen to be involved. You know that doncha. He's workin' to get an early trial 'cause there ain't no way he can pay for you in here forever. The lawyer will be there in court wif ya, OK? Just sit tight and keep ya gob closed."

It was three long weeks before Mary appeared at the Old Bailey on July 4th, 1833. No lawyer arrived to defend her, and so the trial did not take long. Back in Newgate Mary was inconsolable.

Not only had she expected to have a lawyer to defend her, but had prayed that Ed would be there to support her.

Panic gnawed at her.

She was sure she had been abandoned and that the madhouse of the common women's yard was her next stop.

"I will not go there" she told Louisa, "I will die first."

The next day Big Martha made a brief appearance in the ward, an evil smirk on her face.

"Well, Miss high and mighty seems to have fallen a few perches" she gloated.

"Me thinks you may soon be looking for that new protector I spoke of some weeks ago. Unless you have some money or other goods hidden away to pay your way, it looks like you may have to step down in the world somewhat. Ain't nuffink free m'lady; nuffink. But if you are good there just might be a place for you keeping my room clean and tidy, and some nights you might even be able to stay there, if'n you're good that is.

"Might even be some new clothes in it for you," she said, looking Mary up and down appraisingly.

A few days later a visitor in the form of another of Ed's bogus gentlemen arrived with a message from Mary's 'husband'.

"Mary, your husband sends his fondest affection and has asked me to assure you he is heart-broken at your unjust conviction. We have no idea of how the judge reached that verdict. We tried to intervene, but our lawyer was not even allowed in the court. Edward wants me to tell you he has tried all in his power to change the verdict, but unfortunately it will stand. He has ascertained that you are to sail to New South Wales soon after Yuletide and wants to assure you all your needs will be taken care of until then."

"Unfortunately once you leave our shores, his ability to help you will be made much more difficult, but he wants you to know that he will keep trying to free you. All he asks is that you respect the confidentiality of his, ah, business interests."

After he had left Mary rushed to Louisa and her small group of friends, telling them through her tears what he had said. The women looked at each other, but it fell to Louisa to tell her.

"I fear you have been deserted" she said, also crying. "I'm so sorry, but the fact is men have no use for us in here. He will pay for a while, most do, but then he'll stop. Most do. There's any number of stupid young girls out there to fall in love with a flash man or a soldier or whatever, and I'm sure many of them are good - but …"

The older women just looked at each other. Then one girl confessed she was actually looking forward to being sent to the colony.

"I'm told it's warm all the time" she said.

"I think it would be grand to be warm all the time. To never be cold again. I will marry a rich farmer with lots of land - I'm told everyone has lots of land - and have children and they will never go hungry."

"Listen to me luvvie" said Grace, at 24 one of the older women in the group, her face scarred by the pox, "the sad fact is that you cant't trust 'em.

1063. MARY Mc WILSON was indicted for stealing, on the 13th of June, at St. Mary's, Woolchurchhaw, 1 handkerchief, value 1s., the goods of Jonathan Clark, from his person.

JONATHAN CLARK. On Wednesday, the 13th of June, I was opposite the Mansion-house, a little before three o'clock; I perceived a crowd caused by the Queen paying a visit there—I immediately secured my pocket-book, and while I was doing that, I felt something at my other pocket; I turned round, and saw the prisoner hiding my handkerchief under her shawl; I took it from her.

Prisoner. It is false, I had the handkerchief in my hand; I picked it up before I came into the mob, and when I came into the mob, the gentleman said it was his— I gave it him, and he said no more; but about a quarter of an hour afterwards in Old Jewry, the gentleman came up with an officer, and gave me in custody. *Witness.* I followed her down Princes-street, and it occurred to me after I had taken it from her, that she might have taken a pocket-book from somebody, I immediately gave her in charge.

COURT. Q. Did she have it in her hand, and give it to you? A. Certainly, she did not; she was concealing it under her shawl—I took it from her; I felt a pressure at my pocket just before.

Prisoner. I had it in my possession five minutes before it was claimed. *Witness.* I had not missed it an instant; I had it safe immediately before—I had not left the Bank two minutes; she was tucking it under her shawl.

Prisoner. The mob was so great, I was obliged to turn back, and I got into Goldsmith's, at the bottom of Old Jewry. *Witness.* I let her go the length of Princes-street before I saw an officer—I kept her in sight all the time.

WILLIAM JEWELL EDWARDS. I am an officer, and produce the handkerchief.

GUILTY. Aged 20.—Transported for Seven Years.

33 The actual account of the all too brief trial of Mary McWilson on July 4, 1833. A chilling record of how a life can be destroyed in just minutes, it is eloquent in its very brevity. Online Proceedings of the Old Bailey. Sixth Session. 1833.

It's all luvvie duvvie when you're young and pretty and able to give 'em what they want, but as soon as that changes, when the babies come along or you lose your looks, well then it's out with the old and in with the new."

"I had to turn to stealin', and worse, after my Alfred ran orf. One night, while I was out workin' to keep 'im, he just packed his bag, an' all me valuables, and disappeared."

"Left me to fend for meself. Lucky I 'ad some stuff hid I did, so I've bin able to pay me way. Now it's nearly all gone and I want to go to the colony as well. The men down there can't be any worse'n they are 'ere, and besides, I 'ere there's a shortage of women. I might get lucky," she said, breaking out into a raucous laugh that quickly spread.

Despite the women's stories, deep in her heart Mary still believed Ed would come to rescue her. It took more than a month without any contact for the scales to finally fall from her eyes, and only then did she fully realise the bargain that had been made. In return for keeping quiet about Ed and his many 'interests' she would be spared.

Break her silence and she would be thrown to the wolves.

For the moment she was safe, at least until she was put on board the ship that would take her away to where she could no longer be a danger. After that she would be on her own.

It was a deal with the devil, but one she could not refuse. It was to be five long months before the news came that she, along with many of the younger women in Newgate, were to be transported within the week. For those five months she had secretly believed in the fairy tale that Ed would rescue her from the nightmare she was living, but when the dream finally died, a resilience emerged that Mary never knew she had. She had forged bonds of friendship with women facing the same living hell and among them a sense of solidarity and togetherness had grown, a devil-may-care attitude that no matter what, they would survive.

That was when Mary also began looking forward to leaving the dank cold grey of Newgate for a land that was always sunny and warm.

The *Numa*
November 1833

Despite having lived her life in the busiest port in the world, Mary had never been on a ship in her life until the day she was marched in chains to the docks at Woolwich to board *Numa*, a ship which to her untutored eye did not look anywhere near big enough to take her and 140 other women half-way across the world. On the wharf the women lined up silently looking up at the ship, however its crew looking down at the women and anything but silent.

"Hey darlin, have you got your ticket ready" one sailor called out.

An older woman near the front took the bait.

"We don't need a ticket to board that stinking boat just to sail to the other side of hell" she shouted back.

"No, it's the ticket to my heart you need, the one you have inside your skirts" the sailor shouted back to roars of laughter from the crew.

"You've never had a heart you toothless piece of shit, and if you ever found your way into a woman's skirts you wouldn't know what to do there, too many cabin boys methinks."

That brought forth an even louder roar from the crew.

"Don't worry darlin" an older tar shouted, "I'll be there cradle your head when you get seasick, and you will, believe me."

"If my 'ed ends up in your lap you might find yourself missing a small part of your life you whore's kidling" she shouted back. The crew literally fell about laughing at the woman's use of the flash talk to call the man a bastard.

The old tar gave up and went below.

The *Numa* was a three-masted barque of 325 tons, a shade under 150 foot long and 25 foot across the beam. A former whaling ship, it had the big blunt nose and low midships common to the vessels that hunted the leviathans of the ocean - and the smell that came with the catch.

"What is that foul smell" one of the women said as she boarded the ship an hour later. The *Numa* stank. It really and truly stank.

Whale ships were renown to forever carry the pungent, sickly smell of whale blood mixed with whale oil that crept into every crack and crevice as blubber was sliced from the whales to be rendered to oil in huge vats set in a brick stoves on the deck. The whale oil was stored in barrels on the lower deck while crew lived on the upper deck, so unlike most convict ships, *Numa* had just two decks. Because this was her first voyage transporting convicts, the lower deck had been hastily converted into barracks, with tiered bunk beds built in three sided, open-ended areas called a 'mess' - much the same as the men's ships - the one change being the addition of tables to sit at and shelves to stow away their personal possessions, especially the tea served in lieu of the beer enjoyed by the men. A kettle was supplied to each mess and a tin-pot to each female, tea being usually made each morning and night. Food rations were the same as those served to the men.

Being mere women the powers that be had decided that no soldiers were required to guard the convicts and consequently there was no bulk-head across the upper deck in midships, so at sea the women had the run of the ship's entire deck.

As was the standard with men, below decks women-warders were selected by the captain or the surgeon to run each mess.

As the women filtered down into the spacious lower deck there was an outbreak of 'oohs' and 'aahs' as the women saw they would have the luxury one bunk for each prisoner. Importantly, the women got to choose those they would mess with.

"Oh my Lord, this be heaven" said one of the veteran prisoners had been in 'every gaol from Bristol to Newgate', "except for that smell."

As the women explored their new surroundings and found places to store whatever clothes or goods they had brought with them, slowly the fear, anger and violence that had been a constant companion in Newgate began to dissipate. It took another week for all the prisoners to arrive and at the end of that period Captain John Baker called the prisoners on deck to acquaint them with the rules for the voyage.

"Good morning. My name is John Baker and I am the master of this vessel for the journey to Sydney Town." Nodding at the uniformed naval officer on this left, a distinguished-looking older man sporting a magnificent grey moustache, he continued; "this is our Royal Navy Surgeon-Superintendent, Mr Edward Bromley, a man of vast experience in this field who has made many voyages to the southern seas and who, I assure you, will take excellent care of your health on this voyage.

"All of you will have heard many different stories of the land to which you are headed and probably all of them are both true and false in equal measure. What I can tell you is that I have been to the colony of New South Wales and I can assure you it is a land of opportunity. A land where past sins can be expurgated and a new life begun for those who make the effort."

"The voyage can be expected to take about four months, depending on the weather, of course. We are due to set sail as soon this bad weather abates. As soon as we are in the channel your shackles will be struck off. During daylight hours, again weather permitting, you will be allowed the run of the deck provided you do not interfere in any way with the crew."

"The rules aboard this ship are few, but are inviolate."

"Any form of fighting and violence toward other convicts or the crew, any theft of any property, and any refusal to obey orders or carry out daily work, will not be tolerated and will result in the perpetrators being shackled below deck. There is to be no fraternising between the prisoners and the crew, and any infractions of that rule will result in dire punishment."

"What you gonna do Luvvie, send us to the colonies" an anonymous voice piped up.

"Well may you ask", Baker shot back, "but I assure you, you do not want to find out what I can do. In the case of minor offenses prisoners may be placed on reduced rations and be publicly caned. In extreme cases, a prisoner's hair may be publicly shorn off - entirely."

The thought of having their hair shorn brought forth a unified exclamation of horror from the women, followed by a swell of noise and each women turned to talk to their neighbour.

Baker let the response run for a minute, then spoke, getting the attention of every woman.

"I hope that none of these punishments will be necessary. Good day."

Back below deck Mary and her mess friends huddled over a cup of tea.

"Cut my hair orf? I'd like to see 'im or anyone else be try ta do that and live to tell the tale," said Mary McPherson, one of the many Scots lasses on board.

"Anyone who tries will be eatin' a dirk, that's for sure."

"They'll no be doin' anythin' like that" said Caroline Brown, another Scot, "there'd be a bloody mutiny." Everyone laughed a nervous laugh. Outside the wind howled, generating eerie whistling flute sounds as it rushed through the rigging, air vents and iron bars that had been secured to the portholes to prevent escape.

The wind would continue for another three weeks until *Numa* finally weighted anchor the day after Christmas, 1833.

Three weeks of inactivity had given the women time to sort out who their friends were, who they could talk to, who they could trust and who they could not. During the weeks ahead the women began to look at each other as friends and confidantes rather than as enemies. Soon that long unheard sound - laughter - quietly began to waft through the ship.

A few of the older women moved out of Mary's mess to join women of their own age, to be replaced by a number of the younger girls. Ann Connor, just 14 but hardened and wise beyond her years was one newcomer, as was Sarah Burroughs, also 14, but still a child. Jane Christian and Ann Carruthers were about Mary's age and the women bonded and vowed that, no matter what the future had in store, they would stay together.

"The Cap'n might say New South Wales is a fine place, but if it be filled by anythin' like those I met in Newgate then I have no doubt we will all be needing friends" said Jane.

The next day, as the tiny ship head-butted its way down the channel, the shackles were struck from the women just as the first cases of sea-sickness appeared. Mary was one of the first to go down with the incapacitating cramps, quickly followed by more than three dozen others as the ship reared and bucked its way through a howling gale and steadily building seas. Deciding caution was the better part of valour, Baker ducked *Numa* into cover behind the Isle of Wight at St Helens, where he was quickly joined by dozens of other ships until more than 100 were huddled together to sit out one of the worst storms in living memory. After three weeks of boredom two of the older women who messed together, 44 year old Liz Shull and

Ann Smith, 30, both well acquainted with the prison system, were enticed to spend some time with two members of the crew in their quarters.

Rum was produced and within a short time a lively party was underway which soon led to blows being exchanged as the men vied for the favour of the two women.

Word inevitably reached Captain Baker. Normally not in favour of corporal punishment, as indeed were most commercial maritime captains, as opposed to Naval captains who seemed to relish it, Baker was convinced by the experienced Surgeon Bromley that strong action was needed less he face the prospect of a complete collapse in discipline and repercussions from authorities once the ship reached Sydney. Baker agreed provided Bromley did not report the infraction. Four crew members were quickly identified as the culprits and paraded before a muster of crew and convicts where they were given 25 lashes apiece and, of more concern to them, were docked half their wages for the voyage. The two women were also paraded and given 25 strokes of a light cane, but then - as threatened - both suffered the ignominy of being lashed to chairs and having their heads shaved. In addition all the women were re-shackled, confined below decks until further notice and, more importantly, had their ration of tea stopped indefinitely.

That night injury was added to insult when the two bald convicts were beaten by a group women infuriated at having their tea stopped.

Three weeks later on January 29, 1834, the voyage recommenced, as did the sea-sickness, followed by diarrhoea and the wracking sound of the dreaded catarrh. Soon the ship reeked not only of whale oil, but of vomit and worse. Those women not confined to the ship's over-crowded surgeon's ward were forced to holystone and scrub the decks. After two weeks of this tough regime *Numa* eased into warmer climes. Captain Baker again called a muster, addressing crew and convicts.

"You will have noticed that the weather has improved and this will continue now as we head to the equator and below. I have decided that your shackles will be removed and your tea rations restored ..." before he could continue women spontaneously erupted into cheers and hurrahs. Baker could but smile.

"Be aware that I will not hesitate to reintroduce punishment should there be any further infractions of the rules. Surgeon Bromley has ordered every alternate mess to bring their bedding on deck to be aired daily and this will begin immediately."

Mary and her friends immediately hugged each other and across the deck other groups did the same. Helping to lift the air of despondency which had hung over the *Numa,* the sun broke from behind the clouds. As the temperature rose steadily so the humour of the women brightened. Under the direction of Surgeon Bromley, classes were organised for the women in reading, writing, arithmetic and basic accounting - the later which most of the women grasped immediately. Plays were produced, with the women playing all the roles while the crew, initially sceptical, became a rapt audience, demanding encore upon encore.

Ten uneventful weeks after waving goodbye to England, *Numa* sailed serenely into Cape Town harbour, the fabled port at the bottom of Africa beneath the majestic vision of Table Mountain. For the crew, who had been in the port many times, it was business as usual as they set about putting the ship to rights and began the long list of repairs and maintenance normal after such a voyage. The women were mesmerised by the beauty of the white-washed Dutch houses nestled beneath the towering backdrop of the grey-green mountain.

Used to the flatness Britain they were astounded that such beauty could exist. Well aware of the lure of the town to both crew and convict alike, Baker ordered that all the women were to be shackled for the time they were in port. On the second afternoon, under a warm clear blue sky, a 'sheet' of white cloud was seen to suddenly roll over the flat top mountain, only to literally appear to disappear into thin air as it poured down the grey stone mountainside.

Within minutes every woman was on deck, teas left sitting on tables, to stare in wonder at the marvel unfolding before them.

"It is indeed a wonderous thing to see" intoned the surgeon-superintendent saw the women gathered at the side of the ship.

"What is it?" one woman asked at last.

"Well, in scientific terms it is warm winds meeting cold winds. Air from the warm earth meeting air from the cold sea. But I like to think of it as an invitation, an invitation to see beyond the mountain at the glorious hinterland that lays behind the mountain."

Most of the women were now looking at the normally silent and severe old man who had barely uttered a single word to them in the entire voyage, even when treating them. Seeing them looking at him, he was taken aback, but stumbled on.

"I have been lucky enough to travel outside of the town to the farms and vineyards beyond and it is indeed a paradise."

"There are wild animals to hunt, deer aplenty for everyone, and wine to please even Bacchus."

The classical reference bypassed most the women.

"The god of wine" he said to the blank looks. This was the doctor's first voyage with women convicts and he had been amused to find that the common ship wine, which the male crew mostly spat out, was greatly appreciated by the women. So much so that he had been forced to cut down the normal daily ration of a gill a day which was commonly issued to the men because it had been enough to produce a high level of inebriation in the women. In such inequality lay opportunity, as the crew had quickly discovered, and the doctor had been forced to discontinue the men's ration entirely and curtail the women's in order to end the illicit trade which had sprung up. Suddenly aware that the eyes of most of the women had turned toward him, the doctor retreated to bluster.

"Yes, well. Ah, I, ah. I suppose I might get on with it. I need to track down some medical supplies."

No one said a word.

"And, ah, I might ask the captain to secure a supply of the local wine. Did I mention they make fine wine here. In the Cape?"

With that he turned and retreated toward the poop deck.

"I'll be buggered, it talks" said one of the older women.

Bromley paused halfway up the steps to the poop deck to look back. All the women had burst into laughter as one and were hugging each other.

"Strange creatures" he muttered. The idyll in Cape Town lasted barely a week, just enough time for the slickly efficient merchants of the town to restock the vessel with everything from livestock to wine, after which the Numa returned once again to head-butting its way south, this time into the brutal Southern Ocean.

As the women's shackles were removed, Captain Baker took the time to warn the women of the trial that lay ahead, and sure enough the trial started almost immediately. The southerly winds howled without let and the seas poured over the pug nose of the vessel almost continually - and the women revelled in it.

The ship leaked and the lower deck was nearly always awash in icy cold water; sea-sickness returned with a vengeance and coughing became the companion of the howls of the wind, but through it all the women remained not only generally healthy, but in good spirits.

"I have no idea what's going on in the minds of the women, do you Bromley?" asked Baker over dinner one evening. "It's as if they think they are off to a country fair instead of going to a prison in a strange country. What do you make of it?"

The old surgeon pondered the question for some time for venturing to answer, slowly sipping a fine Cape port.

"Sadly, New South Wales will be a country fair compared to what these women have gone through. I have heard them speak freely to each other as I treated them, as if I did not exist! Their tales have made me question how we treat them as women. Believe me, it does us no honour as Englishmen, no matter what their crimes."

Eight weeks later *Numa* swung its nose north out of the Bass Strait towards Sydney Town. Like every convict before them, the women were aghast at the sheer size and apparent emptiness of the coastline that sailed past them as they headed north.

"Wot I don't understand is, wot's 'appened to everyone? I aint seen so much as a campfire, let alone a village or a port on the entire coastline" one of the women eventually offered.

"Ave the bloody army killed 'em all or wot? There's not even been a sail spotted. It's a bit of a worry I don't mind tellin' you. Maybe we made a mistake comin' ere."

"Your mistake was getting caught wif that man's purse in your pocket Mary Bardon" someone shot back, "that an' sleeping wif the gent beforehand."

Sydney Town
June 13, 1834

Exactly one year to the day after her arrest in London Town and six months after stepping gingerly on board *Numa,* Mary McWilson and her fellow convicts looked at the line of warehouses interspersed with nondescript hovels that made up the shore of Sydney Cove. A sombre sense of disappointment and dread settled over the women as they looked at a dreary port town seemingly devoid of any grace or style.

"Well, it's not Cape Town, that's to be sure," said Ann Smith, breaking the silence. As the crew quickly set about securing the ship, one eye on the pubs and bawdy houses that could be seen and heard just short distance away, the women were silent for a change, each lost in their own thoughts on what life would be like in this new world? Their calmness came from the understanding they had no control over what lay ahead, a state of affairs which had been their fate ever since being born female.

Their lives would be decided by men.

They remained quiet the next morning as the Captain and the Surgeon-Superintendent boarded the ship's boat to be rowed ashore to see the Governor; and they were still quiet when the Colonial Secretary, a short bubble of a man with fat legs who could barely walk up the gangplank, arrived to inspect the ship and its human cargo and make a short meaningless speech about hoping the women had been treated well and asking if anyone had any complaints they wished to make.

"As if anyone would bloody listen" Mary Bardon said out loud, causing a ripple of laughter which clearly disconcerted Secretary Macleay, who snorted in disgust and left. In Sydney Town the process of assigning and transporting convicts had long been refined and refined again and now operated with sublime bureaucratic mixture of efficiency and indifference.

While the women watched the goings-on along the harbour, ashore lists were being drawn up, debated, and discussed. Very quickly agreements were struck and decisions made, a handshake between friends forever changing the lives of 140 women.

Deals were done, arrangements made.

The next day, June 17, Captain Baker ordered the women to collect their possessions and muster on deck to be informed of their fate

"I have good news" he began, "almost every single one of you have been assigned to settlers here in the colony, the exception being those women with children who will be transported a bit further inland to the town of Parramatta where you will work and where there is proper accommodation for you to be with your children. A number you, 50 in total, are to be transported by another ship to the settlement of Newcastle and will be further assigned from there. A few of you, 22 in number, who have skills in demand are to be assigned to businesses here in Sydney Town.

"The remainder will be assigned to individuals in small villages or on farms throughout the hinterland of Sydney Town. Given the good behaviour of the vast majority of prisoners during the voyage I have involved myself in the assignment procedure and can report to you that in most cases those women who messed together on Numa have been, wherever possible, assigned to the same general area."

At that news the women began to hug each other, bringing Baker's talk to a premature halt.

For six months the women had lived together, worked together, cooked, cleaned and sewed together. They had sung and danced and gossiped together; helped each other through pain and sickness and the mystery of arithmetic. Most importantly, they had listened to each other as they told their truths, recalled their fears and voiced their longings.

They had become friends and the news that they might be able to remain friends was the best possible news they could have been given.

"Once again I want to say that you have a chance here, in this new land, to redeem yourselves in the eyes of the law and your fellow citizens of the realm. I would urge to you lend yourself to your new lives with vigour and diligence and if you do, you can succeed."

"Now, please line up and present yourselves to Mr Thomas, the deputy superintendent of convicts, who will mark your name and let you know where you are to be assigned.

"Those of you who are being forwarded to Newcastle will remain here on board until your transport arrangements have been finalised.

"Good luck."

Within two days Mary and 44 other women, along with a skeleton crew of unhappy and sullen sailors and Captain Baker, were the only people left on board Numa. For the women, the extra space meant they had a gift none felt they would ever have again, the long-forgotten luxury of being able to be alone after years of being squashed together in over-crowded cells. That, plus the extra food and wine that was suddenly available, created a feeling almost of euphoria, a feeling amplified by the fact the women on board were all friends.

On the second evening Mary was on deck, alone apart from two sentries on the poop deck, watching a spectacular sunset, when Captain Baker strolled past. Emboldened beyond any measure she could have imagined just days ago because of the unique situation she found herself in, and without thinking of the possible consequences, she addressed herself to him.

"Excuse me Captain," she said, as if speaking to an equal. As Baker came to a halt Mary suddenly realised what a momentous mistake she had made and recoiled back against the gunwale, her hands flying to her mouth, far too late to stop the words.

"I'm so sorry" she said, tears welling up in her eyes, her horror so clearly written on her face that Baker's stern face melted and he could only smile.

"That's alright. What can I do for you?" Then seeing that the woman literally could not speak, he held his hands out toward her.

"It's alright, I won't hurt you."

"I was wondering sir, 'ow are we, myself and the other girls, 'ow are we going to go to, um the, ah that settlement. Was it Newcastle? Like the one back 'ome?"

Turning aside for a moment, he looked about, then looked back at her.

"See that ship over there? That's the paddle streamer Sophia Jane. The very first one of her kind in the colony. She will be taking you."

"Paddle Steamer?" Mary asked, a loss as to what he was talking about.

"Yes, well. See that tall chimney between the masts? That's the chimney of a steam engine that drives those two big wheels that push the ship through water. So even when the wind doesn't blow, or blows the wrong way, the ship can still go where it wants to go. You are very lucky to have the chance to sail on her. She is the future of shipping."

Then he tipped his hat and bid her "Good night".

"Yes, he did so say good night to me" she almost shouted with excitement after running below decks and telling her friends of the strange encounter. "He was ever so nice and I wish I could have said something clever, but I just stood there like a statue. I am such an idiot.

"I wonder if that is how it is here in this new country, that we can just say whatever we like to whoever we like?"

"You're lucky he dinna order you to his cabin and ravish you" laughed Caroline, the Scots girl who had become her best friend, "or is that what you were really asking?"

The dozen or so girls gathered around the tea pot laughed and laughed, happy and for the moment at least, content. Compared to the *Numa* bulldog, *Sophia Jane* was a greyhound. Only about half the size of *Numa,* its sharp bow and sleek rakish lines shouted speed. Early the next morning as the women tramped up the gangplank, each struggling under the weight and bulk of all their possessions, they were astounded at the polished decks and brass fittings of the ship, not to mention the huge wheels attached to both sides of the ship.

Then, when they trooped below deck, their astonishment doubled. *Sophia Jane* had initially been built for the enjoyment of wealthy passengers travelling between Britain and France, so no expense had been spared in its fittings.

Descending the stairs the women entered a spacious drawing room fitted with leather couches running along the walls, each wall decorated with looking glass panels.

Mary was one of the first women who ventured below decks and once her bare feet touched the deck she stopped dead in her tracks, the rest of the women spilling around her before also stopping in amazement. Soon all the women were bunched in the middle of the drawing room doing something most had not done for years - looking at themselves in a mirror.

Ann Smith, still recovering from having her hair shaved at the start of the voyage, was the first to break the silence.

"Well, I'm going to have to do something with my hair if this is the way we are to live."

The raucous outburst of laughter even startled the crew on deck. Spreading out to explore, the women found that the ship had three large separate sleeping rooms, one for gentlemen, one for ladies and one for steerage passengers, all fitted with a double tier of single beds lining the walls. Normally the ship could sleep 54 passengers in relative luxury, and the squealing and laughter from the so-called harden criminals as they fell into luxurious bunks or paraded in front of mirrors would have befitted a troop of schoolgirls on a holiday excursion.

No sooner had the women settled who was to sleep where than the ship shuddered and shook and the engine began to roar, the paddles began to churn and the ship began to move. No one seemed bothered as the women surged as one to the deck witness the magical moment.

The only issue the women had with the voyage to Newcastle was that it was over so quickly. Just under seven hours after *Sophia Jane* pulled away from the government wharf in Sydney Cove, she eased in beside the King's Wharf in Newcastle.

Newcastle
1834

If the women had been disappointed with Sydney Town after the delight of Cape Town, Newcastle left them bewildered.

"Is that it?" one woman asked as the town hove into view as *Sophia Jane* slid past Coal Island and the uncompleted breakwater connecting it to the mainland.

"Surely that's just the port, the real town must be further up the river?"

"That's not even a bloody village."

In 1834 Newcastle boasted about 80 houses and various official buildings stretching back from the narrow wooden wharf and scattered across a barren sandy peninsula. Directly up from the wharf sat the Commandant's official residence, while to the left was the lumber yard adjoined by the convict's barracks.

To the right was a stable block and a military barracks with a watch tower. A windmill sat on the skyline. Dominating the bleak scene was the prison - the only double story structure to be seen - squatting ominously on a hilltop overlooking the town. On the wharf a detachment of sorry looking soldiers lounged about.

On board ship the women were not backward with their opinions.

"Blimey. What on earth are we gonna be doin' 'ere?".

"It's the bloody end of nowhere. I'm thinkin' Newgate looked better."

"We might be the only women in the whole bloody place."

"Well, couldn't ask for a better place then, could we?"

On and on went the comments, using humour to cover despair in a desperate situation as the British always did. Once the ship was secured the women were ordered to form up and, carrying their baggage and following the lead of the soldiers, began tramping along a sand track. Although it was late afternoon, the sun beat down on the bonnetless women, the heat only partly relieved by a strong wind off the sea that whipped sand into bare skin. The track wound between the lumber yard and the home of the Superintendent of Works, then opened onto a path up steep incline towards the prison.

"Don't wanna be helping me carry me load does ya darlin'?" Mary Bardon quipped to one of the soldiers.

"I could make it worth your while."

"I doubt it" he shot back, "and besides, it would be worth all the skin off me back to be seen 'elpin' the likes of your luverlie self. Sergeant's got nuffin' to do up 'ere 'cept whip us."

It was but a 700 yard walk to the gates of the prison, but in soft sand under a hot sun, all of the women were played out and collapsed when they reached the gates.

The prison they looked up at was an imposing two story building sitting atop a small rise overlooking the town and port on one side and a white beach and endless expanse of ocean on the other.

The building had initially been reserved for men only, but in the past few years as more and more prisoners had been assigned to farms in the fertile Hunter Valley, sections had been converted to hold the female convicts assigned to landowners or businessmen.

Given the shortage of women in the area, they didn't wait in prison for long. Once a consignment of women had arrived word would quickly spread through the town and men would come from far and wide to collect the woman or women assigned to them.

Mary didn't have long to wait either. Early the very next morning the man she had been assigned to, and who was to play a large role in her life for the next year, arrived at the prison gates.

James Reid was, at just 35, already running to fat. Short and short-tempered, he had puffed his way to the gates himself because his male servants were all occupied elsewhere and he wanted to ensure he secured the female help he had been promised before she was poached by anyone else, a not unheard of occurrence.

Born in Newry in the north of Ireland in 1799, at just 23 he had married well to 17 year old Rosanna Macartney of the ancient and wealthy Macartney clan. Reid described himself as a lieutenant of the 56th Regiment of Foot on half pay, however the little actual service he had seen had been in India, seconded to the East India Company for a brief policing campaign where his main occupation had been abusing the local population.

Arrogant, authoritarian and uncompromising, the soldier who had never seen battle had an absolute belief in his own right and righteousness. Vindictive in victory, sullen in defeat, he ruled his family and servants with a hard and unforgiving hand and was in almost perpetual conflict with his neighbours and virtually everyone who did business with him.

He had arrived in Newcastle in 1823 and immediately began acquiring property. By the time he trudged through the sand to Newcastle Gaol on that cold and windy winter morning he had been in New South Wales for over ten years and had become one of the largest land-owners in the district.

Initially granted 5000 acres of fertile and productive land along the banks of the Hunter, he had since added many more acres to that, buying land as it became available, mostly from grantees unwilling or unable to put in the effort to make a success of farming in a new land. In addition he had been granted an allotment in the town where he had built a large house facing the ocean.

It was there he deposited Mary into the custody of his wife, stomping off without bothering with any introduction. At first glance Mary could see that Rosanna Reid was not well. Heavily pregnant, she had dark rings beneath her fearful eyes and a slight nervous tremor to her hand. She was thin, too thin Mary thought, her skin almost translucent. Instantly empathetic, Mary put down her possessions to go to her side and reached out a hand, forgetting the cultural gulf that separated them.

A cold voice stopped her. "What is your name?" Rosanna said.

"Mary ma'am. Mary McWilson."

"Odd name" Rosanna said, in a strong Irish brogue.

"Through the kitchen" she nodded to towards a closed door, "you will find Mrs Saunders, the house-keeper, who will explain your duties. You will not enter this room again unless summoned, do you understand?"

'Two can play that game' Mary decided, nodding but saying nothing. Rosanna in turn looked Mary slowly up and down.

Even in her travel-worn, dirty clothes, with unkempt hair and dirty bare feet, Rosanna immediately saw that Mary was younger and prettier than her and displayed an obvious insouciance she knew all too well would attract the attention of her husband.

She decided there and then that this woman needed to be put in her place at the beginning and then made to stay there. The problem was, she was just so tired. Every year a new child came, some merely to pass quickly to a better place, their short lives never leaving her a day of rest. She knew her husband was looking elsewhere and with so many convict women of loose morals flooding into the town, she knew he did not have to look far.

"Needless to say, you must try and make yourself presentable. For a start, have a good wash, especially those feet," she said, disgust and disdain written on her face.

"You are not to fraternise with the male staff, or indeed with any other of the convicts on this or any of our other properties. Is that understood?"

Mary nodded but said nothing. The battlelines had been drawn and war declared. Rosanna's eyes steeled.

"At no time and under no circumstances are you to be upstairs without Mrs Saunders or myself. There is to be no consumption of alcohol on or off the premises and if any alcohol is discovered you will immediately be turned over to the prison for reassignment. That's all."

Mrs Saunders, her surname was actually Sanders Mary later found out, but Rosanna gave a tin ear to all attempts to rectify her mistake, turned out to be a former convict from London, now wife of a soldier, who had been over two decades in the colony. She knew everything about everyone in the town and was happiest talking about them.

"Well, you're a pretty little thing aren't you, that could be a problem," were her first words. Pleased to have another Londoner to reminisce with, Mary immediately bonded with the older woman and over the next few days 'Aunt Betty', as everyone except the Reid family called her, filled Mary in on her new situation and her new 'master'.

"Well, the money is all hers needless to say" she said after detailing all the various properties Reid owned both in the town and hinterland.

"All the 'little general' does is strut about the bluddy place playin' the Lord of the Manor to which he were not born. I once 'eard the madam say that he secured a fortune in India he didn't have before, but of that I know nothing. Fortune or not, a right little tyrant 'e is, and I'm warnin' ye, e's known to 'ave wanderin' hands, if you get me drift.

"Consider yourself warned me darlin'. He has a grand farm out in the Valley called Rosebrook, not that 'e stays there much anymore, not since Jacob's Mob burnt it to the ground."

"What!" Mary said, aghast at the thought.

"Well, it was a right affair that" said Aunt Betty, settling herself comfortably into her favourite chair near the stove for what promised to be a good long yarn, "the little general 'as always had a rough tongue with those wot are under his control; 'im and his friend Vicars Jacob learned that in India methinks."

"Both of 'em always putting their servants up on charges, men and women alike, wot didn't jump to it with a 'yes sir, no sir' quick enough. And with 'im being a magistrate, well, let's say 'e gets wot he wants from 'is mates on the bench."

"Lot of good men have lost the skin off their back 'cause they didn't bend the knee to the little fella, and women sent to gaol for not doin' as he wanted", she added, raising her eyebrows to add weight to the obvious meaning of her words.

"Well, it were a few years ago now that Magistrate Reid ordered Jacob's man, young Patrick Riley, get 50 lashes for losing a couple of sheep in the bush, sheep wot turned up later safe and sound so's I hear it. It was excessive, everyone knew it was excessive, but that's the little general for ye; and he made it worse by quoting the bible at the young Patrick, saying he was bound for eternal damnation. Well, Pat, being a good Irish catholic lad and all, well, he'd just had enough. Everyone had had enough, but young Pat was a bit wild. So he escaped custody, got a few mates, and they went to the little general's fancy big farmhouse and burnt it to the ground they did, thinkin' he was inside. Caused a hell of a ruckus."

"The little general was lucky to escape with his life he was."

"Came back here wif his tail 'tween 'is legs and ain't left for more'n a few days ever since."

Mary was listening wide-eyed, totally engrossed.

"And what happened to Patrick?"

"Same's wot happens to 'em all. He ran wild for a time, but pretty soon they all got tracked down by those black devils and the police shot some dead and hung the rest. A shame it was. A real shame. They weren't the only ones mind you. Just this last year gone the men at Castle Forbes, James Mudie's farm, rebelled and went wild because they couldn't take a minute longer the daily floggings and beatings from Mudie's overseer, an evil tyrant named John Larnach. I heard before they fled they fired their guns at Larnach as he swam the river to escape, but sadly missed."

"They whipped one magistrate they caught to within an inch of his life they did, and a good job it was. They would have done the same to Mudie if he'd been brave enough to actually live on his farm, but like our little general, he be too scared to venture out of the town, rather getting his magistrate friends and the police to do his dirty work."

"Sadly, in the end they were also caught and hung. Tis a lovely land out there luvvie, but hear me, there also be some devils that live there."

The Devil Within

While there might have been devils and wild highway men in the countryside, for Mary life in Newcastle proved to be boring. Confined to the house, she cooked, cleaned, washed, ironed, looked after children, ran errands and was on constantly on call. She had met several of her former *Numa* shipmates in and about the town, it was a small town after all, and the women would contrive to get together in their free time to share experiences. One Sunday afternoon after church Mary was sitting on the beach with two *Numa* friends, Grace Denham and young Ann Connor, aged just 15, all having managed to escape the confines of their assigned homes for a few hours.

Grace, the oldest, complained at having to fend off the advances of the man in the family she worked for, who saw providing sexual favours as part of her assignment.

"I'm sure even his wife must know about his behaviour. I swear, I will run him through with a knife if he persists" she said.

"I have said I will report him but he just laughs. Says he is friends with the police and the magistrates and they will do nothing and I will end up out on the street for my trouble. The bastard!"

Suddenly young Ann burst out crying. Both women instantly put their arms around her and asked what had happened, but nothing could console her. Finally, exhausted, she confided that she had been beaten and then raped by the master she was assigned to, almost from the time she had arrived.

"His wife isn't there. There's no one there, just me. What can I do?" she asked, deep sobs racking her slim body again and again.

"He says if I report him no one will believe me and I will be sent away and forced to be a whore just to live. What can I do?"

The next day Mary spoke to Aunt Betty, pleading with her to come up with some solution, but the older woman could only shake her head.

"The poor child. I hate the bastards! They say they are gentlemen, but they are all bastards! I can only pray for her. It happens all the bloody time. I am so glad I married, it's the only escape, if escape it is."

She grabbed Mary's arm so fiercely the girl winced and tried to pull away, but was held fast.

"Tell your young friend to seek permission to marry! It doesn't much matter which man she chooses, one's as bad as the next, but only then will she be allowed to leave that miserable low bastard. Same goes for you Mary McWilson, sooner or later you will also have to choose a man to look out for you. And I warn you, don't you expect any mercy from Mrs Reid should you tell her that you have been ravished by the little general."

"She will not give a fig and will throw you to the wolves quick as a wink. It's happened before as sure as I stand here before you."

Just a month later her prophecy almost came true. In a rare visit upstairs to fetch some soiled bedclothes after aunty Betty had told her the family were out, Reid unheard came up silently behind her and before she could react had her one arm caught against her back while he held the other fast in his hand, leaving both her arms trapped while he still had his one hand free. In an instant he had ripped free the strings holding her bodice and was groping her breasts.

It happened so quickly that Mary had not even had the presence of mind to struggle or shout.

"Yes my little whore, you like that don't you" he gasped, reaching down to lift her skirts, "Been a long time since you have had a man I take it, well we can easily fix that".

"Let me go or I'll scream this house down" Mary eventually managed to hiss, at the same time struggling to free her arms and kick him at the same time. When he merely laughed she lunged at his neck with her teeth, just failing to find flesh. Again Reid merely laughed.

"Go ahead, scream, there's no one to hear and even if there was, there's nothing they could do."

"Come! Do as I want or it will be the worse for you."

Young, healthy and strong after months of good food, instead of surrendering Mary set to the fight with a fury that momentarily stunned Reid and she managed to break free, spinning backward into a cupboard and bringing a wash basin crashing to the floor.

"Mary! What on earth are you up to up there" shouted Aunty Betty, the question followed by the sounds of her tramping up the stairs. She burst through the doorway to a terrible tableau. Leaning back against the cupboard amid the remains of the porcelain washstand Mary was rearranging her blouse, her eyes blazing. Reid stood in the middle of the room red-faced and heaving to catch his breath.

Instantly she understood what had happened, or nearly happened.

"What have you done you clumsy girl" she said brusquely to Mary, walking forward to grab her arm.

"I'm sorry about this Sir," she said, squarely facing the man and looking him straight in the eye, "do you want me to call the watch Sir, or perhaps the soldiers. My husband is just nearby I believe." Reid looked at her, a puzzled expression on his face.

"Ah. No, that won't be necessary."

Then, gathering his wits, he went onto the attack.

"I don't know why you allowed this stupid, clumsy hussy upstairs when you know it has been strictly forbidden by Mrs Reid. Well!"

The older woman held the man's gaze a moment before answering.

"Yes Sir. It won't happen again Sir, I promise you that. Perhaps it's time for Mary her to spend some time at Rosebrook Sir, away from temptation … Sir."

A moment of understanding flashed between the two before Reid answered.

"Yes. Good idea. See to it!.."

Downstairs Aunt Betty took the girl into her arms and instantly Mary began to cry. Between deep sobs she managed to speak.

"I'm not that kind of woman. I'm not! I am NOT"

Aunt Betty said nothing until the crying stopped.

"My girl, you were lucky I came back when I did. Next time you might not be so lucky. You are going to go out to the farm for a while. While you are there you need to look to your future and find a man to look after you. It's the only chance you have in this country."

Three days later Mary found herself bouncing about on the hard wooden seat of one of the ox-drawn drays Reid ran between Newcastle and his country estate. As uncomfortable as the seat was, the journey was both exciting and illuminating. The driver, a personable young former convict named Thomas Clifton, explained that despite having not long ago received his Ticket of Leave, he still worked as a shepherd and driver, or 'bullocky' as he called it, at Rosebrook.

"It's not a bad place to work" he explained, "the boss stays away and doesn't bother us. The overseer is a good man. Food's good and so t'will do 'til I decide what I want to do."

Mary nodded. He seemed like a nice man. At least he was respectful and well-mannered. The oxen moved steadily, slowly leaving Newcastle behind, initially moving through open scrub bush along a well-defined track running parallel to the Hunter River.

Having spent most of her life in London, the countryside was revelation to Mary, full of strange looking birds and even stranger sounds.

Her innocent laughter at Thomas' explanations of each animal and sound was infectious and soon Thomas was having as much fun pointing out the oddities as she was in looking at them and trying to pronounce their names.

Then, as Thomas had said she might, she spied her first kangaroo. It was standing not far off the road in the shade of a tree, chewing and looking straight at her.

Mary jumped up pointing as the startled animal bounded away in giant leaps that had Mary laughing and squealing with delight.

"That is the strangest thing I have ever seen in my life".

"It's like a bloody giant big rat. Are they dangerous?"

"Do they eat people?"

"No" Tom laughed, "but people sure eat them. Never got the taste for 'em meself, but the black fellas sure love 'em. They know everything wot can be et and wot to leave alone."

"I've not seen any of the black people."

"What are they like?" asked Mary.

"Well, to tell the truth, I don't know much about them at all. They stick to themselves mostly. Can't recall ever seeing one on this road in all the time I've been drivin' it, probably 'cause we scare all the game off. They do come down to Rosebrook and the other farms a fair bit in the winter though, to work at harvest time or to pick up blankets from the government."

"There's lots of stories of how they've speared people, but seems to me it's mainly those blokes wot mess with their women that are speared. Pardon me for saying that, but the fact is I've not had a bit of trouble with any of them. Live and let live I say."

As the sun began to settle the dray arrived at a crossroads which was obviously a regular camp site, dotted with stone-lined fire pits beside a small stream with grass for the oxen. Tom, Mary called him Tom now, was all efficiency as he hobbled and outspanned the animals, gathered several armfuls of wood, lit a fire and pulled out a chest of food and cooking equipment. Soon the evening meal was under way.

"Aunt Betty has put in a few goodies for you that I never see, that's for sure. You can travel with me anytime" he laughed, blushing as he realised what he had said. After wolfing down the food he had prepared, a homemade bread with a conserve and some mutton chops, the pair sat around a roaring blaze exchanging their stories.

Mary was surprised at how at peaceful she felt just sitting and staring up at a sky full to overflowing with stars, surprised that she felt absolutely safe despite being out in the forest, miles from anyone, with a total stranger.

Soon Tom was yawning and laying out his bedroll next to the fire.

"You sleep up on the dray" he said, "sometimes the odd snake will come to the fire."

"What!" Mary screamed, jumping to her feet and on to the dray in one movement.

"No! No! No! That doesn't happen. I mean, it does happen, but hardly ever. Never in fact. But just to be on the safe side. I'll be here and I'll keep the fire going all night. Promise."

Stretched out across bags of flour, wrapped in a smelly blanket, with no roof over her head for the first time she could remember, Mary slept like a log.

As the sun rose she lifted her head to see Tom busy making tea to go with last night's leftover bread for breakfast, and as soon as that was consumed he cleared the campsite and in-spanned the oxen with the same speed and efficiency he had displayed doing the reverse last night. Soon they were on the move, Mary wrapped in her blanket against an early morning chill that did not last the hour before the sun slowly began to bake her.

Tom had said they would reach Rosebrook mid-afternoon and despite the dray having to get through some swampy ground early on in the journey, he was as good as his word.

Rosebrook Farm
Hunter Valley

Long before they got to Rosebrook Mary noticed the countryside begin to change from dense forest to grassy plains and rolling hills that even to her ill-informed eye looked like fine farmland. From the road Rosebrook appeared as a cluster of small buildings which looked far from impressive. Along one side of the road leading to the houses in the distance were row upon row of a bright green shoulder high broad-leafed plant Tom explained was tobacco. Mary was astounded.

She had only ever seen tobacco as small brown bits of weedy stuff.

On the other side of the road were fields of corn and wheat spreading as far as the eye could see. Tom explained that it wasn't all wheat, that the farm produced other cereals and fodder crops such as sorghum, lucerne, millet, rye, hay and barley.

"But most of the land is used for grazing sheep, mainly for the wool, but we also run cattle and horses. The farm grows everything it needs and sells the rest at market, some in Maitland or on to Morpeth, but the stuff like the tobacco and wool we ship down to Sydney Town and from there it goes back home to England."

Closer to the farmhouse Mary saw fruit trees and rows of vegetables. As a city girl she had never even imagined such masses of food. The dray stopped outside the main house Tom said had been rebuilt, albeit somewhat smaller, after the disastrous attack by the Riley gang that saw burnt it to the ground. The house was low and wide, with a pitched roof to help those inside to escape the heat Tom said, and was built in a 'U' shape, with the wide frontage facing across fields to the river in the distance and the rolling hills beyond. All three sides had a covered verandah which kept the house in deep shade.

To Mary it looked like a palace.

"Nice house" said Tom, off-loading some of the supplies "pity it's hardly ever lived in."

To one side were a number of open-sided sheds with tobacco leaves hanging in them and some stables, as well as one large cottage, a few smaller cottages and a long building she correctly took to be a shed for workers. An air of quiet and calm hung over the whole scene and Mary had no doubt that while life here might not be exciting, it would at least be safe.

A woman came out of the main house and Tom introduced her as Caroline Foster, the overseer's wife. Mary thought she looked like a very capable and no-nonsense kind of woman and that impression was confirmed as she gave Mary a slow and thorough examination from to toe, taking in the once fashionable clothes, now travel-worn and threadbare, and reaching the obvious conclusion.

"Have you ever worked on a farm before" she asked.

The confusion on Mary's face was answer enough.

"Righto, well in the beginning you will work here around the house. There are cows to be milked, chickens to be tended and lots of food to be cooked. Don't worry" she said in response to the look of shock that passed over Mary's face, "I'll teach you."

"But be warned, there are almost twenty men here and just a few women, so that's a lot of cooking. There are twice as many cows as people and that is a lot of milking, and after all that there is a lot of cleaning up to do."

Seeing the look of absolute horror on Mary's face she could only laugh.

"Please, don't worry. There are lots of people to help and provided we all jump in and do our share it all gets done and there is time to rest and enjoy what this life has to offer. My husband Alan is away for a few days, in the meantime let me show you where you will sleep."

Caroline was as good as her word and while Mary found the work at Rosebrook hard, especially in the beginning when she had to learn how to milk cows and cook huge stews. And the first time she found a snake coiled up in the kitchen her screams could be heard for miles, bringing the men running only to fall down laughing once the retile had been safely despatched. There was plenty to eat and drink and long lovely sunsets to be enjoyed over a cup of tea chatting to

Caroline and the few other wives. Most of all she felt safe, perhaps safer than she had ever felt in her life. She hadn't been at Rosebrook two months when Tom asked her to marry him. He had barely left her side when he wasn't working and while Mary did not feel about him the way she admitted to herself she still felt about Ed McWilson, he was kind and gentle. More importantly, the hard reality had dawned that she needed a husband and 'Tom is here and Ed is not'.

Caroline agreed. The two women had become friends so before answering Tom, Mary asked her opinion about the match.

"Aunt Betty wrote me a note about what happened in Newcastle. I'm so sorry, but the fact is that kind of thing will only continue until you are married. There are so few women out here and the terrible thing is, it's worse for convicts. You are not a loose woman, I know that, but the fact is many women convicts are, and so that is how men will see you."

"Tom is a good fellow, we both know that. He is young, very young in some ways, but the harsh reality is that out here good men are few and far between. If you wish I will ask Alan to speak to the Magistrate for permission for you two to marry."

Mary thought on it for a short time and then nodded her assent. A month later, in December of 1834, permission for the pair to marry was granted.

To celebrate, early in the new year Caroline took Mary on her first trip to the hamlet of West Maitland. Until recently known as Wallis Plains, the boom town of West Maitland was literally mushrooming up on the banks of the river about six miles from Rosebrook and was the closest thing to civilisation for many, many more miles. Truth be told it was little more than a collection of timber slab houses, shops and businesses, interspersed with a few brick buildings, all clustered atop a hill which over the centuries had been half eaten away by the often rampaging Hunter River below. On the day Caroline and Mary arrived, recent rains had turned the main street, almost the only street, into a quagmire. Despite the fact that it was a Sunday, shops were doing a roaring trade with outlying settlers cannily using their rare visit to church to stock up on goods and supplies.

Mary was astounded at the activity.

A constant parade of ox-drawn drays sloshed through the streets, while on every corner knots of pipe-smoking men bantered and bargained. Few women ventured out on the muddy street and those that did were often dressed like the men, wearing trousers and high boots beneath their dresses. Wearing the one dress she had managed to save from her days in London, days already at the edge of her memory, Mary was ill-at-ease - fearing not only that the dress would be ruined by the mud, but certain her borrowed shoes would not last minutes in the mud. Luckily, dealing with such days was old hat to Caroline. She expertly guided Mary along planks laid between buildings to the Cohen and Company General Store without a drop of mud landing on their dresses. Inside the dank building a timber slab counter ran down both sides of the single room separating shoppers from shelves bending under the weight of a surprisingly wide range of farm and food goods. There were several men serving, but no women. Looking around Mary was astounded to see that the far end of the room had a double door hung beneath a sign that proclaimed it to be the Rose Inn! From inside that room came the distinct sounds, and smells, of a public house.

Mary had never seen the likes of such a contradictory combination before and she was standing spellbound at the counter when she heard the words that would change her life.

"Good morning Mrs Foster" a voice said brightly.

Caroline turned and smiled. "Hello Mr Cooke, how nice to see you."

Mary turned to the voice, seeing a pair of deep blue eyes beneath blond hair atop a blonde beard, but as she took at the man he visibly blanched and stepped back, shock written on his face.

"Rebecca?" he said softly.

The Meeting

It was a typically sweltering December Sunday in West Maitland and Cookie decided a cool beer was in order before having lunch and doing the weekly shopping. Putting on his Sunday best clothes, he took the short walk from his home cum workshop down Main Street, past Phil Cohen's soap and candle factory to the grocery shop cum public house of his friend Solly Cohen.

The Cohen family were well on their way to becoming one of the wealthiest families in the district and Cookie had made it his business to foster a neighbourly acquaintance with the family who, being Jewish, were shunned by a lot of the district's English gentry.

Shortly before Cookie had arrived in town the Cohen family had acquired the licence to run a public house and the rear section of the store was now known as the Rose Inn.

Cookie knew that all too soon church services would end and those who had confessed their sins would quickly empty into the street seeking an ale or more to wash the bad taste of contrition away. Standing at the counter were two ladies, one of whom he recognised as Caroline Foster.

"Good morning Mrs Foster" he said brightly, but when her companion turned toward him he stopped in mid-breath, shock written on his face.

"Rebecca" he said softly.

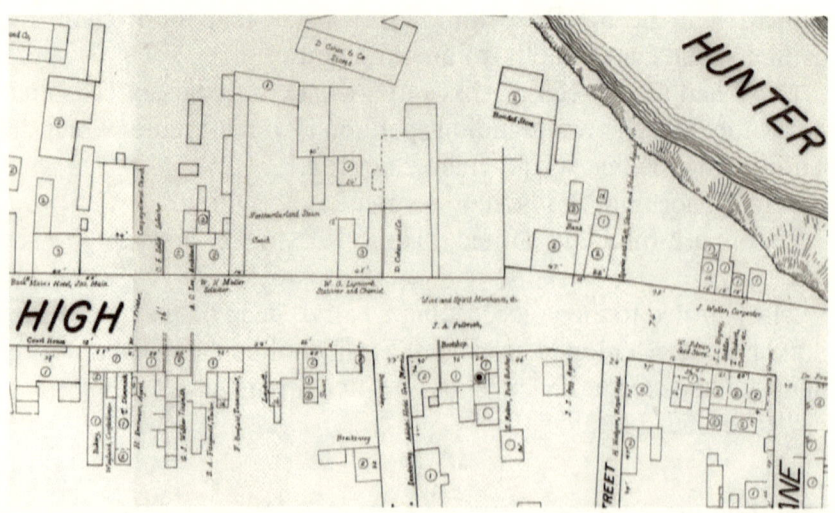

34 Town Plans of Maitland West circa 1833. In an extract from the Deeds Registration Branch of the NSW Registrar General's Office. Cookie's plot is described as "Bordered on the East by a line of five chains (100m) adjoining land belonging to Mr Cohen; on the South by a line of two chains (40m) forming its frontage to the Main or High St." To the west and north his land was bordered "by that portion of Nowland land now purchased by and in the possession of Mr Waller ..."

"Hello Mr Cooke. How nice to see you," Caroline said, extending a hand to take the one that would normally be offered to her, but no hand was extended.

Instead Cookie stood, arms at his side, his face deathly white.

"Are you alright Mr Cooke," Caroline asked.

Cookie said nothing. He stood stock still looking past Caroline, his attention focussed solely on Mary. Caroline turned to look at Mary, who for her part was coolly returning Cookie's stare, then looked back and forth between the pair, the trio locked in a confused silence.

Mary was equally confused by the actions of the man standing wide-eyed at her, but quickly gathering her wits simply returned the man's gaze, saying nothing. Appraising the man in front of her it was obvious to Mary that he was not a convict. Well-built and muscular, he was just a bit taller than her but seemed much bigger. He was wearing brushed cotton moleskin trousers tucked into high boots, a simple white shirt and a bush hat, which he now fingered nervously, seemingly unsure whether to take it off or not.

He had close cropped blond hair atop a trimmed blond beard and the most piecing blue eyes Mary had ever seen. In that instant she knew.

Eventually Cookie managed to croak out a few words.

"I'm so sorry. Please. Please forgive me. For an instant I thought you were someone else" he said speaking directly to Mary, ignoring Caroline completely. Mary, equally taken aback, could only manage a crooked smile. Caroline again looked first at Mary and then back to Cookie, her feminine intuition spinning at high speed.

"Mr Cooke, please allow me to introduce you to Miss Mary McWilson, who has arrived to work at Rosebrook for a time. Mary, Mr William Cooke, known by everyone as Cookie."

For an embarrassing few seconds neither Mary nor Cookie said a word. Caroline's eyebrows rose as yet again she looked from one back to the other. It was Cookie who eventually broke the silence.

"Miss McWilson, I'm honoured to make your acquaintance."

Not trusting herself to speak Mary again merely nodded and smiled. Not sure what he should to do or say Cookie said nothing, so the silence dragged on.

"Ah, have you been in the colony long Miss,…ah…" More silence.

"McWilson" Caroline answered when it seemed Mary would not.

"Miss McWilson has been reassigned" - a code word signalling to Cookie that Mary was a convict without having to say the word - "from Newcastle and loves it so she wants to stay here, don't you Mary?"

Mary nodded. Cookie nodded. Caroline nodded.

Then Cookie nodded again.

"Well, I have to go. I hope to see you again Miss McWilson" he said, putting emphasis on the surname he would never forget.

All three laughed.

As soon as Cookie had half stumbled, half run out of the store, Caroline turned to Mary.

"Well, there's no need to ask what you're thinking is there?" she laughed. "Before we go any further. No, he is not married, so yes, he is eligible. He is a cabinet-maker and a builder and he has his own business and is successful. No one knows much about his background, and no one in this part of the country ever asks such questions, but he is a serious man, very serious, and not easily distracted. He has done some work at Rosebrook and so I know him fairly well. It's a small community. More importantly, he is a good man, not at all frivolous and there are not many of those around these parts."

Mary looked forlornly at Caroline.

"What am I going to do?"

"Well, young lady, I think I know, in fact we both know, what you are going to do. I just don't know how you are going to do it."

A week later Cookie leaned up against the bar at the Rose Inn, an ale in front of him, Alan Forster beside him.

Neither man had said a word for almost ten minutes.

"I don't know what to do" Cookie finally volunteered. Foster, sent on what he called a 'fool's errand' by a wife who would not brook no for an answer, shook his head.

"I know what you have to do" Al replied, "I just don't know how you're gonna do it."

Foster had told him he was under orders to have this talk with Cookie to ask what his intentions to Mary were, hinting that Mary's mind was already made up. He also had a secret second set of orders - depending on the outcome of the first mission - to visit the magistrate in East Maitland to cancel Mary's permission to marry Tom Clifton and obtain a second permission for Mary to marry William 'Cookie' Cooke.

"For goodness sake Al, I have only just met the lady once, for a few moments. She looked lovely and, ah, well, lovely. Very lovely. And nice. Very nice. Reminded me of a lovely lady I once knew. And, well, I would love to see her - Mary McWilson - again. That's for certain."

Al Foster was a big man and he looked down on Cookie slowly shaking his head.

"Well you are going to see her again, take my word for it. My orders are clear. Caroline wants to know your bloody intentions, doesn't she. The fact is, Mary is betrothed to young Tom Clifton" he merely nodded at Cookie's surprised look, "I know, but Caroline, and myself, well we don't see much hope for the match. Tom's alright, but to tell the truth I think Mary said 'yes' a bit quick. She is just over from the old country and it can all be a bit intimidating. So, it's up to you."

Cookie looked up at him.

"Well, I don't know what to do. What do you think I should do?"

"Well I think I know what you should do, and Caroline is very, very certain about what you should do. The thing is Cookie, you've been here a few years now and so you know the lay of the land; there's not many women about, at least not women like Mary I'll be sayin'. If it were me, I'd marry her in a shot" he laughed, then looking seriously at Cookie added "you tell Caroline I said that and you'll be wantin' a new set o' teeth."

The men finished their ales in silence and then went their separate ways. After Alan returned that evening to admit what seemed to be failure, Caroline decided to take matters into her own hands. The next day she had a horse saddled and rode into Maitland to sort the issue out herself, finding Cookie hard at work in his carpentry shop.

"Cookie! Come here to me" she said, sternly enough so as to allow of no excuse. Getting straight to the point he told him that it was clear he was 'entranced' by Mary, and adding that, in her opinion, Mary felt exactly the same way about him.

"The thing is, Mary has accepted a proposal of marriage from Tom Clifton, so what are you going to do about that? Are you just going to let it happen?"

"Well!!" she exclaimed at Cookie's continued silence.

Cookie's confused look told Caroline all she needed to know.

"Exactly. Now, you know as well as I do that a woman, a good and virtuous woman, cannot be long unmarried in this wilderness. Now, there is nothing wrong with young Tom, 'cept he is young, younger than Mary; that and the fact is he is never going to be more than what he is now - a farm hand. Nothing wrong with that either, my dad was a farmer, but I believe Mary is worth more than that and in due course she will need more than that, whether she knows it or not. Let me be tellin' you, Mary is a fine young woman, and smart as a whip. She would be a fine asset to your business that's for sure. And children would be no problem for her."

At that Cookie blushed bright red, as did Caroline once she realised what she had said.

"So" she rushed on, "the question is, do you want to marry Mary? If you don't you're a bloody fool. I understand that this is sudden, but really, there is no time to waste. The magistrate has given permission for Tom and her to marry, but I don't think that after meeting you she wants to go through with that marriage. What do you say?"

Cookie was dumbstruck.

'Do I want to get married?' he asked himself. He realised that until this very instant he had never given the idea much thought. While he hadn't wanted to marry young Liz, he had wanted to marry Bec, so he wasn't against the idea of marriage as such. And the fact of the matter was he was not getting any younger - soon no one would want to marry him! And it wasn't as if the Hunter Valley was swarming with eligible women. His head spinning, he sat down at his work bench. Thinking back he wondered if the attraction he had felt to Mary was simply because she had reminded him of Bec. 'The question is, is it right to want to marry someone just because they look like Bec? The question seemed preposterous, but the instant he asked it of himself he knew the answer. 'Yes' he thought. 'Yes. Why not?'

"Cookie!" Caroline's shout shocked Cookie to his feet.

"Wake up you dolt! This is not the time to daydream! Tell me! What do you have to say for yourself?"

"I, ah. I wonder. Is it ... Ah, could I meet her again. Is that possible?"

"Of course! I will bring her here tomorrow, about mid-morning. I need not say again you have very little time, so there's no point in dilly-dallying. Fact is, you need a wife, she needs a husband. You are both suited to each other, so just get on with it. "

"Now good day to you," she said, stomping out of the workshop.

Cookie stood and watched as the woman walked out and away, remaining in the same spot for a long time, his mind in turmoil.

'Could it be; should it be; so easy to marry someone?' he wondered. Sitting down heavily he realised that he had no one to discuss the question with. He was lonely, and suddenly aware he had been lonely for some time.

"How is it I didn't know this before?" he wondered aloud. After a while he looked around the cluttered sawdust-strewn building that was both his workshop and his home.

"It isn't much is it?" he asked himself aloud, "certainly not near enough or good enough for a wife is it?"

But even as he voiced the question he knew that in all probability it was enough. He assumed that as a convict such a home would be a big step up for Mary. Not only would she have her own home, and perhaps her own family, but she would be safe and secure - he would see to that. Closing the shop he trudged up to the Rose Inn. He needed a rum. The next morning he rose early after a night of much thought and little sleep, dressed in his best clothes, and then sat quietly on his only chair watching the sunrise work its way down the Hunter Valley and across the Hunter River.

At Rosebrook the reaction to Caroline's intervention was slightly different.

"You did what!" Mary all but shouted.

"How could you do that? Oh my Good Lord, what must he think of me? I can never see him again! I will never ever be able to look him in the eye again. I would rather die than marry that man now! I am so embarrassed I could die."

Caroline had expected the outburst and merely sat quietly, letting the torrent of words swirl over and around her, biding her time to speak. When the torrent finally dissolved into a flood of tears, Caroline stepped forward, putting her arms around Mary's shoulders.

"Mary. This is not the time for hysteria. The fact is that you are in charge of this. When I spoke to Cookie he actually shed tears for fear he may have lost you" she lied smoothly.

"He was so grateful that I had spoken to him. He said he had been just waiting for the right time to come out to Rosebrook, but when I told him that Tom had proposed and that permission had been granted, he was beside himself with grief and wanted to rush here straight away to try to dissuade you! I said he should wait until I spoke to you and that I would try to persuade you to speak to him. Mary, you need to be sensible here. I know you were attracted to Cookie - William - and I know he was attracted to you."

"Tom is a fine young man, but he is not for you and deep down you know that. He is a farm hand. Has always been a farm hand and always will be. He has stayed here at Rosebrook, where he was first assigned, though he has his ticket and could leave at any time!"

"Cookie is a mature man with assets and skills and he is ready to settle down, he even told me so!" she again lied easily.

Straightening her shoulders she went in for the kill.

"I have told him we are going into town tomorrow and I told that if you so wished, I would let you drop in to see him, and you will Mary McWilson. You most certainly will."

That night Mary also lay awake for a long, long time, running her mind back over the terrible chain of events that had dragged her away from her life in London, through the cells of Newgate and the putrid holds of a whaling ship to here, the uncivilised far end of the world.

And she cried.

She cried for her lost love of Ed McWilson; cried for her lost parents; cried for the sure knowledge that she was destined to live the rest of her life in this vast unknown land. She cried and cried until eventually her tears took her exhausted mind to sleep, awakening to a clear cold morning with a clear cold mind.

She did not know Cookie, or William she resolved to call him, but there simply was no other choice.

She would be a good wife and mother, of that she had no doubt, and should it happen that William was a less than good husband and father. Well, he would pay a dear price.

That resolved, she bathed, brushed her hair and again put on her one fine dress and sat watching the sunrise while waiting for Rosebrook to stir and for Caroline take her to her fate.

When she told Caroline of her decision the older woman simply nodded. There was nothing more to say.

The ride to Maitland was quiet, neither Mary nor Caroline had anything to say. The events of the morning would unfold as they would.

The meeting, when it came, went better than either Caroline or Cookie or Mary had expected. Dropped at the workshop while Caroline went shopping, Mary stood, unsure of what to do next, but Cookie appeared at the door almost immediately.

"Good morning Miss McWilson" Cookie said brightly, "you see, I managed to remember your name."

He laughed a nervous laugh. Mary remained silent. Cookie coughed.

"Ah, I have something to tell you," he said. She looked sharply at him.

"No! Nothing bad I imagine. Well not too bad."

He walked her into the workshop, stopped and took a large breath.

"The fact is I am an ex-convict. No one around these parts knows that about me 'cept you now. And you should know that. Seven years. Served my time. I'm a free man. But the thing is, I think I know what you have been through."

"I don't need your pity Mr Cooke" she replied.

"No! No. No, that's not what I was trying to say. I was trying to say that, well it's a very hard country. And it can be a very lonely country. Just last night I realised that I have been, am, lonely."

Cookie saw by the look on Mary's face that he had walked into another dead end.

"Not that that is any reason to be married. No. No, not at all."

At a loss for words he looked around for a distraction.

"Ah. Mary - can I call you Mary?" he asked, the pleading in his voice clear. Sensing his confusion matched hers she nodded.

"Thank you. Thank you. Ah, I was wondering, just across the road is Mrs Pulbrook's bookshop, just over there" he pointed.

"Well Mrs Pulbrook, I know her very well, her and her husband" he quickly added, "well, Mrs Pulbrook serves a wonderful cup of tea. And cake, she has cake. So I was wondering, could I perhaps offer you a cup of tea. And cake."

By now Mary was fully at ease, in charge, and sure her decision was the right one. She would marry William Cooke and they would be happy. She would see to it. Over tea she asked Cookie about his work in the valley and the people he had met. Given something to talk about that he knew lot about, Cookie very quickly regained his composure. Soon they were talking freely and Mary was laughing at his description at some of the pompous characters he knew in the valley. A real laugh, not a fake one. As he walked her back across the street to show her the 'home' part of the workshop, she slipped her arm through his. In the middle of explaining how a treadle lathe worked, Cookie asked her to marry him, and she accepted, and they both laughed.

Three months later, on April 6, 1835, Cookie and Mary were married by the newly arrived Reverend George Keylock Rusden in the newly consecrated St Peters Anglican Church in East Maitland.

As was the system, shortly after the marriage Mary Cooke was reassigned into the custody of her new husband.

35 Mary and William Cooke, circa 1881.

Epilogue

John Haynes looked across the small room at Cookie and Mary. At some time while Mary had been speaking, her husband had contrived to quietly move and sit next to her on the two-seater divan and was holding her hand now as she gently sobbed.

Caroline was also wiping tears away and there were even wet streaks on the journalist's cheeks. For a long time no one spoke. Caroline - it was now obvious who the daughter had been named for - had moved to stand behind her mother and her hand now rested on her shoulder. Mary put her other hand up to hold her daughter's. Haynes pulled out his pocket watch to check the time. Mary had been speaking for almost two hours non-stop, the words tumbling out as if they had been walled in for a long, long time and the wall had suddenly been breached.

"That is the first time I have told that story Mr Haynes. Not even my children have heard it all and I suspect some of it even came as a surprise to William" she said, casting a quick look at her husband.

"I don't know what came over me. I vowed no one would ever know the secrets of my past and so now I have to ask you to keep those secrets as well Mr Haynes."

The journalist nodded.

"It's a compelling story. I am ashamed to say that while I obviously know much of the sad tale of the transportation of thousands of men and women to Australia, I never really grasped the full import of just how wrenching it really was for those caught in its deadly jaws."

"To be torn from loved ones, from mothers and fathers, husbands and wives and even children, all for the crime of just trying to get something to eat, or stealing some trivial thing, such as a handkerchief worth just a few coins ... well, it astounds me. That women like

yourself were subject to such degradation and abuse fills me with anger."

"To hear it come from your lips Madam, as I have heard it from Cookie's, pardon, Mr Cooke's, over the past days, has greatly affected me I assure you. It has reinforced my desire to have stories such as yours told for all Australians to read so that the real history of this country can be appreciated."

In response to the sudden shock on the faces of Cookie and Mary, he held up a hand.

"I understand and there is no need for concern. As I have said, I have given my word and your stories are safe with me, thought I must admit I would dearly love to tell them. Can I ask, briefly, for I fear the hour of my departure approaches, what happened to bring you to Morpeth and what transpired in the past forty years?"

Mary looked to her husband, who answered for both.

"Well, very briefly, after we married we stayed in West Maitland for a while, but the economy there failed and I was forced to move on. I closed my business and Mr Keppie, the engineer of the Sophia Jane who I spoke of, bought my land. Then he and I worked together for a while at Paterson, where we build a steam-driven mill among other things. I had a plot in Morpeth's High Street so once Caroline was born, followed by Eliza, we - Mary and I - we decided it was time to settle down. I built a house and later bought some land here in Morpeth and, well, here we are."

"It has not been easy, Mr Haynes, not at all. We have had to keep to ourselves so as to not invite discussion of our past. We did not lie, we simply didn't tell the whole truth."

"Then why tell your story now, may I ask? What had changed?"
Cookie hesitated.

"Well, I need hardly remind you that it was yourself who approached me, but that said, I agree there was no necessity for me to speak. I suppose the fact is that I - we" he amended, looking at Mary.

"We decided it was time."

"I am not a young man Mr Haynes and I feel my time in drawing to a close. Yes, yes, I know" he said, stopping Caroline's protest

36 Morpeth circa 1865.

with a raised hand "it may not be polite to speak of it, but the end is coming for me as it does to all of us. So be it, I believe I can face that day with my head held high."

"I have had a full life and even if not all of it was good, the end result most certainly is."

That thought brought an end to the conversation. Sitting there with the kind of family who had brought with them the determination and dignity that would build the new Australia, as opposed to the landed aristocracy who had brought nothing but their ill-gained wealth and their ingrained prejudices, Haynes more certain than ever that it was the stories of ordinary men such as 'Old Cookie' and of ordinary women such as Mary Ms Wilson that he wanted to tell to other Australians.

'They are ordinary people yet their stories are extraordinary.'

'Who knows' he pondered, 'there might even be a book in old Cookie's story one day.'

37 Extract from The Bulletin, page 4 of August 20, 1881.

www.ingramcontent.com/pod-product-compliance
Lightning Source LLC
Chambersburg PA
CBHW020352080526
44584CB00014B/1000